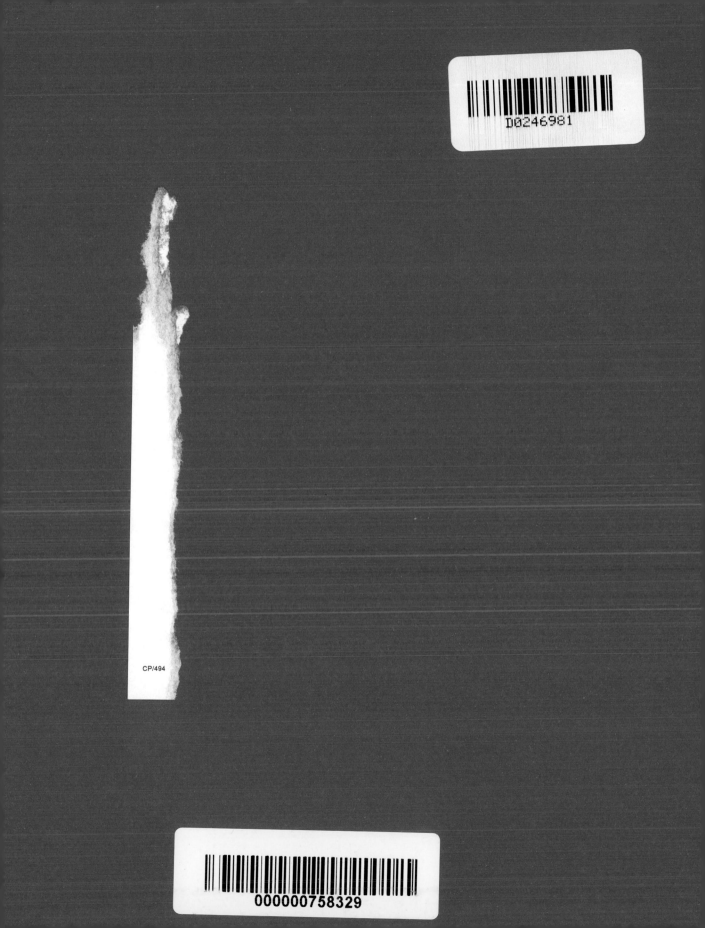

CP/494

D0246981

000000758329

THE GOOD GARDENER

Simon Akeroyd

THE GOOD GARDENER

EXPERT ADVICE FOR EVERY GARDEN FROM THE NATIONAL TRUST

National Trust

DUDLEY LIBRARIES

000000758329

Askews & Holts	04-May-2015
	£25.00
SED	

contents

1. Garden basics 12

2. Designing your garden 28

3. Lawn care 76

4. Planting 100

5. Propagation 126

6. Pruning 144

7. Garden maintenance 176

8. Grow your own 198

9. Greener gardening 252

Hydrangea Paniculata with Sellick
1895

Introduction: modern gardening in an historic landscape

Gardening at the National Trust: Forever for Everyone

I sit writing this in the Edwardian Head Gardener's office at Polesden Lacey, adjoining the potting and tool sheds at the back of the walled garden. It is 7.20 in the morning and I am waiting for the team of gardeners to turn up for the day. Many of the original tools used more than 100 years ago still hang on the walls and racks that surround me. Copies of old seed catalogues and planting diaries dating back to this period are filed in the drawers behind me for posterity. The shelves by my head are stacked with terracotta pots, placed in order of size, ready for the gardeners to sow into, and the original soil sieves sit out on the potting bench. Stepping into the office each morning is a sensory overload as the evocative musty smell of compost and damp crocks mingles with whatever plants are flowering in the window display of the potting shed. Today there are hyacinths and miniature narcissus perfuming the fresh, cool air. A shard of light from the early spring sunshine is thrown across the tiled floor from from the door, which has been left ajar. I feel a cool breeze on my face and I catch a sweet-smelling waft of Christmas box (*Sarcococca humilis*), flowering just outside the door.

On the face of it, very little has changed in the world of gardening over the last few centuries. I can imagine that a past head gardener would have walked into this very office 100 years ago, sat down in the same chair and written up a list of jobs for the day almost identical to the one I wrote earlier. They would have looked out of the window at a scene very similar to the one I see today. He

Far left Sellick, the Head Gardener at Saltram, Devon, in 1895 stands in front of his hydrangeas.
Left The author at the desk in the Head Gardener's office at Polesden Lacey, Surrey.

too would have seen the frame yard where vegetables are being forced on under glass for taking up to the house for guests to enjoy. The main difference today is that the guests are not part of the aristocracy, but National Trust visitors and members who have come to enjoy and be inspired by the gardens.

Of course there have been many changes in the world of gardening, such as the mechanisation of equipment and the development of disease-resistant plants and varieties with better fruiting or flowering qualities. Accepted standards on the best techniques of how to plant and prune have also changed substantially, as have methods of propagation and the feeding of plants. National Trust gardeners have always been at the forefront of the latest gardening practices, and the gardens they look after have thrived from it.

However, despite these technical advances, there is a gradual change which in some cases is almost bringing us full circle, back to the heyday of the great British gardens and landscapes. Driven by a desire for long-term sustainability, gardeners are rediscovering the rustic skills of their forefathers and reviving many lost gardening techniques. Petrol-driven strimmers are being traded in for scythes, and rotavators swapped for spades. Modern gardeners now prefer to use homemade comfrey or nettle tea rather than artificial fertilisers and to adapt green methods for managing pests and diseases rather than reaching for a chemical treatment. Wildflower meadows are once again flourishing and a richer biodiversity of the planet is something to be enjoyed and celebrated rather than looked on with suspicion. Fuel-guzzling garden mowers are being switched off while we enjoy longer grass instead of perfectly manicured lawns. Suddenly gardeners are once again in love with nature and no longer at war with it.

Awareness of the environment and the importance of the conservation of places of historic significance is the key driver to these changes. A long-term vision of a sustainable future is the core principle to a greener world. Minimal intervention and working with nature as opposed to working against it is now very much the principle underpinning the work of contemporary gardeners.

The biggest growth area in modern gardening is without doubt the revival in growing your own food. Not since the Dig for Victory war campaigns has there been such a wish to reconnect with the soil and produce homegrown food like our ancestors would have done on the allotments or in their gardens. In twenty-first-century gardens the desire to reconnect with other like-minded gardeners is evident as more community kitchen gardens appear on National Trust land than ever before.

Sustainability and supporting a rich biodiversity

The symbol of the National Trust is the oak leaf, probably the most majestic and magnificent plant species in the country. Its mighty trunk supports weighty boughs that stretch out in all directions, almost defying the laws of gravity. Whether it is standing alone in open landscape or in a mixed woodland, it stands head and shoulders above other trees and plants. It epitomises strength, standing upright and proud, ready to face any adversity. Chances are it will still be standing there still in hundreds of years. Over the centuries it will see the landscape around it evolve and will adapt to it. From its lofty heights it will witness gardening styles and fashions change around its mighty girth. It will support a rich biodiversity teeming with wildlife, supporting a rich community, whether it is birds nesting in the trees, insects living among the bark or toadstools living on the roots. And when it finally dies, it will have produced thousands of acorns which will have grown into trees for future generations to enjoy.

The National Trust is a conservation charity looking after one of the greatest collections of historic gardens and cultivated plant collections in the world. The oak tree is an apt symbol for the National Trust, which also supports a rich and diverse society, teeming with a wide range of people from all walks of life – more than 4 million garden-visiting members, 1,000 modern and historic gardens, more professional gardeners than any other conservation charity in the country and thousands of garden volunteers.

Learning from our past

The gardens cared for by the National Trust stretch back more than 400 years. The charity was originally formed in 1895 and was the vision of three environmental pioneers, Octavia Hill, Sir Robert Hunter and Canon Hardwicke Rawnsley, with the intention of preserving the green spaces that were being encroached upon by the late-Victorian urban sprawl. The National Trust is now custodian to some of the most important landscapes and historic gardens in the country. Gardens such as Hidcote, Sissinghurst, Stourhead, and Bodnant are some of the most beautiful gardens not just in the UK but worldwide, with some of the most impressive plant collections and demonstrations of horticultural excellence.

The thousands of historic gardens cared for by the Trust reflect fashions, styles and social changes throughout the last few centuries. They support a diverse range of plants, as well as the wildlife that depend on them. These historic gardens are an important slice of social history, for their creators include Capability Brown, Gertrude Jekyll, Humphrey Repton, Vita Sackville-West

and Graham Stuart Thomas – a list which reads like a Who's Who of the world's most influential gardeners. They probably never imagined the enduring influence they have had on gardening in the twenty-first century.

This book describes many of the gardening techniques used by the modern National Trust gardeners within their historic landscapes, and there are tips from some of these experts on how to garden for a sustainable and greener future. The book takes you on a typical horticultural journey from the preliminary assessment of your site through to considering various design principles, followed by chapters on how to keep your garden looking good throughout the year. There are also inspirational photographs from National Trust gardens. Although most of us do not have the vast spaces of some of these gardens, there are always elements that can give you something to replicate on a smaller scale in your own garden.

Basics The first chapter introduces you to the main elements that are needed to develop a garden. It looks at the importance of aspect, climate and soil. This knowledge is the bedrock for creating a sustainable living space.

Design Once the basics have been mastered the creative fun can begin. Designing a garden is about functionality and practicality but also about putting your individual creative stamp on it. If you are short of inspiration there are plenty of National Trust gardens, ranging from eighteenth century landscapes to modern chic urban spaces. In this chapter you will find a plant-picker section to help you choose amazing plants that will look great in your garden.

Lawns Most people have a love/hate relationship with lawns, which are a prominent feature in most gardens. They are great for playing and picnicking and useful in design for linking various other elements of the garden together, but are considered by many to be hard work and not environmentally friendly. This chapter looks at how to create and maintain a lawn, and suggests other alternatives.

Planting techniques Methods used for planting have changed over the last few years, as have the techniques for staking trees and even the types of pots that plants are sold in. This chapter explains how to ensure that you give your plants the best possible chance of survival once they are delivered to your doorstep or brought back from the garden centre.

Pruning There are many different reasons for pruning, including plant health, shaping a topiary bush or just encouraging a plant to produce more flowers. Whatever your reasons, with a few extra tips such as what tools to use, and the best time of year to make your cuts, this chapter explains how to get the best results.

Propagation You do not need to spend a fortune on buying large established plants – in fact you can often stock your entire garden with plants for free if you are willing to be patient and collect seeds or cuttings from friends' gardens. There is nothing more magical than growing your own

Far left The June borders at Nymans, West Sussex.
Above, left Thinning apple trusses at Westbury Court Garden, Gloucestershire.
Below, left A reminder of traditional gardening methods used at Godolphin House, Cornwall.

plants and this chapter will provide you with some tips and suggestions to make the best of nature's free resources.

Maintenance Once you have created your outdoor space you will need to know how to maintain it and how to keep it healthy. This chapter explains some of the methods needed to keep it looking good all year round. It includes advice on staking, deadheading and the importance of staying on top of weeds.

Grow your own The desire for sustainable living, reducing air miles and the life-affirming pleasures of harvesting and eating your own food have brought huge popularity to the art of growing your own vegetables and fruit. This chapter explains how you can get your own slice of the good life.

Greener gardening Environmental concerns have made sustainable gardening the mantra for gardeners at the National Trust. This chapter explains the importance of gardening with an eye to the future and ensuring that our wildlife as well as our plants are here for future generations to enjoy.

Conservation and inspiration: looking to the future

Sustainability is not just about the way we physically garden. It is also about ensuring that there is a future generation that can use tried and tested methods to continue maintaining and creating gardens and open spaces for the public to enjoy. Without the skills of gardeners our horticultural, heritage and plant collections will be lost forever. The National Trust plays a key role with its programme of events for the public to attend and of course with publications such as magazines and even this book. They have the largest collection of gardens and the biggest team of gardeners in the UK, spread right across the country.

Gardening must be one of the most satisfying careers available. Playing a part in greening the landscape and making it look colourful and beautiful fills many hearts with happiness and joy. It involves ensuring there is an abundance of plants which will provide the breathing lungs for the planet. Playing a part in maintaining the fresh air we breathe is no small undertaking for a school-leaver deciding on a career choice. It is hoped that National Trust gardens inspire some of our young visitors to become gardeners and form an affinity with plants and nature that should provide a lifetime of satisfaction. For those wanting tasters in the outdoor world, the National Trust provides opportunities with academies, internships and work experience. These experiences can inspire the younger generation to become gardeners and therefore custodians of future outdoor spaces.

For people at a later stage in their career, or who have come to the end of it, there are opportunities to volunteer. Without their time and effort, the exceptional standards of the gardens could not be maintained. The National Trust have thousands of gardener volunteers. At Polesden Lacey alone there are more than 130 garden volunteers, without whom the gardens could not be enjoyed by more than 300,000 visitors each year.

Like the symbolic oak tree, hopefully there are thousands of acorns that the National Trust has sown, to help sustain a greener future and continue with the vision that Octavia Hill had when she first co-founded the National Trust. And it was she who wrote, 'The need of quiet, the need of air, and I believe the sight of sky and of things growing, seem human needs, common to all men.'

Left A bright collection of flowers in the border at Powis Castle, Powys, in July.

garden basics

Above, left
Foxgloves growing at Monk's House, East Sussex. Formerly home to Virginia Woolf and her husband Leonard, it is said to have been a huge source of inspiration for the author. **Above, right** A mix of shade-loving herbaceous plants and shrubs at Woolbeding Gardens, West Sussex.

Right plant, right place

Unlike humans, plants tend to enjoy relatively uncomplicated lives, with just a few basic requirements such as light, water and nutrients. However, like humans they are fussy about where they live and if planted in the wrong place among surroundings they don't like they have a tendency to sulk. In plant terms, that means they stop developing. Many plants are destined for failure in the garden from the minute they are taken away from the garden centre. Very often, that inspirational, colourful plant that looked so healthy when it was bought is wilted, brown and struggling to survive within just a few weeks.

One of the key reasons for such a poor success rate is placing the plant in the wrong site. Many are adapted to specific climates or soils and understanding the plants' requirements is vital for a sustainable garden. Many garden centres these days have information on the labels advising on the 'hardiness' or 'zone' that is suitable for the specific plant. This is very useful information, but it's only part of the story; within every garden there are microclimates and these are the determining factors as to whether a plant will survive or not.

Most of us understand the macroclimate of our country. As a very rough rule of thumb, if you live in the north of the UK the climate is colder and even slightly tender plants will struggle to survive. In the south, although the climate is still not balmy, a few sub-tropical plants may survive in a very sheltered site, but tender plants certainly won't without protection from a greenhouse or conservatory.

However, there are many anomalies. For example, there are some very mild places on the west coast of Scotland where sub-tropical plants survive, partly due to the warm air of the Gulf Stream. My allotment on the North Downs in south-east England sits in a valley in a frost pocket and during some winters the temperature has plummeted as low as –12°C (10°F), when some of the toughest vegetables struggle to overwinter.

Identifying the microclimates

It is understanding the microclimates and subtle nuances of your own garden that is the real secret to the survival of your plants. Knowing where the frost pockets are, where the shade is at midday and which areas of the garden are a real sun trap is key. Look for dry shade under tree canopies and damp sections in the flower border. Once these areas have been discovered, your understanding of what plant will grow where suddenly becomes a lot easier.

Thankfully, nature has a way of guiding you. Look at the existing plants in the garden, even if they're weeds, as these are great indicators of the growing conditions. Nettles are always found in the most fertile areas of the garden, while creeping buttercups or cowslips thrive in damp conditions. If there is moss on a wall or fence, that is a sure sign that it is facing north or permanently shaded.

The best way to discover the light in the garden is simply to spend time there and observe where the sun reaches it at different times of the day. Note which walls and fences can be used to train sun-dwelling plants on and which are north-facing and cold. Remember that the sun is much lower in the winter and an area will not necessarily be bathed in sunshine all year long.

Aspect

- A south-facing garden will receive sunlight for most of the day – great for sun-dwelling plants, but will require the most amount of watering.
- A north-facing garden will receive very little light, particularly in winter.
- An east-facing garden receives the cooler early-morning sunlight.
- A west-facing garden will be bathed in light at the end of the day.

Above The south-facing border at Hardwick Hall, Derbyshire.

Wind

It doesn't take long for wind to decimate plants and shred foliage to pieces. Large trees can be brought down by strong winds, particularly evergreens during winter when the winds are usually at their most powerful. Furthermore, the soil can rapidly dry out if constantly exposed to the elements.

The easiest method of avoiding problems is of course to plant wind-tolerant species, such as shrubs from coastal areas that are adapted to being battered by the wind or low-growing plants that hug the ground for shelter. Avoid shallow-rooted plants such as beech trees and ones with ornamental leaves that will rapidly shred, such as acers.

Another way to reduce damage is to create windbreaks. The best are those that allow the wind to filter through them, since solid structures tend to force the wind over the top, generating more speed as it drops into the garden. For this reason, walls aren't always the best option. Trees and particularly hedges are ideal as their natural structure gently funnels the wind through, slowing its force down, yet still enabling it to gently circulate around the garden. A moderate amount of air movement is important as this reduces pest and disease problems. Trellis is also suitable, again because it allows the force of the wind to slowly dissipate.

Above Yew tree hedging provides shelter from the wind at Nymans. **Opposite, above** The north-facing border in the West Court at Hardwick Hall. **Opposite, below left and right** Many hardy winter plants can be found on the Winter Walk at Anglesey Abbey, Cambridgeshire.

Directions of the sun
Consider the movement of the sun
around these features:
• Shady wall
• North-facing slope
• Front garden
• Frost pocket at end of slope
• Water where it will be warmer
• South-facing walls
• Hedges for wind breaks
• Pond where it is warmer
• Near house – more sheltered if
  at top of slope, but frost trap if
  house at bottom.

Frost

Many garden plants are vulnerable to frost damage, which causes the moisture inside the plant cells to rupture. This results in blackened foliage and flowers, or, in the case of bedding and tender plants, death. An early frost can damage fruit crops such as the blossom on pears and peaches or the emerging shoots on grape vines. Vegetable seedlings can also be damaged or killed by frost in spring, or finish prematurely in autumn with the arrival of an early drop in temperature. The emerging buds of early-flowering plants such as camellias can be damaged after a frosty night if the sunlight hits them first thing in the morning, so it is often advisable not to site these plants in an east aspect.

Check the garden for frost pockets. These are often at the bottom of a slope, particularly where there is a impenetrable barrier such as a wall or fence, as the cold air will remain there. Trees can often filter the cold wind and offer some protection from the cold, and the temperature is often warmer closer to water such as ponds, lakes and particularly the sea. The altitude of the garden will also drastically affect the temperatures at which those plants can grow. As a rule of thumb, for every 300m (985ft) in height there is a drop in temperature of approximately ½°C (1°F).

Gardening with the environment

Ideas are changing within the gardening world, and most people now consider sustainability when they want to create and enrich their outside space. In the past, for example, if someone wanted a rockery, limestone would have been extracted from Cumbria or Yorkshire and driven down the motorway, or if a small rhododendron copse in a back yard was required then trailer loads of peat extracted from the peat bogs would be imported, along with ericaceous compost to create the right environment for acidic soil-loving plants.

This happens less often now as we have a much better understanding of the environmental consequences of our actions when materials are shipped from around the world and minerals, rocks and peat are extracted from the finite resources available. With such a wide choice of plants now available, people are tending to buy plants that suit the existing environment rather than import an environment that suits their plants. If you have a boggy area in the garden, for example, rather than try to conquer it, maximise it and buy bog plants that will look amazing when in flower. Building boardwalks through it will give an attractive effect and allow you see the plants from close quarters.

Work with the contours of the garden, too. If you have a slope, it isn't always necessary to import tonnes of soil to level the ground and put in concrete to support the retaining walls. Instead, use it to your advantage by creating areas of interest and attractive curving paths.

There are no hard and fast rules, however. While it is not ideal to chop down mature trees to make flower-beds, sometimes removing a dense tree planting will let in light and encourage more flowers to flourish. Dispensing with overgrown conifer hedges such as leylandii is usually advantageous as they tend not to sustain much wildlife, and a different species will be more beneficial and look more attractive in the garden. Generally, though, it is possible to work around the garden trees and hedges, make features of them and have a beautiful outdoor space to enjoy.

If the garden has impoverished soil there are plenty of plants that can be grown there, including herbs, prairie plants and wildflower meadows. Many trees and shrubs are as tough as old boots, some of them accustomed to growing in very scanty soil in the wild. You only need to look out of a train window as you travel through both rural and semi-urban landscapes to witness how trees and shrubs reclaim the land without the use of compost and fertilisers.

Of course, there will always be a desire to tweak a garden – after all, that is what gardening is about. We shall always want to add a patio, buy exciting plants, create a pond or build a pergola for sitting under, and grow vegetables, roses, fruit, or sub-tropical plants that mean the soil must be improved with organic matter. Yet it is usually better for the environment if the integrity of the garden and its soil and composition remains, so go with the flow, try not to fight nature too much and embrace the natural resources of the garden.

Above, left Water-loving plants, including *Darmera peltata* and candelabra primulas, thrive by the stream at Coleton Fishacre, Devon. **Above, right** A curved path lined with box hedging draws the eye through the Herb Garden at Buckland Abbey, Devon.

Below The wild flowers at Polesden Lacey, such as this white achillea and the dark blue cornflowers, create a stunning colour contrast.

Understanding the soil

Apart from the weather, the other major consideration for the gardener is the type of soil. This is defined by the percentage of clay, sand and silt that the soil is composed of. If it has a good balance of these ingredients it is referred to as 'loam'.

Clay soil

The type that gardeners like least when it comes to digging, clay soil is usually very heavy and sticky, making it back-breaking to work with. Its fine particles retain moisture, causing waterlogging and and sticky clumps on gardeners' boots and tools. It is usually advisable not to work on any soil in wet weather because it destroys the structure, but this is particularly the case with clay. It also tends to bake hard and even crack in dry weather. Adding organic matter will improve and enrich the soil, bringing additional fertility and improving drainage, as well as making it easier to dig and work with.

Sandy soil

In gardens with sandy soil, digging can be as easy as on a sandy beach. The difficulty is that the large particles in the soil (the largest of which are 1,000 times bigger than clay soil) do not retain any moisture at all and are low in fertility and nutrients. Sandy soil may also be unstable, which means that the ground surface could shift beneath patios and lawns.

Silt soil

With larger particles than clay soil, silt soil drains far better, yet it does have good water retention. It is more fertile than sand so in many ways is the happy medium between the two other soil types.

How to tell what soil you have

Clay soil rolls into a ball and feels sticky in your hand. It retains its shape when rolled into a long thin cylinder.

Sandy soil does not mould into any shape at all and feels gritty to the touch.

Silty soil moulds into a ball, but when rolled thinly starts to crumble.

Tip

'We put pine needles on beds to bring on acid-loving specimens as well as to keep our hydrangeas bluer. We manure other hydrangeas heavily to get pink.'
Simon Walker, Head Gardener at Emmets Garden, Kent

Right Pink hydrangeas in a walled garden at Gunby Hall, Lincolnshire.

Where a soil is predominantly clay or sand you can improve it if necessary by adding organic matter such as garden compost or well-rotted manure. This helps to improve the soil structure, improving drainage in clay soils and slowing it down in sand. However, there are plenty of plants that tolerate these conditions (see pages 24-27), so you do not necessarily have to change the soil type.

Checking the depth of the soil

Knowing the type of soil is important, but it is useful to discover the depth of it, too. There are usually two layers: the topsoil and the subsoil. The topsoil is the looser material on, or closest to the surface. It is usually higher in organic matter than the soil below, which is referred to as subsoil. Subsoil is more compacted, making it harder for plants to grow. Ideally the topsoil should be about 30-60cm (12-24in) deep for perennial plants and shrubs to be able to really thrive and develop a decent root system, although many annuals and wild flowers will cope in just a few centimetres. The best way to find out the depth of the topsoil is to dig out an inspection pit, about 1m (3¼ft) across and 50cm (20in) deep. In a large garden, it is worth making holes in different areas. Have a look at how deep the topsoil is as this will guide you as to the quality and potential of your garden. Leave the hole overnight when no rain is forecast and inspect it in the morning. The height of the water in the hole will inform you as to how high the water table is in your soil, although do remember this will vary at different times of the year, with late winter being the highest point, and early autumn being the lowest. This will indicate a high water table and therefore a moist soil, which will inform your choice of plants.

The pH of the soil

The acidity or alkalinity of the soil also dictates which plants will grow successfully. This is described by the pH number of the soil: a pH of 7.0 is neutral, with pH numbers below that indicating acidity. Above 7.0, the soil is alkaline.

The easiest way to find out what type of pH you have in the garden is to look at your neighbours' plots or the surrounding landscape, as the soil type will usually be the same. For example, if there are plenty of rhododendrons, bilberries, heathers or pine trees in the wild, and camellias, magnolias and acers in the gardens, the chances are that the soil is predominantly acidic. If those plants are not present, and instead there are plants such as lilacs, *Choisya* species and irises, the soil is probably alkaline.

A more accurate method of finding the pH of your soil is to buy a soil testing kit from your local garden centre or online. They are inexpensive and simple to use – just follow the instructions on the packet.

Ideally, you should grow plants suited to the soil. Although it is possible to grow acid-loving plants such as blueberries and cranberries in neutral soil by adding plenty of acidic activators such as sulphur chips and rotted pine needles, it is not a particularly sustainable method of gardening. In addition, the soil will need regularly topping up each year. An alternative is to grow acid-loving plants in containers or raised beds with acidic compost or soil improvers of some type.

Above You can tell what type of soil you have by moulding it in your hand.

Case study: Working with the environment at Polesden Lacey

Once you have established what soil type you have in your garden, you can set about choosing the plants best suited to the environment.

Polesden Lacey has a 12ha (30 acre) garden perched on top of a hill on the North Downs in Surrey. The soil is almost solid chalk and in some areas of the garden it is virtually impossible to dig without using a pickaxe to break through the ground. In the Edwardian period, tonnes of soil and compost were imported to create areas such as the rose garden, the kitchen garden and the 150m (492ft) herbaceous border.

In a bid to garden more sustainably yet maintain the high horticultural standards expected of a National Trust property, the current garden team carefully select plants that will thrive in extreme chalky conditions, avoiding those that require imports such as fertilisers, soil improvers and of course the impact of delivering them to the site. The result is a garden that still looks glorious and opulent, but is much more in tune with its environment on top of a chalky hill.

One anomaly in the garden is a 1.2ha (3 acre) area of woodland on the east side of the house, where the soil is lighter and wild rhododendrons thrive. The soil was tested and found to be slightly acidic. As the garden team were keen to expand the diversity of the plants at Polesden Lacey and develop the horticultural experience for the visitors, this was really exciting as it meant a much wider range of plants could be grown in this area. Many beautiful woodland trees and shrubs enjoy this soil, so it has been planted up with species for autumn colour that include a collection of acers, sorbus, stewartias, ornamental birches and cherries and many more. Spring-flowering shrubs such as camellias and a large collection of magnolias have also been added to the collection.

By working with the natural elements and soil conditions, the team have created a horticultural paradise that will hopefully be enjoyed by visitors for hundreds of years.

Left *Verbena bonariensis* is among the wide variety of plants grown in the garden at Polesden Lacey.

Tales from the Potting Shed

Soil biology by Ed Ikin, General Manager at Morden Hall Park and Rainham Hall and former Head Gardener at Nymans

Could your garden actually look after itself? This is an appealing thought for many gardeners and the answer is yes, for a biologically active 'wild soil' suppresses disease, makes its own fertiliser and enables plants to take up water more easily.

It is all down to an interlinked foodweb of microscopic soil-dwellers: bacteria, fungi, beneficial nematodes and protozoa. Bacteria break minerals down to release fertiliser in 'useful' ionic form and are kept in check by 'grazing' protozoa. The mycelia tendrils of fungi associate with plant roots to increase their effective surface area and exert antagonistic influence over undesirable disease. If you have always believed that a garden is in regular need of input to thrive, this knowledge may inspire you to try a different approach where you replicate the biological harmony found in a wild soil.

The most fundamental difference between wild and garden soils is disturbance. Our desire to work the soil, exposing it for frost and wind to 'break it down', is an ingrained tradition we should challenge more often as it degenerates desirable microbes. Sowing a green manure to cover the soil during winter could be a simple step towards a better soil foodweb, as could a move from annual bedding (with associate soil disturbance) to perennial designs.

Herbicides and inorganic fertilisers both contain salts, the enemy of desirable soil microbes, and reducing their use or embracing organic methods will encourage a healthy soil flora to build. Finally, there is no finer ally for a garden soil than organic matter. Mulching twice a year and incorporating composted manure when planting or cultivating makes the soil a more welcoming environment for desirable biology to thrive.

Plants to suit your soil

It is worth noting that some of these plants are listed because they are capable of tolerating extreme conditions while many will cope with either sand or clay if their soil is improved with the addition of horticultural grit, garden compost or well-rotted horse manure. (ac = acidic, al = alkaline, n = neutral)

Plants for clay and silt soil

Acer (Japanese maple) Tree ac/n
Aconitum Perennial ac/al/n
Aster novi-belgii Perennial
Astilbe Perennial
Astrantia Perennial
Berberis Shrub
Calamagrostis Perennial
Camellia Shrub
Carex elata Perennial
Deschampsia Perennial
Digitalis (foxglove) Perennial
Filipendula Perennial
Hosta Perennial
Hyacinthoides (bluebell) Perennial
Hydrangea Shrub
Laburnum Tree
Magnolia Tree
Mahonia Shrub
Malus Tree
Ophiopogon Perennial
Paeonia (peony) Perennial
Pyracantha Shrub
Rodgersia Perennial
Rosa Shrub
Rudbeckia Perennial
Sambucus Shrub
Solidago Perennial
Syringa (lilac) Shrub
Vitis (grape vine) Shrub
Weigela Shrub

Astilbe This moisture-loving herbaceous perennial produces fluffy plumes of flowers in summer.

Rodgersia Stunning herbaceous perennial suitable for damp soil, bearing creamy-white or pink flower panicles.

Peony A popular, brightly coloured, perennial producing large, showy flowers. It will tolerate a heavy soil.

Acer palmatum (Japanese maple) This tree is grown for its attractive foliage and autumn colour.

Mahonia An impressive foliage shrub producing attractive flower spikes during winter.

Magnolia This tree produces creamy-white or pink flowers. There are both evergreen and deciduous species.

Rudbeckia Also known as 'Black-Eyed Susan', they can be an annual, biennial or herbaceous perennial.

Aconitum This herbaceous biennial or perennial plant produces purple flowers. All parts of the plant are toxic.

Filipendula Commony known as 'Meadow Sweet', this is a damp-loving perennial with sprays of white flowers.

Hosta Popular foliage plant suitable for shady areas of the garden. Produces long flower spikes in the summer.

Pyracantha A vigorous, spiky evergreen shrub that is ideal for screening and winter interest.

Elder This small tree produces showy white flowers in spring and dark berries in winter.

Hydrangea This shrub produces ornate pink or blue flowers in late summer and often holds them well into winter.

Crab apple A tree that produces white-pink blossom in spring and small fruit in autumn, ideal for making jam.

Lilac A distintive, fragrant flowering shrub that is also suitable for limey, chalk soils.

Plants for sandy soil

Acacia dealbata (mimosa) Tree
Achillea Perennial
Allium Perennial
Anthemis tinctoria Perennial
Buddleja Shrub
Cotoneaster Shrub
Dianthus Perennial
Echinops Perennial
Erica carnea (heather) Shrub
Eryngium Perennial
Eucalyptus Tree
Festuca glauca Perennial
Hamamelis (witch hazel) Tree
Helianthemum Shrub
Gaillardia Perennial
Iris Perennial
Juniperus Tree
Kniphophia Perennial
Lavandula (lavender) Shrub
Oenothera Perennial
Osteospermum Perennial
Perovskia Shrub
Pieris Shrub
Pinus (pine) Tree
Papaver orientale (poppy) Perennial
Rhododendron Shrub
Rosmarinus (rosemary) Shrub
Salvia officinalis (sage) Perennial
Salvia microphylla Perennial
Sedum Perennial
Stipa Perennial
Thymus (thyme) Perennial
Verbascum Perennial/biennial

Achillea A herbaceous perennial popular in borders, with a fern-like foliage and tall flower heads.

Allium Related to the onion, this bulb produces large purple or blue flower balls and is great for borders.

Cotoneaster There are many different types with varying growth habits, but most of these shrubs produce berries.

Erica Carnea A low-growing evergreen shrub typical of acidic heathlands. Some varieties produce winter colour.

Eucalyptus These trees grow quickly and their ornamental trunks make an attractive addition to a large garden.

Witch hazel Ideal for producing a splash of colour in the garden during the winter months.

Gaiilardia A herbaceous perennial producing large, daisy-like, fiery blooms well into autumn.

Kniphophia Also known as 'Red Hot Pokers', these herbaceous perennials flower in the summer months.

Lavender A small-growing shrub with evergreen foliage and scented blue flower spikes in summer.

Osteospermum This low growing herbaceous perennial is ideal at the front of a sunny-coloured border.

Perovskia Commonly known as 'Russian Sage', this shrub produces purple-blue flowers on white stems.

Poppy Often spotted in wildflower meadows and very easy to grow, they thrive in well-drained, sandy soil.

Rhododendron A classic shrub that thrives in acidic soils, grown for its showy flowers in spring.

Salvia There are a few different species of salvia, the most common being the culinary herb, sage.

Stipa This ornamental perennial grass is ideal for low-maintenance, prairie-style planting.

designing your garden

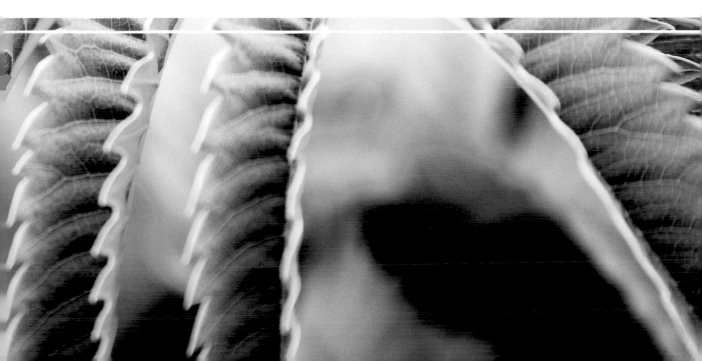

'We all need space; unless we have it we cannot reach that sense of quiet in which whispers of better things come to us gently.'
Octavia Hill, co-founder of the National Trust, in *Homes of the London Poor* (**1883**)

Once you have mastered the basics of gardening, the fun can begin. Designing your garden is an opportunity to get your creative juices flowing. It is where you can express yourself, let your imagination run riot and put your personal stamp on your outside space. Creating a garden takes you on an exciting journey as you create your own visual masterpiece that takes place just outside your back door.

To most gardeners, the outside space is all about the plants. To designers, it is the question of the overall feel of the garden and how the different elements fit together. Then there are the other mundane, practical but nevertheless important considerations too, such as areas for seating, dining al fresco and for kids to play in, and of course the working parts of the garden – compost heaps, sheds, paths, greenhouses, places to keep bikes and so on.

It's becoming a bit of a cliché, but many people consider the garden to be an outside room, making the design of it just as important as in the rooms indoors. In the warmth of summer, it will indeed be the most popular living space in the house. If you're lucky enough to have a large garden, then it can be designed as a series of outdoor rooms, such as at Hidcote Manor Garden in Gloucestershire. Whether it is one space or several, it essentially has to flow well, be functional, and also be a beautiful and inspiring place to sit and relax in.

Above The White Garden at Sissinghurst Castle, Kent, in winter.

Working with what you have got

When you are designing your garden, bear in mind that it is much easier and more sustainable to work with the existing soil type and contours rather than importing materials and making drastic changes. There are gorgeous plants to suit every type of soil and aspect, and beautiful designs to fit into any garden no matter what shape or size. Of course you will need and want to buy some plants and materials, but working with what you already have will minimise your environmental impact and, of course, the amount of money you spend.

Above, left Nepeta, astrantia and iris grow in the Old Garden at Hidcote. **Above, right** The Ornamental Vegetable Garden at Osterley Park and House, Middlesex. **Below** The White Garden at Hidcote in June. Yew hedging and box topiary provide year-round interest.

Working with the landscape

Even if your garden is largely a bog, it can still be transformed into a horticultural haven. Boardwalks or decking from recycled timber can be used to make seating areas or walkways above the damp conditions. There are impressive architectural plants such as *Gunnera manicata* with its huge foliage or *Rodgersia aesculifolia* with large palmate leaves like those of horse chestnut and plumes of white flower spikes. Other plants that love damp conditions include hostas, trilliums, astilbes and primulas.

Conversely, if the soil in your garden is sandy and completely devoid of nutrients there is no need to despair – there are thousands of plants that will thrive in dry, infertile soil including many wildflower species. Many famous gardens have turned barren soil and lack of rain into an advantage. Felbrigg Hall in Norfolk, for example, has a nutrient-poor soil which is extremely free-draining, yet there is a wide range of plants that thrive in these conditions. They include Chusan palm (*Trachycarpus fortunei*), to add height and give a taste of the exotic, while gazanias, Californian poppies (*Eschscholzia californica*), argyranthemums and many other plants that love a dry spot thrive in this popular National Trust gravel garden.

Below Californian poppies thrive in dry soil and provide a lovely splash of colour to your garden.

Above, left Bold and architectural in form, the Chusan palm will grow in dry and nutrient-poor soil.
Above, right The Bog Garden at Great Chalfield Manor, Wiltshire, is an ideal site to grow lush greenery, such as hostas.

Getting started

Begin by assessing what you already have. Herbaceous plants may be worth digging up and dividing to produce more, while existing trees may make attractive features and focal points. Patios, decking and fences can sometimes be revamped by pressure-washing or painting; if they are in the wrong location, they can be removed and placed elsewhere. Tired-looking lawns can be revamped, reseeded and easily reshaped.

An entire garden can easily be made to look beautiful at no cost by simply recycling other people's 'rubbish'. Items such as patio slabs, bricks and timber can be found in skips or discarded on building sites (always ask permission, though). Old sinks and bathtubs make fantastic plant containers, with the plug holes providing drainage. Pallets can be made into a whole range of furniture and features in the garden, including decking, picket fencing, sheds, outdoor coffee tables and garden benches. They also make attractive wooden planters.

Ask your friends and neighbours if you may visit their gardens armed with a spade. Most herbaceous perennials benefit from being divided, so you can take a few clumps home with you to fill your garden without causing any damage or loss. Alternatively, take hardwood cuttings from their trees and shrubs.

If you have just moved into a new home, though, do not rush into the garden with your planting plans in one hand and a spade in the other. Instead, wait for a couple of seasons as you may be pleasantly surprised by the plants that are already present.

Self-seeders

The following self-seeders may already exist in your garden. If they are on your shopping list, cross them off, as these promiscuous plants usually spread themselves about everywhere, so you will save lots of money by letting them propagate themselves. All make beautiful plants, though their ability to self-seed is very climate-dependent, and what works well in one area of the country may not be so successful elsewhere.

Aquilegia vulgaris (columbine)
Alchemilla mollis (ladies' mantle)
Centranthus ruber (red valerian)
Chrysanthemum parthenium (feverfew)
Deschampsia cespitosa (tufted hairgrass)
Digitalis purpurea (foxglove)
Foeniculum vulgare 'Purpureum' (bronze fennel)
Galanthus spp. (snowdrops)
Helleborus foetidus (stinking hellebore)
Meconopsis cambrica (Welsh poppy)
Nicotiana sylvestris (tobacco plant)
Oenothera spp. (evening primrose)
Sisyrinchium striatum (pale yellow-eyed grass)
Stipa tenuissima (feather grass)
Verbena bonariensis

Columbine Pretty 'Granny's Bonnets' are one of the more welcome self-seeding plants.

Stinking hellebore This plant has green foliage and lime-green flowers and regualrly seeds under hedges.

Red valerian A classic opportunist, this plant will cast its seeds anywhere, even in small cracks in walls.

Feverfew This plant produces daisy-like flowers and aromatic foliage.

Snowdrops (above) A welcome self-seeder, bringing attractive white flowers to the winter garden.

Verbena bonariensis (below) An attractive self-seeder, it can be tricky to eradicate.

Tobacco plant Guaranteed to spread its seed in the garden, producing white or pink flowers.

Pale yellow-eyed grass This self-seeder produces attractive spires of white flowers.

Know your limits

The starting place for any garden is your boundary. This clearly defines the area into which your garden is going to be enclosed. If the current boundary structure needs to be replaced, for reasons of either disrepair or unsightliness, you have a choice of ways to mark out your patch, the most obvious being a fence.

Overlap panel fence

The most common type of fence is a traditional 1.8m (6ft) tall overlap panel fence, which is cheap, easy to erect and creates an instant screen. Panels are available in a range of different sizes and qualities, including half-size panels.

Split chestnut fencing

This type of fencing consists of vertical strips of chestnut with pointed ends, wired together and attached to sturdy round or square posts about every 1.5m (5ft). It is not particularly attractive as it stands, but it can be disguised and used in conjunction with evergreen hedges. It makes a great barrier for keeping dogs and livestock in or out and creates a safe area for children. A further benefit is that it can be used around tight curves and other tricky shapes.

Feather edge or closeboard fencing

Renowned for strength and versatility, this type of fence is more expensive than a standard fence panel but has a nicer finish. It is called feather edge because one side of the individual boards is thinner than the other. It can be constructed to fit into a gap of any size, as opposed to a panel fence which generally just comes in one length.

Woven hazel or willow fencing

This is one of the most appealing boundaries as it has a natural, rustic feel. There are various different patterns and styles, usually with a lifespan of five to six years.

Split post and rail

While this does not offer much privacy, it is ideal for defining boundaries where a view is to be retained, such as overlooking fields or a lake. It can be expensive but is usually made from hardwood which makes it very durable, and it is perfect for creating the impression of a rustic idyll. Chicken wire mesh can be secured to the lower section to keep small children or pets safely in the garden without losing the transparent effect.

Above A rustic post and rail fencing made from sweet chestnut. **Opposite, above left** Feather edge fencing. **Opposite, above right** Woven hazel fencing. **Opposite, below** A split post and rail fence at Nymans allows a view into the fields beyond.

The vernacular style: keeping it local

When considering the materials for your boundary, take into account the surrounding landscape and where possible use local materials from a sustainable source. For example, if there is a woodland coppice, woven hazel fencing would be ideal, or dry-stone wall boundaries would look great if there is natural stone nearby as they would blend into the surroundings. In urban locations, wrought iron fencing can look more appropriate and suit the specific period of the property. Look at neighbouring architecture for guidance as to the local style of the period.

Above The ha-ha is a feature often found in gardens designed by Lancelot 'Capability' Brown, such as Stowe Landscape Gardens in Buckinghamshire. **Opposite, above** Slate fencing, using local materials at Snowdownia, Wales.

Ha-has

The ultimate status symbol in the garden, a ha-ha is not commonly seen in private gardens, but the National Trust have many surrounding their stately homes. It is a classic design element in which a hidden ditch is created, usually retained by a wall, to keep livestock out of the garden. From the house the effect is of a seamless, flowing landscape incorporating the idyllic countryside with no physical barriers.

Walls

Whether it is made from brick or natural stone, nothing beats the feel of durability and security that a wall gives. Walls can range from low, knee-height boundary markers to huge 3.6m (12ft) structures such as those found enclosing traditional kitchen gardens attached to stately homes.

If you have an unsightly wall, disguise it with climbers. These take up hardly any space, making them ideal for small gardens. Austere walls can be transformed into lush green havens just by using a clever bit of 'climber staging' – using climbing plants will help or soften vertical or upright hard landscaping materials. Ivies are particularly effective climbers as they are fast-growing, evergreen and their foliage comes in a range of different colours.

Three top ivies to try

Hedera colchica 'Dentata Variegata' This ivy has large green leaves with an attractive creamy edging around the outside.

Hedera helix 'Goldheart' Add a beautiful, rich splash of colour to a wall with this variegated evergreen climber.

Hedera helix 'Midas Touch' An ivy with attractive red stems and small triangular or heart-shaped, golden-yellow leaves, this produces black berries in autumn.

Step-by-step: Making a woven fence

I created this low woven fence at Polesden Lacey to give definition to a small section of garden. The beauty of working with hazel rods is that they are flexible, so I could make a curvy, rustic fence with an appealing informality. This fits in well with the overall feel of this garden with its culinary and medicinal plants.

1. Bang sturdy upright hazel stakes into the ground at approximately 40cm (16in) intervals along the area of your fence.

3. Keep working your way up to the desired height. Use secateurs or loppers to trim off the excess lengths of hazel, keeping the edges looking neat.

2. Start to weave your hazel lengths between the uprights, making sure to alternate the side you start from each time.

Living on the edge

Planting climbers on a wall or fence will encourage wildlife to visit your garden. Berries will provide a source of food for many garden birds, while ivy is a fantastic source of late autumn nectar for honey bees when there is little else flowering.

Other options for disguising walls and fences include the impressive foliage of *Actinidia kolomikta*, climbing and rambling roses, or a climbing hydrangea such as *Hydrangea petiolaris*.

Hedges

A hedge is the natural solution to marking out your boundary, creating a living wall. Evergreen hedges such as yew and box will create permanent screens that can be clipped into formal shapes, or even elaborate topiary.

Mixed wildlife hedges are a good alternative, with a wide range of plants that will encourage greater biodiversity than a single-species hedge. Choose a combination of trees that provide berries, such as elderberry (*Sambucus nigra*), hawthorn (*Crataegus* spp. *monogyna*), *Viburnum opulus* and blackthorn (*Prunus spinosa*). Plants such as holly provide an evergreen habitat and berries too.

Deciduous hedges offer seasonal interest through the year. Beech and hornbeam have attractive foliage, form a dense hedge and turn a beautiful buttery colour in autumn, holding onto their leaves well into winter.

For quick-growing, flowering, seasonal hedges, try tall plants such as sunflowers (*Helianthus*), *Cosmos bipinnatus* 'Purity', *Nicotiana sylvestris* or *Verbena bonariensis* to give splashes of temporary colour. Structures such as bamboo or hazel canes with annual displays of sweet peas or runner beans make beautiful displays and also effective impermanent screens.

Left An archway made from yew makes for an attractive entrance to the Mulberry Garden at Bateman's, East Sussex. **Above** Fragrant sweetpeas grow on a cane wigwam at Avebury Manor, Wiltshire.

The inside view

Once the boundaries are in place, you can start to focus on what lies within the garden – but before you rush out there with a spade or set off to the garden centre, take some time to plan out what you really want. A more leisurely approach will result in a better garden and no money wasted on unsuitable plants.

Finding inspiration

To prompt some ideas of how you would like your own garden to be, compile a scrapbook with photographs you have taken of gardens you have visited, or images in magazines that have captured your imagination. Best of all, visit as many garden shows as you can to see how professional gardeners and designers have created magical, inspiring spaces. At the biggest shows, these may range from large show gardens for people with big budgets to much smaller courtyard and urban examples. It is always a delight to see these little oases of gardens and plants in such small areas.

Also, visit plenty of National Trust gardens. There are inspirational gardens all over the UK with just about every style of planting and landscaping imaginable. Although most of us do not have

Tip

'Think carefully about where you site plants. If it's an eye-catching plant, place it in a prominent spot; often a good plant ends up just getting lost among the general planting in a garden and people will walk right past it.'
Martyn Pepper, Assistant Head Gardener at Coleton Fishacre, Devon

Above The walled garden at Wordsworth House and Garden, Cumbria, with elegant alliums and foxgloves. **Opposite** Lush foliage helps to disguise the brick walls at Polesden Lacey.

such large outdoor spaces, there are always design elements or planting combinations that can provide plenty of food for thought, and can easily be translated into smaller spaces.

The practicalities

Necessary features such as pathways, compost and rubbish bins, a shed, a patio, a pond, a place for barbecues and a greenhouse may not be such fun to plan as the planting, but it is still important to think about how they may best be sited. Make a sketch of the shape of the garden, then list the practical elements that need to be incorporated. Add them to the sketch, noting the amount of space required. Once this has been done, the creative and magical elements of a garden such as plants, focal points and other features can be woven into the design.

Use a tape measure to mark out the size of the garden and then draw it on graph paper to help keep it to scale and ensure the proportions are correct. Alternatively, there are numerous software programs and apps that are useful tools for designing your outside space.

Once you have your design ready, start marking it out in the garden. Use string or sand to mark out where the flower-beds are going to go. Alternatively, if there is long grass currently there, the shapes of the distinct garden areas can be mown out. Stand back and check that you are happy with the shape and that the area feels balanced and in proportion. What looks good on paper often feels very different to the reality once you are outside, so the overall look may need a lot of tweaking before the actual physical transformation can take place.

The time-poor culture

Most of us seem to lead hectic lives these days, with less leisure time than ever before. When planning your garden, give careful consideration to how much time you can realistically spend looking after it. Some types of planting require much more maintenance than others, and you need to make sure your garden does not begin to represent stress as you look out on to tasks that badly need attention you cannot give.

Features to avoid if you are time-poor

Lawns Traditional lawns usually need cutting once a week during the height of the season.

Hedges While they are great for wildlife, hedges can grow quickly and will need cutting once the nesting season is over.

Containers Depending on the types of plants grown, they may need watering up to twice a day.

Bedding plants and annuals These can mean a lot of work as they need planting or sowing each year and regular watering.

Vegetables Growing your own food can be very time-consuming, requiring regular watering and sowing.

Fast-growing trees and shrubs The most obvious are leylandii and eucalyptus, but any rampant plants in the garden will need regular pruning to keep them under control.

Features to go for if you are time-poor

Wildflower meadows These will only need cutting once a year, in late summer, and provide a beautiful display of wild flowers.

Fences They do not need regular cutting like a hedge, and a sturdy fence should last a good few years.

Patios Easier to maintain than a lawn, patios also provide a good solid area for sitting or walking on.

Herbs and Mediterranean plants Most herbs and silver-leaved plants are drought-tolerant, which will reduce the amount of watering required.

Succulents These are usually slow-growing and require minimal watering as they retain water in their fleshy foliage.

Slow-growing trees and shrubs Plants such as yew and box require less pruning and maintenance than more vigorous species.

Prostrate plants Plants with creeping, low-growing habits will cover the ground and reduce the need for frequent weeding.

Mulch Layer material such as gravel, slate or bark on the beds around shrubs as this will reduce the need for weeding and watering.

Left Wildflower meadows provide fantastic colour and fragrance, and require very little effort.
Opposite The curved path leading through the Winter Walk at Anglesey Abbey.

Paths

In terms of design, a garden without paths can seem to lack direction. This is particularly the case with large spaces, as paths help to divide and coordinate various sections of the garden. Smaller courtyard gardens do not necessarily need a path, but you may find one a useful feature in its own right, such as three stepping stones across a small lawn. There is of course a practical side to having a path in that you can reach areas of the garden such as the shed or bins without getting your shoes muddy.

Paths also entice you into the garden and take you along a journey on which the other elements of the garden can be enjoyed. A garden will seem much larger if the path zigzags or has a serpentine curve to it – not just when viewed from the house, but also because it extends the time taken to walk through it, enabling you to dwell among the plants for longer.

You can make your garden feel much bigger by creating a path that leads around a corner and out of sight, such as behind a hedge or trellis. This immediately tricks the mind into thinking that the space is larger than it really is, even if there is nothing behind the corner except a compost heap or a seating area. It also creates a sense of intrigue, enticing visitors to travel the full length of the garden, even if it is only a few metres long.

In a narrow garden, paths and straight lines crossing the lawn horizontally make the area seem a lot wider. One of the most famous examples is Vaux-le-Vicomte in France, where the great garden designer André le Nôtre (1613–1700) exaggerated the width of a very long garden by transecting

it with numerous paths running at right angles to the full length of the garden. He was a master illusionist and loved to play with perspective.

Types of paths

Grass While grass paths are one of the simplest options, they are among the most high maintenance as they need mowing and edging. They can be used formally, in straight lines, or informally to weave between flower-beds and through wildflower meadows.

Brick There are many different patterns that can be used to make brick paths, herringbone being one of the most popular. They can be expensive to lay, but provide an attractive, solid base to walk upon. Brick paths are very flexible in design, ranging from attractive rustic paths in kitchen gardens and potagers to formal walkways in grander gardens.

Woodchip This is great way of recycling material from your own garden if you have a wood chipper. Woodchip paths are easy to make and perfect for informal woodland gardens. They will need regularly topping up with fresh material once a year, and will benefit from wooden edging, such as re-used lengths of trunks or branches, or you could buy gravel boards to help prevent the wood-chip from spreading onto lawns.

Gravel If you like the crunch of gravel under your feet, this is the perfect material for you. It needs a membrane underneath to prevent it from working its way down into the soil below, but is a very, simple easy path to lay.

Concrete A very cheap, practical, hardwearing path, concrete may not seem exciting but you can mix in materials such as seashells or gravel to provide additional interesting textures.

Decking and boardwalks These wooden paths give an authentic feel to woodland areas or groves of sub-tropical plants and bamboos. Their disadvantage is that they can be slippery when wet.

Recycled material Materials such as crushed and washed glass or slate can give a contemporary feel to a garden and are environmentally friendly.

Paving and stone These create a hardwearing surface. Choose materials that fit in with the surrounding buildings, otherwise the path could look out of keeping.

Left, above A gravel path runs through the garden at Dunham Massey, Cheshire. **Left, below** The meadow grass at Nymans has been mown to create a pathway. **Opposite** The gardener Gertrude Jekyll and architect Edwin Lutyens collaborated on many projects to ensure there was a strong link between the hard landscape of the buildings and the materials and style of the garden. Lindisfarne Castle in Northumberland is a great example of Jekyll's striking garden design style.

Plants for screening

Unless you are unusually exhibitionist, one of the essential elements to enjoying your garden is a sense of privacy and seclusion. It should be a tranquil spot where your outside space can be enjoyed either on your own or with family and friends, away from the gaze of neighbours. Many gardens are overlooked, particularly in urban environments, but by carefully selecting a few choice plants, it is possible to screen them without impinging too much on either your light or that of your neighbours.

Right Beech foliage provides attractive coverage at Fountains Abbey, North Yorkshire.

Evergreen plants are usually the most effective as they will provide a screen all year round. However, some deciduous trees such as beech do retain their leaves well into winter, too. Copper beech makes a particularly attractive choice with its purple foliage.

Leyland cypress, *Cupressus × leylandii*, commonly referred to as leylandii, has received a lot of bad publicity on account of its rapid, vigorous growth that can quickly block out the light. Used appropriately in large gardens, it can be a useful, almost instant plant for screening, but think carefully before planting it. Also bear in mind that leylandii does not react well to hard pruning, particularly cutting into hard wood, so if you do need to prune it back hard, you may end up looking at a lot of unsightly bare wood.

Bamboos and grasses

As an alternative to trees and shrubs, bamboos and grasses can also make effective screens. They provide all-year-round, semi-permanent screening but tend to be less dense than most evergreens, so they allow more sunlight into the garden. They also add an element of movement, as many of them sway in the wind.

The grass *Miscanthus sinensis* is suitable for this purpose as it reaches heights of more than 2m (6½ft). The cultivars 'Silberspinne' and the slightly smaller 'Morning Light' are good choices as they both have narrow, arching leaves and produce attractive flowers in late summer and autumn

There are many bamboos available, but go for a clump-forming type as other forms can be very invasive and will quickly take over your garden. The best include *Chusquea montana* and *Fargesia murieliae*, which will reach more than 2m (6½ft). The beautiful black bamboo *Phyllostachys nigra* is also worth considering – while it is generally described as clump-forming, it may need its roots restricting by planting it in a large, non-perishable pot before sinking it into the ground.

As with any form of screening, try to choose plants that suit your garden style. Clumps of Asian bamboo as a backdrop could look slightly out of character in a traditional English cottage garden, for example. This not to say that styles cannot be mixed, but a clipped yew or privet hedge might look more appropriate in this type of garden.

Some fairly large evergreen plants to consider are:

Arbutus unedo (strawberry tree)	8m (26ft)
Eucalyptus gunnii	up to 25m (82ft)
Ligustrum lucidum (Chinese privet)	10m (33ft)
Magnolia grandiflora	15m (49ft)
Photinia x fraseri 'Red Robin'	5m (16ft)
Prunus laurocerasus 'Rotundifolia' (laurel)	5m (16ft)
Quercus ilex (evergreen oak)	25m (82oft)
Taxus baccata (yew)	15m (49ft)

Making the most of your space

Not many of us are lucky enough to have exactly the garden area we would like, but there are ways to improve the appearance of any plot. Garden designers have been creating illusions of space and grandeur with simple visual tricks for centuries. Here are just a few of them.

Let there be light

Ponds and lakes are perfect for reflecting and increasing the light in a garden, but if you don't have a water feature, then mirrors can be used to reflect light. It is particularly effective in small gardens and if they are strategically placed, they can also give the sense of doubling your actual outdoor space. Do be aware that birds may fly into mirrors, as they think it is part of the extended landscape and not realise it is a physical surface. To prevent them harming themselves, site mirrors behind trellises or low down near the ground, which should be out of their flight paths.

Framing views

If you are lucky enough to have a beautiful view from your garden, use it to your advantage. Creating holes in hedges or walls helps to frame the view and bring in the view from beyond. Create the hole at eye level so that the framed view feels natural. If it is an area where you sit, adjust the height of the hole accordingly. The hole can be as large as you like, and can be any shape, so long as it feels right to you, and gives the intended effect. If the hedge is deciduous then it is best to wait until winter to make the hole, as the tree will be denuded of leaves, and you will see where the cut should be made. Evergreen hedges are harder to get the hole in the right place because you

Below The parterre at Westbury Court Garden is an eye-catching feature. You could consider making your own, scaled-down version with box hedging and colourful herbs.

Above, left
These bright
tulips in a copper
planter draw
the eye through
the hedging at
Sissinghurst
Castle. **Above,
right** A hole in
the wall creates
a focal point at
Polesden Lacey.

are cutting 'blind'. It can be lined up with the potential framed view by pushing a long bamboo stick through the hedge, then checking on the other side to see where it is aligned to. If you are making a hole in an existing wall, rather than building a wall with an intentional hole design, seek advice from a structural engineer before starting to remove bricks or stones.

Focal points

Not every garden needs a focal point. It is possible to have a lovely space surrounded by your favourite plants and a wide variation of garden objects or even clutter. However, a focal point helps to give a garden a sense of direction, adding structural elements to the feel of the place. It draws the eye, creates intrigue and gives a purpose to an otherwise empty space.

A focal point can be more or less anything, but is usually a distinct object that stands out as a feature in the landscape. It often may catch the eye because of its colour, size or texture, or even because of its starkness or quirkiness. It may be a formal sundial, bird bath, statue or even a garden gnome, but can just as easily be a natural feature such as a beautiful tree or shrub. Even a lawn or flower-bed can be a focal point if it is distinguished in shape and colour from the surrounding landscape.

A focal point does not have to be there purely for aesthetic purposes – it can be practical too, for example a bench or other seating area, or even a compost stack. It is equivalent to interior design – a room can lack interest if there is no fireplace or painting, so place something in the garden that will give your eye something to rest on and offer a momentary extra pause of pleasure.

Using perspective

An avenue is a useful method of leading the eye and the direction of a walk through an open space. Most of us do not have enough space for an avenue, of course, but paths lined with repetitions of upright plants can have the same effect. To trick the eye and mind into thinking a distance is greater than it is in reality, use taller plants at the start of the row and smaller plants at the other end. Alternatively, make the path taper as it recedes, just as a road in the landscape appears to narrow as it reaches the horizon.

Create some height

Creating features in the garden that will direct the eye upwards instantly expands the visual experience. It extends the available area, allows colour and texture to be provided in an otherwise dead space and, most importantly, allows you to cram more plants into your garden. Boundary walls are an obvious place to site climbing plants, but there are other options too.

Pergolas and arches

Creating upright structures within the garden breaks up a flat horizontal space. Pergolas are ideal for casting some shade over a seating area, giving some respite from the midday sun and making al fresco dining much more comfortable. Available in kit form, they are easy to construct. Many climbers can be trained over the structure, but if you want to add a touch of the Mediterranean, grow a grapevine. The large ornamental leaves are perfect for creating some shade, while the bunches of grapes that form in late summer and autumn can be picked and made into delicious homemade wine.

Arches not only provide attractive uprights to walk through, they are also fantastic extra places to grow climbing and rambling plants. They encourage you to walk through from one space to another, helping to redefine different areas of the garden. Usually made from metal or wood, they are easily available from local garden centres or online.

Above The varied plant heights in the borders and hedging at Hinton Ampner, Hampshire, keep the garden visually interesting.
Opposite Roses trained over an archway at Mottisfont, Hampshire.

Step-by-step: Making a simple rustic arch

1. Drive two 2.4m (8ft) wooden stakes into the ground on each side of the pathway, ensuring that a length of at least 60cm (2ft) is below ground.
2. Cut about five flexible willow withies or hazel rods to a length of approximately double the width of the path.
3. Fasten them into a bundle and then tie them tightly to the post on one side using wire or garden twine. Arch them over the pathway and tie them to the post on the opposite side. There should be about 2.4m (8ft) head room from the centre of the path.
4. Finally, put in plants on each side of the path and train them up the archway. These could include apple trees trained as a single cordon – if you plant different varieties at each side of the arch they may naturally graft together when they reach the top, enabling the archway to be taken away. Rambling or climbing roses will smell beautiful every time you walk under the arch, or you might like to plant blackberries or hybrid berries such as boysenberries.

Right plant, right aspect

South-facing
Actinidia kolomikta
Solanum crispum
Rosa – climbers and ramblers
Vitis vinifera (grapevine)
Wisteria sinensis

North-facing
Akebia quinata (chocolate vine)
Hedera helix
Hydrangea petiolaris
Parthenocissus tricuspidata
Pileostegia viburnoides

West-facing
Campsis radicans
Jasminum officinalis
Lonicera tellmanniana
Passiflora (passion flower)

East-facing
Clematis montana
Hedera colchica
Jasminium nudifolium (winter jasmine)
Lonicera japonica
Parthenocissus quinquefolia (Virginia creeper)

Seasonal attractions
Very often, climbers will provide you with more than one season of interest. Plants such as Clematis 'Bill Mackenzie' have beautiful flower displays in summer as well as very impressive seedheads later in the year. Some climbing roses have very attractive rose hips, while the Japanese wineberry provides delicious red berries in late summer and also has a stunning display of red stems in winter. Many grape vines such as 'Brandt' and 'Purpurea' have attractive autumn foliage as well as fruit. Also consider golden hops (*Humulus lupulus* 'Aureus'), which have scented white flowers in summer and bright yellow foliage for most of the year.

Tip
If you have an old tree in your garden that is looking past its best, leave it for the wildlife to enjoy rather than cutting it down. Train a climbing plant such as the rampant rose 'Rambling Rector' up it to provide an extra layer of interest in your garden.

Rose – climbers and ramblers The quinessential cottage garden flower.

Wisteria Gives out an intoxicating scent from its long blue racemes of flowers in spring.

Chocolate vine A quirky climber with chocolate-coloured blooms that give off a vanilla fragrance.

Jasmine This plant produces pretty star-shaped flowers and gives off a wonderful fragrance, particularly in the twilight hours.

Virginia creeper This creeper creates a striking fiery autumn display.

Hydrangea A climber with attractive foliage and white flowers, useful for covering unsightly walls.

Passion flower This plant produces stunning flowers and, if in a warm situation, attractive fruits in autumn.

Colour tricks

Warm colours such as reds, oranges and yellows are full of vibrancy and energy. In a large garden they can feel warm, cosy and inviting, but be careful when using them in a small space as they can make it feel even smaller. As they are attention-grabbing, warm colours are also useful for diverting the eye from practical features such as sheds and compost heaps.

The cooler colours are blue, purple and green, which tend to merge into the background. They imbue a sense of tranquillity and are useful colours for making a small place feel bigger.

Colour can really play tricks with the mind, and good garden designers will use that to their advantage. If you want your garden to feel bigger or longer, for example, use soft pastel colours such as blue, mauve and white towards the back. Immediately those plants will seem further away than if you had used bright colours.

In a herbaceous border, this trick can be used by planting brightly coloured plants towards the start of the border and pastel-coloured plants further away. This gives the impression that the herbaceous border is much longer and more impressive than it really is.

Paul Farnell
Head Gardener at Waddesdon Manor, Buckinghamshire

'Waddesdon Manor is renowned for its seasonal bedding displays. The parterre alone can use up to 200,000 bedding plants annually. The beds are raised up in the high Victorian style to create maximum impact from the bedding displays.'

Opposite Some gardens rely on a simple palette of just one colour, with subtly different shades. The famous white garden at Sissinghurst, designed by Vita Sackville-West and Harold Nicholson in the 1890s, uses just shades of whites, silvers and greys to create a peaceful and enchanting atmosphere. **Left** Kniphofia, crocosmia and echinops bring vibrant colour to the garden at Killerton, Devon.

Colour and mood

It is amazing how colour can affect an atmosphere and in particular your mood. Blue is said to be a peaceful and relaxing colour but some research has shown that it can cause people prone to depression to feel low, hence the phrase 'feeling blue'. However, bright yellow colours are said to lift the mood, so by incorporating bright yellow in the composition the whole feel of a garden can be changed.

Combining colours

Deciding upon your colour combinations should be something instinctive that just feels right. The choice of colour is a very personal decision; there are no hard and fast rules. Basically, if it looks right to you, then it is right for you.

However, if you are unsure about your colours, use a colour wheel for guidance. Very simply, colours that sit opposite each other on the wheel usually make the biggest contrasts and the most impressive statements, so if you want to create a flamboyant and exuberant floral display, those are the one to go for. For example, in the herbaceous border at Polesden Lacey, yellow achillea 'Gold Plate' is next to the blue *Salvia* x *superba* is a classic plant combination by plantsman and designer Graham Stuart Thomas. In a similar way, a flint wall with orange-yellow narcissus and purple trailing aubretia works well, or a lavender garden with purple-blue lavender spirals, contrasting with a vibrant golden thyme in the centre.

Finally, when colours are next to each other on the colour wheel, they tend to create a harmonious atmosphere, for example blue with green or orange with red. Choice of colour is very personal but it is one of the most important decisions in the garden. It can reflect your mood, your personality and your personal taste, making the garden your own individual space that you can enjoy and relax in.

Below, left Yellow achillea and blue asters contrast in the herbaceous borders at Tredegar House.
Below, right Yellow achillea against a backdrop of deep red roses at Tintinhull Garden, Somerset.

Texture

Another integral element of garden design is texture, which is just as important as colour. Plants create a deeper field of vision, making a space feel less 'flat.' Leaves are the best providers of texture, ranging from the bold and coarse to the fine and delicate. Getting the right balance is important, as too many small flowers can look messy and lack focus, whereas too many of the bigger plants can be overwhelming. Experiment with a range of plants in different shapes and sizes.

Above In the east garden at Ham House, Surrey, box hedges, santolina and lavender provide textural contrast to the gravel paths

Above left The fernery at Greenway, Devon, includes bergenias and saxifrage, providing a tapestry of rich green foliage.

Plants for texture

• *Gunnera manicata* has huge, bold, rhubarb-shaped leaves and loves a slightly damp soil. Other plants with impressive textural foliage include yuccas (which also provide bold flower spikes) sea kale (*Crambe maritima*), ferns, cardoons (*Cynara cardunculus*) or, for a subtropical feel, the lush foliage of the banana plant (*Musa basjoo*). For damper, shady areas, hostas provide texture around the base of trees.

• Ornamental grasses not only provide texture with their delicate foliage, they also provide movement and noise when they sway and rustle in the wind.

• Succulent plants such as sedums and sempervivens provide a fleshy patchwork of foliage that provides an attractive background to contrasting plants.

• Hairy or silvery foliage plants, including lavenders, santolina, artemisia, yarrow and *Stachys lanata* (lamb's ear), will all thrive in dry, sun-baked flower borders, as will sea holly (*Eryngium*). The light captured by the different sized foliage will empahsise the textural qualities, and provide contrast – some having thin, spiky foliage, others soft or coarser leaves. They will also provide a contrast to other surrounding plants with different foliage such as ruffled leaves of heuchera or glossy, shiny leaves of *Canna indica* (canna lilies), or the coarser texture of ground-hugging conifers.

• Fine foliage gives an attractive, fuzzy effect to a garden when viewed from a distance. Plants to consider include baby's breath (*Gypsophila paniculata*), cosmos, coreopsis and amsonia. For something bigger, *Acer palmatum* var. *dissectum* is ideal for providing finely cut foliage. It requires dappled light and shelter from strong winds.

Water in the garden

Most people would agree that a garden only starts to feel like a special place when it has a personality of its own. At the National Trust we talk a lot about the 'spirit of place'. It means the essence of a garden – the features in it that make it unique and seem alive.

Water is a powerful force in the garden in this respect. The noise of running water has an intoxicating quality that, like a warm fire, draws people to it. Perhaps there is some instinctive, primeval sense within us all that recognises water as being essential for life, and for that reason we like to be near it.

Like colour, water can transform the mood of a garden. A fast-moving fountain or stream provides a sense of vibrancy and excitement to what could otherwise be a static space, as well as a refreshing, cooling sound on a hot day – a pleasure in itself, and also a feature that can be used to distract attention from traffic outside an urban garden. A lake or pond, on the other hand, suggests a mood of tranquillity and conjures up images of lazy days and relaxing by the water's edge in the dappled shade of a weeping willow tree.

The other element water provides is light. Water can be mesmerising when it splashes and the sunlight catches it. Reflections from a still lake impart huge amounts of additional light, and even a small pond in the garden can seem to expand the space by reflecting the sky.

Coleton Fishacre is one of the horticultural jewels in the National Trust's gardens. In terms of using natural water features, it could not be better placed as the garden is on a cliff edge, leading directly down to a beach on the Devonshire coast. Every view of the garden has been created to enhance this natural view. Within the garden itself there are magical rills and tranquil pools that create distinctive moods, depending on the speed of the running water. The water also enhances the effect of the surrounding lush subtropical gardens that make Coleton Fishacre feel like a paradise on earth. Not surprisingly, it is a favourite garden with National Trust members.

Below, left An upper concave pool at Coleton Fishacre. **Below, right** A small waterfall in the lower garden at Woolbeding Gardens.

Topiary gardens

Topiary, usually evergreen, can provide structure and a sense of geometry and balance to a garden in a very formal way. However, it also allows full rein to human eccentricity and can be puzzling and humorous, even bizarre. It's also an excellent example of 'slow gardening'. Topiary as a garden art form has a long history and happily is back in fashion again. In Ancient Rome actual gardening work was done by slaves and it was the *topiarius* who looked after the ornamental garden or *topia*. Clipped hedging became hugely popular in Renaissance Italy and by the late Middle Ages in Britain a formal style had developed using hedges in elaborate, geometric patterns, mazes and labyrinths and shaped forms grown as standards. The seventeenth century is seen as the golden age when topiary became an essential part of the formal landscape, culminating in the giddy excess of Versailles in France, whose style spread across the great gardens of Europe. Having been swept away by the landscape movement, only to be revived by the Victorians, topiary continued to thrive into the twentieth century as part of the Arts and Crafts style, as at Hidcote Manor and Mount Stewart where Edith, Lady Londonderry, created the formal gardens in the 1920s and 1930s. There, the parterres are hedged with an unusual choice of species such as heather, berberis, hebe and bay laurel. Huge arches of leyland cypress and large domed bay trees provide a strong Mediterranean, architectural structure.

'Smaller plants are best when creating new hedges or specimens – they acclimatise to local conditions much more quickly than larger plants.'

Phil Rollinson
Former Head Gardener at Mount Stewart, County Down

Choosing the right plant

The most common plants for topiary are yew and box because of their small leaves and dense growth, and their ability to regenerate readily, not only from clipping, but from hard pruning, if necessary. Other evergreens such as holly, privet, Portuguese laurel and even ivy work just as well. You could try deciduous plants, too, for example beech, hawthorn and hornbeam. Why not experiment with more unusual subjects? Try Chinese holly (*Osmanthus delavayi*), mock privet (*Phillyrea*), *Escallonia* and *Euonymus*. Or, for milder locations, try bottlebrushes (*Callistemon*).

Creating your chosen shape

Simple shapes can be cut freehand but the more complex the design the greater the need for a guiding framework. These are readily available to buy or you can make your own using a variety of materials, such as fencing wire, chicken wire, rods, stakes and bamboo canes. Tie in stems to the framework, pinching back any new shoots to encourage branching out and speedier covering of the frame. New growth will have to be trained to fill in gaps, tying shoots in with something that is biodegradable such as tarred string. This is best done in the growing season when the shoots are young and pliable. Topiary doesn't have to be geometrically accurate to be of interest. Over the years they can get pretty wonky, maybe due to bad weather, pests and diseases or mistakes. You might start with a shape in mind but end up with something totally different – go with the flow and make a feature of it.

Clipping: when and how

Ideally, once established, topiary should be clipped every four to six weeks in the growing season to retain a crisp finish. From May through to September is a good guide. Hedges need less regular attention and generally an annual trim is sufficient. Always be wary of late or early frosts, which can scorch new growth badly or even kill plants, especially box. Topiary takes up your time and patience and lots of standing back and looking. For intricate specimens you should use scissors, secateurs and hand shears. Electric hedge trimmers are good for less intricate work and for hedges. Try to avoid petrol-driven trimmers – they are noisy, smelly and generally heavy to use.

Phil Rollinson
Former Head Gardener at Mount Stewart, County Down

'Don't forget you are using sharp cutting implements. Always wear proper personal protective equipment and watch out for those cables when using electric trimmers. Keep the blades well clear of the cables – residual circuit breakers are a must. Make sure ladders and steps are firmly secure. Here, at Mount Stewart hedge trimming can be a great spectator sport; our visitors are always curious but you must always concentrate.'

Routine care

Just as for any freestanding shrubs, weeding, watering and mulching are essential to promote healthy, vigorous growth. Feeding during the growing season with a good, balanced fertiliser, twice if possible, is good practice, particularly if any renovation pruning has to be done. This may be necessary if hedges or topiary have been neglected and have grown badly out of shape. Yew and box are both excellent at regenerating from severe pruning, right back to the trunk if necessary. Be aware that snowfall on topiary can be very damaging because of the extra weight on branches. Gently knock it off any flat surfaces or better still use netting over your topiary pieces to alleviate the problem.

Tales from the Potting Shed

Knot Gardens by Tracey Parker, Assistant House Steward, Polesden Lacey

Knot gardens were one of the first types of 'designed' gardens in Britain, dating back more than 500 years. Their elaborate and intricate patterns are just as impressive today, and the National Trust looks after a number of these historic garden features.

In the sixteenth century, the Renaissance period inspired an element of curiosity about the natural world and a desire to create harmonious forms in the garden – a movement away from the more utilitarian approach of productive garden design. Architectural styles in Italy were becoming very geometric and the shapes and sizes that featured in the design of the grand houses were repeated in the layout of the gardens. In Tudor England, gardeners and designers took their inspiration from Italy and began to create gardens suitable for enjoyment and delight. As a result, mazes and knot gardens were created.

Knot gardens in particular were designed to look very impressive and were often created as a symbol representing an event or a personal connection with the family who owned the house and gardens. At Compton Castle in Devon, the home of the Gilbert family since the early fourteenth century, the knot garden is designed with a topiary squirrel as its centrepiece – an animal that is featured on the family crest and after which one of Sir Humphrey Gilbert's ships was named.

The designs for the knot gardens were inspired by the patterns found on furniture, windows, fabrics and jewellery. They were usually interlacing designs fitted into squares and, more importantly, were always symmetrical. During Tudor times there were not yet many plants that flowered during the autumn and winter months and sources of all-year-round stunning displays of colour needed to be found elsewhere. Scented herbs, such as thyme, lemon balm, lavender, myrtle and marjoram, provided good evergreen colour and texture, and materials such as crushed brick and sand proved ideal to create more colour and make striking patterns with the plants. As a result, from the house windows, residents could see the design and patterns of the knot garden and admire its beauty all year round.

Woodland gardens

A horticultural haven in a woodland glade is a romantic idyll that many of us would love to create in our own back garden if we had room. Many grand houses in the Georgian and particularly Victorian periods had woodland walks in their pleasure grounds. The paths were informal and curving, creating a sense of exploration as they meandered among specimens of new shrubs, trees and other woodland plants that had been brought back by plant hunters from around the world. These gardens were a plantsman's paradise packed with horticultural wonder where the aristocratic owners could show off their specimen plants to their guests. Around each bend in the path would be an exciting new discovery that would draw the visitor to explore further. Very often a woodland garden would lack structure, as the aim was to conjure up a romantic notion of exploration with the possibility of getting lost, yet all within the confines of the safe home garden.

Woodland gardens tend to have two key periods of interest. The first is in spring, when bulbs such as bluebells, snowdrops and other spring-flowering bulbs erupt from the ground and shrubs such as magnolias, camellias and rhododendrons vie for attention with their showy flowers. The second period of interest is in autumn when the ornamental woodland plants such as acers, nyssas and sorbus take centre stage with fiery colours of orange, red and yellow in the canopy of the trees.

Small trees for small gardens

Although there is a wide choice of garden trees, there are far fewer small trees available for use where space is a premium. Suitable small garden trees fall into three groups.

The first group contains clear-stemmed trees that are naturally small or slow growing, or have a distinct habit that limits their size. These include the Japanese maples (*Acer palmatum*), the flowering dogwoods (*Cornus florida* and *C. kousa*) and the weeping silver pear (*Pyrus salicifolia* 'Pendula'), or the traditional conical or pyramidal shape of the garden conifers, such as *Chamaecyparis pisifera* 'Filifera Aurea'.

The second group includes large tree-like shrubs that are commonly grown as small garden trees and are often grown with multi-stemmed trunks that originate from ground level. In many cases regular pruning is required to maintain these clear stems. This group includes the serviceberry (*Amelanchier lamarckii*), Chinese privet (*Ligustrum lucidum*) or the Chilean fire bush (*Embothrium coccineum*).

Mike Buffin
Consultancy Manager (Gardens and Parks), London and South East Region

'Selecting a tree that performs through a number of seasons is important in a garden. For example, the Chinese paper bark maple (*Acer griseum*) has cinnamon-coloured bark that flakes, followed by fiery autumn colour and attractive seeds, so it will grace a garden throughout the different seasons. Trees are very long-lived compared to other garden plants, and their selection, positioning and aftercare requires careful consideration, since established trees can be very difficult to relocate.'

Opposite Woodland gardens do not have to be huge. Gardens such as the Colby Woodland Garden in Pembrokeshire can be recreated in the smallest corner of the garden using just two or three smallish trees such as acers or birches underplanted with spring-flowering bulbs such as bluebells, narcissus or snowdrops.

The remaining group contains trees that respond to regular annual or biennial pruning and due to this pollarding treatment can be kept smaller. The following trees respond well to this treatment: Indian bean tree (*Catalpa bignonioides* 'Aurea'); the silver wattle or mimosa (*Acacia dealbata*) or the small-leaved lime (*Tilia cordata* 'Winter Orange').

The many benefits of planting trees

The visual beauty of a tree is often the main reason why it is planted, and in many cases such a selection will be based on the showiness of its flowers, foliage, fruit, bark or twigs, or even its shape or habit. Trees are also planted to create a focal point, to provide shade or create a microclimate to protect other plants, to screen, to hide or focus on a garden feature, or even to enhance a design feature. For example, a tight conical tree such as Rocky Mountain juniper (*Juniperus scopulorum* 'Skyrocket') can be used to great effect to enhance a Mediterranean design. However, garden trees can also bring many other benefits into the garden, and these may include:

- The shade cast by a tree can help to reduce the temperature in the shade during summer and help to keep the immediate area a few degrees cooler.
- Trees hold pollutants on their leaves, which fall harmlessly when the leaves are shed and the pollutants are absorbed into the soil. As the leaves are broken down they recycle their nutrients back into the soil.
- Tree roots bind the soil together and can help limit the effects of soil erosion, a common problem during rainstorms.
- Trees can filter and slow the wind and thus prevent damage to other garden plants.
- Trees provide habitat and shelter for a vast array of garden inhabitants. In a garden space for trees is always a limiting factor and will govern the size and numbers that can be planted.

Above Dappled sunlight falls on the woodland path at Colby Woodland Garden.

Where and how

Although the selection of a garden tree may seem fairly straightforward, a number of issues may affect the way that the tree will grow in the garden, so it is essential to understand the nature and make-up of the site before selecting your tree. To achieve this, consider the following:

- What is the type and make-up of the garden soil? You will need to record and understand your soil pH and soil type.
- How will local climate and weather affect the tree's growth and survival?
- For what purpose is the tree being planted? Is it to add a sense of scale, to screen unsightly buildings, to create shade for other plants, to add beauty, or for wildlife or shelter?
- How much space is available to plant your tree and allow it to mature?
- Will the tree have seasonal colour, or is it required to provide a foil for other plants, in which case might an evergreen tree be more suitable?

Formal or informal?

Whether you choose to make your garden formal or informal is entirely a matter of what suits your personality and visual taste.

Formal gardens

A formal garden tends to have a rigid structure, suggesting a very ordered and planned area that expresses the human wish to shape and control nature. It often consists of a perfectly manicured and striped lawn, surrounded by perfectly clipped box and yew hedging. Symmetry tends to be an integral part of the design and topiary often makes an appearance, providing all-year-round interest and structure. Many of the early historic gardens had elements of formality to them, featuring patterns with knot gardens and parterres.

Left The formal gardens at Oxburgh Hall, Norfolk.

Colin Clark
Senior Gardener at
Greenway, Devon

'My favourite tip is to design your herbaceous border to finish and go over at same time at year end (rather than finishing at different times) and put the flail over it! Trimmed and mulched in one! This is great if you're short of time'.

Informal gardens

Relaxed structures and loose planting schemes are the key features of an informal garden. Flower-beds are usually packed with plants all loosely growing into each other and jostling for attention with blowsy, brightly coloured flowers. Rustic staking with birch or other types of brushwood is usually seen, with wigwam structures providing height.

This type of garden gives the impression that nature rather than man is in control, with naturalistic drifts of flowers and informal paths weaving and flowing among the beds. Very often fruit trees, bushes and herbs are inter-planted among the flowers, blurring the distinction between ornamental and kitchen garden plants. In smaller gardens, the style referred to as 'cottage gardening' is a classic example of informal gardening.

Other garden styles

There are numerous styles of gardens to suit personal tastes and budgets. Visiting National Trust gardens will give you some more ideas and inspiration.

Kitchen garden design

For some, the most enjoyable kind of gardening is the kind that produces crops they can eat. Today, many people have got the grow-your-own bug – there are more than 300,000 allotment-holders in England alone, with huge waiting lists of other budding kitchen gardeners. However, the desire

Above, left Alfriston Clergy House, East Sussex, has a picture-postcard garden, the informality emphasised by the abundance of plants. **Above, right** Beatrix Potter's garden at Hill Top in the Lake District is a quintessential cottage garden, crammed with traditional garden favourites. Flower spikes such as foxgloves and mulleins rise from the flower-beds, underplanted with sweet william, snapdragons and poached egg plants. **Opposite, left** The foliage of purple continus shrub contrasts well with herbaceous perennials such as white echinacea. **Opposite, centre** Wigwams provide height for traditional climbing plants such as honeysuckle, sweet peas and hollyhocks to scramble over. Hardy's Cottage in Dorset. **Opposite, right** Artichokes and rainbow chard in the kitchen garden at Dunham Massey.

to know where the food on your plate has come from does not necessarily mean a mundane plot, since a bit of creative imagination can make a kitchen garden just as beautiful as it is productive. Some people prefer to grow their veggies in straight lines, while others prefer to mix them up informally among the ornamentals.

Like ornamental plants, edible crops offer seasonal interest, including foliage texture from cabbages, leeks, lettuces and other leafy vegetables and berries from fruit such as blueberries and redcurrants. Some vegetables such as asparagus, peas, runner beans, potatoes and courgettes provide attractive summer flowers, while the seedheads from onions and garlic rival those of the most ornamental allium plants. Colour is also provided by foliage such as purple-leaved amaranth and purple kale.

Japanese gardens

The serenity of a traditional Japanese garden is hard to beat, and Tatton Park in Cheshire has one of the best examples in the UK. Most Japanese gardens include acers, bamboos, bonsai trees, ornamental gravel and wooden bridges, often linking islands in water stocked with Koi carp, but there are many variations. There is a sense of reflection and harmony in most Japanese gardens.

Exotic gardens

You do not need to go on holiday to a tropical Caribbean island to enjoy some of the exotic plants associated with these areas. National Trust gardeners have been experimenting and pushing

Cat Saunders
Head Gardener at
Overbecks, Devon

'Tropical planting is an attitude. It's all about mad huge leaves, spots of searing colour, and a small attempt to mimic natural planting combinations. The trick is not to follow a formal herbaceous border style, but to take inspiration from the jungle, repeating a few plants in a random manner. In a cold garden, combine hostas and ferns and use Impatiens, not bedded in groups, but sprinkled naturalistically throughout to give a flavour of a tropical rainforest. It's a style, and not limited by climate.'

Above The tranquil Japanese Garden at Tatton Park.

the boundaries of some of the more tender plants and the results are impressive. Lush, tropical gardens have been created, particularly in the warmer climate along the south-west coast such as at Overbecks and Coleton Fishacre. These exciting plants can also be grown in urban gardens which are a few degrees warmer than rural ones, creating riots of colour among the flower-beds. To create this look, if your climate is warm enough you can include *Echium pininana*, the hardy banana *Musa basjoo*, species of *Hedychium* (ginger lilies), *Canna indica* (canna lilies) and *Trachycarpus fortunei* (Chusan palm).

Traditional herbaceous borders

Gertrude Jekyll (1843–1932) was considered to be the queen of the traditional herbaceous border, with her style focusing on drifts of plants and colour themes. There are many National Trust gardens with examples of her work, stretching from Lindisfarne Castle in the north of England to Hatchlands in the south-east and Knightshayes and Castle Drogo in the West Country. Barrington Court in Somerset has superb examples of how she interwove her style and colour schemes into many areas of the garden.

Prairie-style planting

Modern herbaceous borders tend to focus more on large swathes of colour, using the texture and movement of large gutsy, perennial plants such as *Rudbeckia, Echinacea purpurea, Monarda, Persicaria amplexicaulis, Helenium, Sanguisorba* and *Eupatorium purpureum*. These are combined with grasses such as *Calamagrostis, Stipa, Panicum virgatum, Miscanthus sinensis* and *Pennisetum*. One of the attractive features of this style of border is the overall effect when they are planted *en masse*, providing an almost ephemeral and translucent quality to the overall scheme.

Tales from the Potting Shed

Restoring a historical planting by Emma McNamara, London and South East Gardens and Parks Consultant

Part of the authenticity of a garden restoration is in the accuracy of the planting schemes. Achieving this is essential and the research of the herbaceous and shrub borders can be done using several different sources to avoid creating a pastiche. The garden's history can date back several centuries and the structure will reflect this; however, the planting in a garden is different as the original scheme may only partially survive or may have been lost altogether. The style and fashion of the era are reflected by the plants that were available at the time. Many plants will be easy to replace but the original names may have changed, perhaps as a result of reclassification, or the plant may have been superseded by a more disease-resistant variety.

Replanting can be simple if plant lists, plans and seed orders are available. If not, paintings, drawings or photographs showing the planted areas of the garden give a great insight into the planting style and overall impact of the design. Old photographs were used as a reference at Morden Hall Park in London for the replanting of the rose garden. Archived photographs and old catalogues from the 1920s showed the roses available to the gardener of the time.

Westbury Court Garden in Gloucestershire is the best example of a complete garden restoration using pictorial evidence, in this case a seventeenth-century Johannes Kip engraving backed up by plant records from the period. Other successful National Trust garden restorations using archive material include the rose and rock gardens at Emmetts at Sevenoaks in Kent, restored using family photographs and letters written by the owner to his contemporaries describing the garden's creation, and the double-sided herbaceous borders at Polesden Lacey, restored with reference to Graham Stuart Thomas's original design and with a re-creation on the west side in the same planting style.

Seasonal interest

When you consider the design and planting of your garden, making sure that it will offer interest all year round is an important point. It is easy to get carried away with planting colourful flowers for spring and summer and then realise that for the rest of the year there is little to attract the eye.

The winter garden

Producing colour without using lots of flowers makes winter gardening both challenging and exciting. Colour can be found in various plant parts. Coloured stems such as dogwoods (*Cornus*), willow (*Salix*) and brambles (*Rubus*) give permanent colour for at least six months of the year even on the greyest of days. The bold leaf colour of oleaster (*Elaeagnus*) and Mexican orange (*Choisya*) (both green and yellow types) will assist in making excellent backgrounds to show off other plants. Careful choices of ground-cover plants are important as you will need to have colours that can complement the surrounding plants such as *Euonymus* 'Emerald Gaiety' with *Viburnum bodnantense* 'Dawn' or colours to give a strong contrast such as *Luzula sylvatica* 'Aurea' with *Mahonia aquifolium* 'Apollo'. Good-sized bold groupings are important for impact as single plants will get lost in the general mix. Activating all the senses is what winter gardening is all about and the sense of smell is a must to be explored. There is a vast choice of shrubs that can be used, including *Mahonia*, *Viburnum*, honeysuckle (*Lonicera*), wintersweet (*Chimonanthus*) and Christmas box (*Sarcococca*) to name a few. Being aware of the sun's direction is the key for showing off some interesting features for plants that have good branch formation such as corkscrew hazel (*Corylus avellana* 'Contorta') or plants with attractive thorns or flaking bark. Remember the winter sun is low and will shine through things rather than directly from above. We use dark foliage backgrounds to lift plants into view as well as the use of the dark layer of leaf mould under plants like dogwoods and brambles. Take advantage of planting spring bulbs under deciduous shrubs so that a good display is enjoyed before new foliage blocks out the light. Taller flowering bulbs can be added to ground-cover areas, for example the use of narcissus with ivy and crocus with *Vinca minor*.

Richard Todd
Head Gardener at Anglesey Abbey, Cambridgeshire

'Aim to experiment with combining bulbs and other plants such as snowdrops with early miniature iris and hellebore, or using the foliage of *Cyclamen hederifolium* or bergenia as a background.'

The spring garden

Spring must be the most exciting time of the year in the garden. It feels as if the great outdoors has finally awoken from its winter slumbers, with plants as well as wildlife coming out of hibernation to greet a new season. For many of us, too, it is our first venture out of the house into the garden for some while.

There are masses of spring-flowering plants to choose from but ideally you should select ones that have more than one season of interest, such as *Cornus kousa*, which provides showy white bracts in spring, followed by attractive fruit in autumn and impressive autumnal displays from its

Above Autumn time is a riot of stunning garden colour, whether it is foliage changing colour on trees and shrubs, or late-flowering plants such as the dahlia (above, right).

foliage. Climbers such as *Wisteria sinensis* and *Clematis armandii* add to the excitement of spring with their intoxicating perfumed flowers. In larger properties, woodland gardens take centre stage with showy flowers from magnolias, camellias and rhododendrons, while elsewhere showy displays of cherry and other fruit blossom appear.

The summer garden

This season really does spoil you for choice, as there is such a wide range of plants and styles of garden available to suit all personal tastes and budgets. Rose gardens will flower throughout the season if repeat-flowering types are chosen. The traditional herbaceous border really comes into its own during summer, making a massive, showy impact including plants such as the stately upright delphiniums towards the back of the border and penstemons and catmints (*Nepeta*) towards the front. Herb and vegetable gardens also reach their peak of perfection towards mid- and late summer. Annuals such as sunflower, love-in-a-mist, sweet peas, cornflowers and poppies create a bright splash of colour in any flower-bed, while island beds, containers and hanging baskets can be packed full of bright bedding plants, such as busy lizzies, petunias and geraniums.

The autumn garden

With the sun lower in the sky, the garden takes on beautiful, subtle colour hues. There is a mellowness and a sense that nature and the garden itself are preparing for a well-deserved rest after the exertions of summer. Before the plants slip into a period of dormancy, though, they have one last trick up their sleeves. It's the crescendo of the year, with trees providing a spectacular display of autumnal foliage ranging from fiery reds and purples to buttery yellow. There are lots of berries on show, too, in a wide range of colours, which provides not only a feast for the eyes but some much-needed sustenance for the wildlife too.

Closer to the ground, there are still some flowers providing a show-stopping finale to the growing season, including dahlias, chrysanthemums and asters. Bulbs also put on a performance, such as *Colchicum autumnale* (naked ladies), *Crocus sativus* (saffron crocus) and *Sternbergia*, while kitchen gardens and orchards are ripe with brightly coloured pumpkins and squashes in the vegetable patch and apple trees laden under their weight of their fruit.

Plant picker: autumn interest

Acer palmatum var. *dissectum*

Acer palmatum 'Sango-kaku'

Aster novi-belgii

Chrysanthemum 'Cassandra'

Colchicum autumnale

Dahlia 'Bishop of Llandaff'

Echinacea purpurea

Liquidambar styraciflua (sweet gum)

Nyssa sylvatica

Rudbeckia fulgida 'Goldstrum'

Plant picker: winter interest

Acer griseum

Betula utilis var. *jacquemontii*

Cornus sanguinea 'Winter Beauty'

Corylus avellana 'Contorta'

Daphne bholua

Eranthus hyemalis (winter aconite)

Jasminum nudiflorum (winter jasmine)

Prunus serrula

Sarcococca humilis

Viburnum farreri

Plant picker: plants for full sun

Achillea filipendulina 'Gold Plate'

Delphinium 'Black Knight'

Helianthus annuus (sunflower)

Eryngium bourgatii (sea holly)

Ceanothus 'Cascade'

Olea europàea (olive tree)

Lavandula 'Hidcote Blue' (lavender)

Philadelphus 'Belle Etoile'

Verbena bonariensis

Plant picker: semi-shade or shade

Ajuga reptans

Camellia x *williamsii*

Digitalis purpurea (foxglove)

Dryopteris erythrosora

Hosta 'Golden Tiara'

Rudbeckia A classic late summer/early autumn herbaceous perennial producing bright daisy-like flowers.

Daphne bholua This upright shrub produces light pink flowers that perfume the crisp, cold winter air.

Sweet gum The foliage on this tree provides a blaze of colour to the garden in autumn.

Cornus sanguinea These shrubs are grown for their brightly coloured winter stems. Prun back hard in early spring.

Dahlia Produces showy flowers in late summer/early autumn. Tubers may need protecting over the winter months in colder areas.

Corylus avellana 'Contorta' This shrubby hazel provides plenty of winter interest with its catkins and eyecatching corkscrew branches.

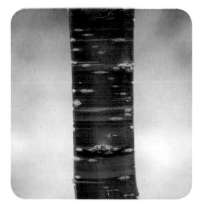

Prunus serrula An ornamental cherry tree with stunning red bark.

Philadelphus This popular garden shrub produces heavily scented flowers in late spring/early summer.

Hosta The perfect foliage plant for a shady corner of the garden.

Sunflower This popular summer flowering annual can grow up to 3m (10ft) in height.

Verbena bonariensis This tall herbaceous perennial has attractive clusters of purple flowers.

Skimmia japonica A lovely evergreen shrub that provides structure and interest to a winter garden.

Sea holly Provides a splash of electric blue to the garden. This herbaceous perennial loves free-draining soil.

Foxglove A tall biennial commonly seen in woodland gardens. The many varieties come in a range of colours.

Viburnum x bodnantense This winter flowering shrub produces clusters of pretty pinkish-purple flowers.

lawn care

Bring back lawns

For many years, lawns were considered an essential feature in the suburban garden – usually a rectangular space given pride of place in the centre of the plot. More recently, they have come under heavy criticism for two main reasons: they are considered to be high maintenance, at the very least requiring cutting and edging once a week; and they are thought to be environmentally unfriendly, requiring petrol-driven machinery to maintain them and a constant supply of water and fertiliser to make them look lush and green.

However, these criticisms are not entirely fair. A lawn in the garden provides millions of tiny oxygenating plants that create a wide range of habitats for bugs and insects, whether they are living in the soil just below the surface of the lawn or within the thatch. If you sit down among the blades of grass you will see that they are host to a huge range of wildlife including ants, ladybirds, bumble bees and beetles. Considering the alternative landscape material is usually decking, concrete or patio slabs, it is not hard to realise that lawns are by far the greener option.

Secondly, lawns have a fantastic absorption quality. A large part of the flooding problem in the UK in recent years has been attributed to the hard landscaping of our front and back gardens, meaning water run-off has nowhere left to go. If there were more lawns there would be less flooding, as the water would be held in the soil layers below the surface for longer.

Lawns do not have to be high maintenance, either. True, if you want a finely manicured lawn it will take some work, but not really any more than having to weed a vegetable bed or a bedding display every week. Cutting the grass much less often will certainly encourage a greater diversity of wildlife, much of which will not only feed on it but also use the material for nesting. Allowing some weeds in the lawn will enhance the garden's green credentials even more, as they will attract pollinating insects such as butterflies and honey bees.

Practical considerations aside, gardens often look better with a lovely green space somewhere. It is enticing to sit on, perhaps with a picnic or a cold drink, and it is a natural soft material for children to play on safely.

Right The impeccably kept lawn at The Courts Garden in Wiltshire.

Creating an environmentally friendly lawn

Mowers are a very useful and efficient tool for cutting the grass, but there are other options that are not dependent on petrol-driven machines. Solaro-powered battery mowers are efficient for cutting small and medium-sized lawns, and small areas of grass can be cut roughly with hand-held shears.

Concepts of lawns are also changing, with some people preferring longer grass that only requires cutting once or twice a year, and incorporating wild flowers into their lawns. Alternatively, you could consider 'fake' or artificial grass and avoid lawn maintenance altogether.

Below The lawn at Polesden Lacey is spiked with wild flowers.

Scything the grass at Polesden Lacey

The grass in the orchards at Yew Tree Farm in the grounds of Polesden Lacey used to be regularly cut each year with a ride-on mower. This was done every couple of weeks, leaving the orchard with short, clipped grass that was easy for visitors to walk on.

However, apart from one or two mown paths, the grass is now cut just once a year, in late summer, using scythes. There has been a huge revival in the popularity of scythes as people increasingly appreciate the benefits of equipment that does not rely on fossil fuels. The grass can still be cut reasonably low and there is no longer the unpleasant sound of machinery in the garden, or the need for ear defenders on a warm summer's day.

Leaving the grass longer has increased the diversity of plant life, with wild flowers such as cornflowers and knapweeds springing up. This in turn has encouraged the wildlife including butterflies, bats and bees. Small mammals are now nesting in the long grass and this has encouraged a pair of buzzards to forage in the area too.

The long grass is raked off to ensure that the fertility of the soil is not increased, as this would encourage coarse grasses at the expense of the more delicate wild flowers. The grass is bundled into piles by the side of the orchard and slow worms, hedgehogs and grass snakes use them for nesting.

Interestingly, the apple trees seem to have become less prone to disease and aphid damage – it would seem that the natural balance of life has been restored to this beautiful corner of the Surrey Hills.

How to create a lawn

The quickest way of establishing a lawn is to lay rolls of turf. This is by far the most popular option for many householders and professional gardeners as the results are almost instantaneous – the lawn looks good immediately and is ready to walk on about two weeks later. It can also be laid throughout the year except for in extreme periods of drought or cold, though the ideal time is autumn as the ground is still warm and the lawn should need only minimal watering to get the roots established before the growing season in spring.

Turf-laying can be back-breaking work, though, and if the idea of hauling heavy rolls of turf around the garden does not appeal you may be better off seeding the lawn instead. However, if you are willing to engage outside help, there will be plenty of garden contractors happy to lay the lawn for you. Always check the rolls of turf before they are laid to ensure that they look healthy and are not stressed and turning yellow.

Tip

'Trim plants that grow over lawn edges little and often so that they don't get hacked back hard and then look awful.'

Martyn Pepper, Senior Gardener at Coleton Fishacre, Devon

Below The immaculate maincured lawns at Coleton Fishacre are set off beautifully with the background of herbaceous perennials and impressive subtropical planting.

Step-by-step: Laying a lawn

It is important to get your timing right when you order your turf, since once it has been delivered it will need to be laid within a day or two. If the work is delayed, unroll as many of the rolls as possible in the shade to prevent the grass turning brown.

1. Prepare the ground by digging it over with a fork and removing any perennial weeds. Rake it level using a landscape rake and then firm down the soil by walking over it slowly to remove any air pockets.

2. Rake over the soil again lightly and then start to lay the turf, butting each roll up tightly to the previous one. When it gets to the second row, cut a roll in half so that the pattern is staggered like brickwork as this makes a stronger bond.

3. Tamp down each roll of turf with the back of a rake. Lay boards or planks to work from, avoiding walking directly on the existing laid lawn. Avoid using small strips at the end of the lawn as these quickly dry out. Instead use them in the middle of rows.

4. Finally, use a besom or brush to sweep a non-peat top dressing into the gaps between the rolls of turf. If rain is not predicted, water the lawn well and then avoid walking on it for a few weeks until the roots have established.

Chris Wilson,
Senior Gardener at The
Vyne, Hampshire

Creating a turf raised bed

'We created our turf raised bed to use up excess turves when creating the vegetable areas of our walled garden. We cut the turves using a 300mm (12in) wide turf cutter (available from most hire shops). They were lifted at maximum machine depth and we cut each one to 1m (3¼ft) long to keep them manageable. Next we marked out the corners of the bed – about 1.5m x 3m (5 x 10ft) for us but any size works.

Then we placed the first layer of turf upside down within the rectangle we had just created. Starting from the corners, we put further layers of upside-down turf on top of each other, staggering the joins in the same way a bricklayer builds a wall.

Once we had reached our desired height of eight layers, we put a final layer on top with the grassy side up. Then we filled the middle with topsoil and planted the vegetables. Our first set lasted about three-and-a-half years before they fell over. Every few weeks we would cut the grass top and sides with shears or a strimmer.

This is a great way of recycling material, and making an enviromentally friendly structure in the garden. It is free to make and avoids any need to import materials.'

Sowing seed

For the more green-fingered gardener, sowing seed is a better option. It is trickier to establish, and patience is required as the lawn may not be ready to use for as long as 12 weeks. However, there are far more choices of grass types available, ranging from shade-tolerant to drought-tolerant, and a bag of seed is far cheaper than rolls of turf. Sprinkling seed is also much less hard work than dealing with rolls of turf.

The disadvantages are that seed needs reasonably warm temperatures to germinate and when freshly sown will need protection from birds. The bare soil is also susceptible to weeds until the grass starts to grow.

Tip

'To reduce the chance of birds eating your grass seed, pre-germinate it in a seed tray so that it grows away quicker.'
Colin Clark, Senior Gardener at Greenway, Devon

Above, left The grass is left to grow wild, and paths mown into it at Westbury Court Garden.
Above, right Sow grass seed first in one direction, and then at 90 degrees to that, ensuring an even coverage.

Micro clovers

The sowing of micro clovers is a relatively new development in lawns. They are simply a standard clover with tiny leaves, and from a distance they look like grass. They can be added into grass seed mixes or sown as pure clover.

There are many advantages to using micro clovers. Because they fix nitrogen from the soil with their roots, they don't require fertiliser – in fact, their supply of nitrogen helps to feed any surrounding grasses. They tend not to suffer from drought like grasses do, are reasonably tolerant of wear, and because they stay small and low to the ground, the lawn doesn't require cutting regularly.

Step-by-step: Sowing a lawn

Sow seed only between mid-spring and early autumn – it will fail to germinate in the cooler temperatures. Avoid sowing on a windy day, as the seed will be blown onto your flower-beds and you will find it difficult to distribute the correct amount on the soil.

1. Dig over the soil with a fork or use a rotavator, removing any perennial weeds and their roots. Also extract any stones in the soil. Level the soil with a landscape rake and then walk over it to firm down and remove air pockets.

2. Rake over the soil again to create a fine tilth. If the weather is very dry it is worth watering the soil, as this will encourage germination.

3. Using string, mark out the area into 1m (3 ¼ ft) square grids. Check the sowing rate on the seed packet and measure the seed out into the cup.

4. Sow half the amount in one direction in a square, and the remainder at 90 degrees to it. Repeat this process in the other squares. Lightly rake the seed into the soil and water.

Alternatively, instead of sowing by hand a seed distributor machine can be calibrated for seed sowing. Seed distributor machines are reasonbly cheap to buy, and are useful for sowing grass on larger areas. By following the sowing rates on the sack or box of grass seed it should be possible to callibrate the machine to distribute the right amount of seed as you push it along. You don't need to mark out squares, but it helps to mark out the rows, using string. The machine will tell you the rate seed will be distributed at, if you walk at an average speed. It is possible to check the distribution rate by walking the machine over a hard surface first, then sweeping up the seed, weighing it, and checking it has distributed the right amount of seed per square metre that you required. If the machine has distributed too much or little, then adjust the machine accordingly and test it again.

Right A rotary mower is the most popular choice for cutting all kinds of lawns, but there are many other options available.

'If you want to put stripes on your lawn but are a bit worried about your ability to get them straight, consider cutting diagonally across the lawn rather than square to the edges. It is easier to disguise wonky lines this way.'

Chris Gaskin, Senior Gardener at Polesden Lacey

Lawn mowers

A mower is probably the most expensive piece of kit you will need for the lawn, if not for the entire garden. There are several different types and which you choose depends on your budget, lawn size and how much work you want to contribute yourself.

Rotary mowers

The most commonly used mower in the domestic garden is the rotary. This has cutting edges like helicopter blades that rotate parallel to the ground. Rotary mowers come in all shapes and sizes, but usually have a collection box at the back to catch the grass clippings, and adjustable height so that a lower or higher cut can be made.

Rotary mowers are tougher than cylinder mowers so are ideal for rougher areas of grass. Many have a roller on the back to give a striped effect to the lawn. Most ride-on mowers and hover mowers also operate on a rotary type of system.

Mulch mowers

The blades of a mulch mower are like those on a rotary mower but are at a slight angle which chops up the grass clippings into tiny pieces and spits them back out onto the lawn. These clippings are an invaluable extra source of nitrogen and will keep the grass looking green. Because the clippings are so small they do not smother the grass, causing brown dead patches. Some ordinary rotary mowers also have a mulch option rather than using the collection box, but the performance may not be as good as a mulch mower specifically designed for the job. Mulch mowers are much lighter as they don't have a roller on the back or use collection boxes, this makes them ideal for using on steep banks or awkward small areas.

Cylinder mowers

Used on fine lawns, cylinder mowers give lawn-fanciers those much-desired traditional stripes. Rotary mowers with rollers on the back will also provide stripes, but they are not usually as pronounced. They are much more finely tuned than rotary mowers and capable of cutting at a considerably lower level, but are not suitable for rougher, coarser grasses or uneven ground. The collection box is usually on the front and the roller is at the back. The cutting action consists of a horizontal rotating drum with blades that trap the grass against a lower, fixed blade. They are usually more expensive than rotary mowers and are not as easy to maintain.

The greener option

Retro push cylinder mowers have come back into fashion. They do not require any electricity or petrol, you will not annoy the neighbours with the roar from your mower, and you will get a good weekend workout in the garden too. Push mowers are surprisingly efficient, inexpensive (you may even find one being given away on a recycling website) and give a lovely finished look to the lawn. Electric mowers are always a better option than petrol mowers in terms of energy efficiency. However, it is usually necessary to have a cable trailing from a power source and is therefore not practical on large areas. At Polesden Lacey we invested in battery-operated rotary mowers which are light to use and still give an exceptionally good quality of cut. We rigged up solar-panelled units on the toolshed, and these charge the batteries each night.

Right Push cylinder mowers are a greener and more peaceful alternative to rotary or cylinder mowers.

History from Polesden Lacey

'The pony used to pull the roller and the mowing machine. We used to put his leather boots on, put one foot in, strap it round each foot... they had flat bottoms to stop them damaging the turf.'

Mr Arthur Thompson, the groom at Polesden Lacey, 1907

Types of grass seed

Most garden lawns are a mix of several species of grass. This is because individual species have specific desirable qualities, but none of them is able to provide everything that is required of a lawn – some species, for example, have a creeping habit that knits a lawn together, while others form clumps but have better disease resistance. Consequently, lawn mixes are designed to provide the best qualities from a range of different species.

Choose a blend of grass that is suited to your lifestyle. Lawn grasses have been developed so that there are tough types able to withstand a lot of foot traffic, while others are more sensitive but can be cut short and look more attractive than their coarser relatives. Agronomists have also developed mixes suitable for specific areas of the garden such as shady or damp areas and there are even some species-rich and wildlife-friendly blends that will encourage insects, birds and small mammals into the garden. You can also obtain wildflower mixes.

The big four

While there are a number of grass species to be found in lawn mixes, there are four most often to be found.

Festuca rubra Creeping red fescue is probably the most common type of fescue found in a lawn. It has thin, needle-shaped blades and is usually found in good-quality lawn turf and surfaces for sports. As the name suggests, it has a creeping habit and is great for knitting a lawn together. It can be cut short and is often blended with bents, which are also fine lawn species.

Agrostis capillaris Commonly known as browntop bent, this is a fine-leaved grass that is used in formal lawns and wildflower mixes and can be cut as short as 3mm (⅛in). It is a very popular choice in formal meadows because of its attractive appearance.

Lolium perenne Perennial rye is a popular grass for lawns for general use. Very tough and hard-wearing, it usually appears in a blend with smooth-stalked meadow grass in family lawns and rugby and football pitches. It will not tolerate close mowing and is therefore not normally used in formal lawns.

Above, left *Festuca rubra* makes for a fine looking lawn at Shaw's Corner, Hertfordshire. **Above, right** *Agrostis capillaris* is one of the finer types of grass, making it ideal for naturalising in an orchard where wild flowers can grow among the grass.

Poa pratensis This hardwearing perennial, known as smooth-stalked meadow grass or Kentucky blue grass, is often combined with rye grass to create a resilient lawn suitable for high footfall and for sports pitches with high wear and tear. It is also suitable for sowing in banks and on slopes.

Some baddies in the grass world

Holcus lanatus Yorkshire fog is a vigorous, coarse grass that quickly seeds into formal lawns, leaving unsightly clumps. The only realistic way to remove it from the lawn is to dig it up, then top-dress the lawn and overseed it with the preferred grass mix.

Poa annua Annual meadow grass seeds everywhere, producing small unsightly seedheads that cause problems in bowling greens, golf greens and tennis courts as they affect the roll of the ball. In gardens, when it dies back in winter, it often leaves bare patches that weeds can seed into.

Hardwearing grass at Polesden Lacey

With more than 300,000 visitors per annum, the lawns at Polesden Lacey were often worn out by the end of the season. Many of them were designed to be formal and cut short, but the existing mix of fescue and bent species was not hardy enough to cope with the footfall. The garden team started to overseed with a new type of dwarf-leaved rye grass that looks like a fine grass but has the tolerance of a normal coarse perennial rye. Now the lawns at Polesden Lacey remain green all year round and are able to cope with the high visitor numbers.

Right and below Yorkshire fog can form unsightly mounds in the lawn and should be removed in order to keep your lawn looking immaculate.

Tip

'If you have a fine lawn it is best to vary the direction that you mow it each week to avoid creating permanent ridges. However, avoid mowing at right angles from one week to another too, as this affects the smoothness of a fine lawn. Instead, mow at 45 degrees.'
Chris Gaskin, Senior Gardener at Polesden Lacey, Surrey

Greener lawns

Making a herb lawn

Thyme and camomile are low-growing creeping perennials that can be used as an alternative to the traditional lawn. They're not as hardwearing as grass but they can make attractive features in garden, and when walked on they release a beautiful scent as the leaves are slightly crushed. Both will produce flowers that are popular with bees and butterflies, although some purists like to use the non-flowering camomile variety called 'Treneague'.

1. Prepare the ground thoroughly by digging it over and removing any perennial weeds. In heavy clay soil, add horticultural grit to improve drainage, as both thyme and camomile prefer not to sit in wet conditions.
2. Use a trowel to create planting holes approximately 10cm (4in) apart, then remove the plants from their pots and place them in the holes. Their fast-growing, creeping habit should quickly fill in the space between.
3. If no rain is predicted for a few days, water them in lightly. Avoid walking on them for a few weeks after planting, and even then, do not walk on them too often as they will start to die back.

Tips for a greener lawn

- Avoid using petrol-driven machinery where possible.
- Allow the grass to grow longer.
- Leave grass clippings on the lawn as an extra nitrogen feed. Alternatively, make sure they are added to the compost heap.
- Consider creating wildflower meadows instead
- Tolerate some weeds in shorter lawns, but do not let them take over.
- Do not water unless absolutely necessary. Grass is amazingly resilient.
- Use natural products on the lawn, such as bonemeal to provide phosphate. Rake in garden compost to add nitrogen and ash from the fireplace or barbecue for some potassium.
- Consider the use of micro clovers.

Below, left Corn chamomile makes a pretty alternative to grass lawns. **Below, right** The lawns in the Victorian Parterre Garden at Erddig, Wrexham, are carefully maintained by their team of gardeners.

Scarifying

To keep a lawn looking in tip-top condition you should scarify it at least once a year, ideally in autumn, to remove some of the 'thatch'. This is the build-up of debris that occurs throughout the year, usually composed of decaying fragments of grass clippings and leaves. Collecting at the base of the blades of grass, it impedes the water uptake in the soil and can smother and kill the grass eventually, leaving dead, brown, muddy patches.

On large areas, scarification is carried out by a scarifying machine. This is usually driven in one direction and then the setting is lowered and the machine is sent across at a 45-degree angle to the original cut. The thatch is then raked up, or mowed up into the collection box and added to the compost heap.

A greener method of scarifying is to use a spring-tined rake, pulling it across the surface of the lawn. Scarification inevitably makes the lawn look ragged, but it will quickly recover.

Above The lawn is scarified with a spring-tined rake to remove all the thatch from the base of the blades of grass.

Above It is surprising how much thatch can come from a small area of lawn. The material can be added to the compost heap to rot down.

Aeration

After a lawn has been scarified, it is often spiked to break up compaction of the soil and encourage air to circulate down at the roots. Compaction is often a major problem in lawns, particularly in public spaces and on desire lines – the paths that walkers make as the easiest way to their destination. When a lawn becomes compacted the roots are prevented from growing downwards, causing the grass to die back as it fails to take up nutrients and water from the soil.

At Polesden Lacey, compaction is an issue because of the large number of visitors each year. The lawns are often used for picnicking, particularly during the summer. To resolve the compaction problems we use a 'plugger', which is a machine that pushes spikes in the lawn and heaves them slightly when it lifts them out.

On smaller lawns a fork can be used for aeration. Simply push it into the ground, give it a wiggle and pull it out, repeating about every 20cm (8in). Once the holes have been made, sweep garden compost or a peat-free top dressing into them.

Above Aerating your lawn means that nutrients and water are able to reach even the more compacted parts, making for a greener garden.

Lawn repairs

Having a good-looking lawn can be as easy or as complicated as you wish to make it. There is no doubt that a smartly striped lawn with clipped edges looks great in a formal setting, but it is equally pleasing to see longer grass with informal, curvy paths snaking through the garden. Whatever style of lawn you have, there are a few tricks of the trade to keep it in good condition.

Bumps and hollows

After a few years lawns become uneven, particularly if there is any mole activity, and need to be levelled out. A very uneven surface can make cutting the grass with a cylinder mower almost impossible.

Bumps Using a half-moon tool (see page 94), make a cross through the bumps and peel back the turf. Remove some of the soil and gently fold back the turf, ensuring it is level. Tamp down the lawn with the back of a rake.

Hollows Make a cross in the lawn, peel back the turf and fill the hollow with good-quality topsoil. Replace the turf and tamp down with the back of the rake.

Worn edging Slice out the worn section of turf. Turn it 180 degrees, aligning the newly cut side with the edge of the lawn. Back-fill the worn section with topdressing and overseed.

'There's nothing more annoying than clipping a perfectly straight edge only to find the mower wheel or roller then bends some stray blades of grass over your pristine edge. Always mow first.'

Len Bernamont, Head Gardener at Bateman's, Alfriston Clergy House and Monk's House, East Sussex

Below From left to right: edging shears; small tined rake; bag of fertiliser (back row); bucket of grass seed (back row); half moon; fork for aerating; rotary mower (centre); besom (for brushing in top dressing); switch; true lute; spring-tined rake; wheelbarrow full of top dressing (back row).

Above Using a shovel to throw your top dressing across the lawn ensures an even distribution.
Below A switch can be dragged across the lawn to remove the morning layer of dew.

Tools of the trade

Acquiring a few basic tools will help you to achieve a handsome-looking lawn. The following are not expensive to buy and provided you give them some basic care they will last a long time.

• **Switch** This tool is swept over the lawn to remove the dew in the morning, pushing the moisture down into the roots where it is needed. Lawns should not be cut when they are wet as the grass clogs up the mower. Dew brushes are also commonly used to brush off moisture on the lawn.

• **Edging shears** As you might expect from the name, these are used to edge the lawn. Use them working in the direction of the open blades, as you would scissors. Keep your right hand still, using your left hand to do the cutting motion to ensure a straight line is maintained.

• **Half moon** For cutting straight lines through turf, this tool has a blade designed to cut through the grass easily. Use a board to stand on to avoid damaging the edge of the turf, and to create a perfectly uniform straight line and neat edge.

• **True lute** While this is not an everyday gadget, it is handy for lawn repairs where there are bumps and hollows as it is used to level out top dressing. It is particularly valuable on lawns where level surfaces are crucial, such as the croquet pitch at Polesden Lacey.

Above Chartwell in Kent is the former family home of Winston Churchill. The croquet lawn was, and still is, kept in immaculate condition. **Opposite, far left** Using a lute to level the lawn after fixing a hollow. **Opposite, left** Edging shears help to keep your lawn looking neat.

Tip

Remember to remove lawn clippings after edging to prevent weed germination.

A wildflower meadow

Creating a wildflower meadow in the garden is a wonderfully rewarding experience. Your meadow does not need to be on a large scale – you can incorporate one in the tiniest of spaces and it will become a nectar bar for thousands of pollinating insects.

The main difficulty in establishing a wildflower meadow is competition from vigorous grasses. Wild flowers generally thrive in poor soils, where they will not be overwhelmed by stronger and taller plants. On very fertile sites it pays to strip off the grass entirely and remove the first layer of topsoil. This can be added to areas of the garden where fertility is required, such as filling up raised beds in the kitchen garden.

Where the soil is moderately fertile, a plant called yellow rattle is often sown. A semi-parasitc plant, it decreases the vigour of the competing grasses, enabling wild flowers to become established.

Wildflower plug plants can also be bought from garden centres, giving the flowers a head start against the grasses. A cheaper option is to buy a seed mix, sow it in modules in peat-free compost and then plant out later in the year.

Andy Lewis,
Head Gardener at Uppark, West Sussex

'We collect seed from the hemiparasitic yellow rattle in the meadow to use in other areas of the garden in the autumn. We cut the grass short, scarify and then broadcast and roll the seed in using a garden roller. We then leave it to germinate and establish over the next few months.'

Step-by-step: Creating a wildflower meadow

1. Use a scythe or mower to cut the grass right down, as close to the soil level as possible. Remove the grass clippings and add them to the compost heap, where they will add valuable nitrogen to the mix and eventually contribute to the fertility of the soil.

2. Pick areas at random for a more natural feel, and use a spade to remove sections of grass and scuff up the soil with a rake.

3. Sow a type of seed mix suitable for the soil. If the soil is fertile, there are some more vigorous mixes that will survive, but be careful that they do not take over the entire garden when they seed or spread.

4. Rake the soil over the seed, add water and leave to germinate. In large spaces it may be necessary to provide some defence against birds taking the seed.

Aftercare

Once a wildflower meadow is established it is very easy to maintain. Cut it down each year after it has flowered and had a chance to set seed. After cutting, collect the grass otherwise it will rot down and increase the fertility of the soil. Either add it to the compost heap or leave the grass in piles at the sides of the meadow as this will hopefully encourage wildlife such as hedgehogs and mice seeking a home for hibernation.

Above A wildflower meadow is easy to maintain and means that your garden will be filled with colour.

Annuals for wildflower mixes

Anthemis arvenis Commonly known as corn chamomile, this classic meadow annual has attractive large, white, daisy-shaped flowers with yellow centres. It is often used in a 'corn' mix with cornflowers, corn marigolds and corn cockle.

Agrostemma githago The corn cockle has vibrant magenta flowers that create an instant splash of colour in a wildflower meadow. It is uncommon in arable fields now as a result of modern agricultural practices, so it is lovely to see it being introduced to ornamental meadows. However, it should be noted that it is highly toxic.

Centaurea cyanus The cornflower is a classic and popular choice in meadows because of its stunning bluish-purple flowers. It is also a very easy flower to naturalise in grass.

Papaver rhoeas There is nothing more spectacular than a meadow full of bright red poppies with their dark black centres. They prefer disturbed ground and can lie dormant in the soil for years.

Chrysanthemum segetum Corn marigolds are a maginificent sight in a meadow, producing golden-yellow flower heads from June until October. It grows in a range of soils and can just as easily be found on a rubbish tip as it can be in a meadow.

Above The corn cockle is a delicate and attractive addition to a meadow.

Below The striking blue cornflower.

Above A sown wildflower meadow at Hidcote.   **Below** Corn marigolds add a sunny cheer to a wildflower mix.

Instant wildflower meadows

If sowing a wildflower meadow sounds too difficult, it is possible to get rolls of wildflower mixes and lay them on prepared flower-beds. This creates an instant wildflower meadow or bed in just a few weeks if done in spring. There is a range of mixes including annual and perennial species that come in lots of different colours and seasons of interest.

planting

Preparing the soil

Before planting anything, you need to prepare the soil in your garden to give your plants the best start in life. You have two choices as to how to do this: the hard way or the easy way! Traditional horticultural techniques teach the importance of digging over the soil prior to planting. However, some gardeners advocate a technique called the 'no-dig' method, whereby the soil is left undisturbed to avoid damaging the structure, and instead the planting areas are built up by adding material to the surface.

Personally, I love the feeling of digging over the soil. It is a workout for my arm and stomach muscles that no expensive gym subscription would be able to provide, and it helps me to feel in touch with the earthy medium that I am working with. However, I am sure that as I get older, the

Step-by-step: Double digging the soil

The most common method of digging is called double digging, but this is very hard work and only really necessary on heavily compacted soil or if you have plants which need a deep root run, such as if you are planting up a long-term soft fruit area or a rose bed. Double digging can help to break up a heavy pan in the soil and improve drainage. Otherwise, digging out the single depth ('spit') of the spade should suffice. As you dig over the soil, remember to remove any perennial weeds that you come across, and keep them separate from the compost bin to prevent them spreading.

1. Using string, mark out your first row to dig. It should be the width of your spade. Dig out one spit depth and place the soil in a wheelbarrow.

2. Use a fork to dig over the bottom of the trench, down to the depth of the second spit (hence the name double digging). If the soil is really impoverished, add a layer of well-rotted manure to line the bottom of the trench.

3. Mark out your second row and repeat the procedure of the first row, only this time place the soil you dig out in the first row, rather than in the barrow.

4. Mark out your third row and then repeat what you did in the previous step. Continue this process until you get to the final row.

5. Once you have dug out your final row, empty out the contents from the wheelbarrow to fill the final trench.

6. Finally, rake the soil level, leaving it as smooth as you can.

no-dig method will begin to ingratiate itself more in my favour. And after all, the results of the no-dig method are just as impressive.

A rotavator can save on backbreaking work, but it does not dig down deeply, uses up a lot of fossil fuel and in some cases the weight of the machine can cause compaction rather than relieve it.

The no-dig method

The theory behind the no-dig method is that the process of digging actually damages the existing soil structure. This affects the natural bacteria in the soil, and of course the activity of worms. Furthermore, by digging over the soil you can slice through perennial weeds, which encourages them to multiply, and you can also end up unearthing what would otherwise be dormant weed seed.

The no-dig process works on the basis of adding copious amounts of organic matter to the area to be planted. If you are planting up vegetables then add at least 15cm (6in) of organic matter, but ideally more. Once it has been added, the no-dig system relies on the natural rotting-down of the material and the activity of the worms below to draw it down into the existing soil, thus improving the depth and quality of the growing medium.

One no-dig method is 'lasagne planting', so called because it builds up layers of organic matter between cardboard, in a similar way that mince and vegetables are sandwiched between sheets of lasagne. Cardboard is rich in carbon, an important component in the decomposition of the material, and combines with the nitrogen which is present in the green and kitchen waste.

Above A rotavator can be used to break up the soil surface. **Below, left** Digging your garden is a great form of exercise.

Tip

Try to keep your back as straight as possible to avoid damaging it. Do not overload your spade, but instead dig out manageable chunks of soil. Remember to take regular breaks, and spread the whole job over a few days or weeks to interrupt the intensity of digging.

Step-by-step: Making a lasagne bed

It will take a good few months for the material to be incorporated, so start the process in late summer or early autumn. The winter frosts will help to break down the material, meaning that by springtime, your planting area will be ready for use. Do not plant into fresh material as this decomposition process can affect the fertility.

1. Place a layer of cardboard on the surface of the soil, ensuring any perennial weeds such as ground elder or bindweed have been removed beforehand.

2. Use a fork to puncture a few holes in the cardboard, and then give the area a good soaking. This should encourage worms into the root area.

3. Add a 15cm (6in) layer of green garden and kitchen waste and then another layer of cardboard.

4. Finally place another layer of green waste on top and leave to decompose over winter.

5. Plant your vegetable seedlings into it and enjoy their bounty.

6. Remove your plants at the end of the season, adding them to the compost heap, and then repeat the process from steps 3 –5 again and continue each year.

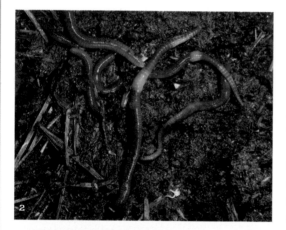

Using herbaceous perennials

Think of your choice of herbaceous perennials as an artist would think of their painting palette. They offer a massive range of colours from which to select your personal preferences. Furthermore, you can incorporate textural and architectural qualities by using ornamental grasses and plants with impressive foliage.

A herbaceous perennial is simply a plant that does not produce woody stems (as a shrub does), and generally dies back below the soil during winter – although there are a few herbaceous perennials such as heucheras and hellebores that usually retain some foliage above ground.

Planting your borders

This is where your dreams turn into reality – all those colours and textures that you had planned in your head or on paper are now finally going to be planted in the soil. If you do not have a planting plan, do a quick sketch before visiting a local garden centre or plant nursery. Just buying random plants to slot in somewhere will result in a border that lacks cohesion.

Herbaceous plants always look best when planted in odd numbers – usually groups of three in smaller borders, but five, seven and nine are more common in large borders. Individual plants look fine, particularly if they are in repeating patterns.

As a rule of thumb, lower-growing herbaceous plants, such as hostas, heucheras and nepetas should go towards the front, medium-sized perennials in the middle, and, yes, you've guessed it, taller perennials such as delphiniums, persicara and cardoons towards the back. However, don't stick rigidly to this rule. More interest and depth can be created by pulling some taller plants forward, creating natural flowing patterns among the plants and their flowers.

Look for patterns

The Arts and Crafts garden designer and artist Gertrude Jekyll famously used 'drifts' in her planting plans, where blocks of plants would seamlessly flow into each other. However, there are many other patterns and techniques that can be used. The National Trust advisor, plantsman and garden

Above, left The attractive bronze foliage of heucheras adds interesting textural qualities to the front of a border. **Above, right** The herbaceous borders at Killerton, have repeats of planting patterns running throughout the design to add interest to the overall scheme.

writer Graham Stuart Thomas, used certain architectural and foliage plants such as santolina and yuccas as repeat plants that would punctuate throughout a planting scheme. He also used repeat patterns of planting combinations and colours, such as yellow *Achillea* 'Gold Plate' and the blue *Salvia* x *superba* (seen opposite).

Piet Oudoulf, the Dutch plantsman renowned for his modern prairie-style planting, sometimes uses blocks or drifts of one just type of plant diagonally from the front to back of a border and then runs another single block of a different plant next to it, repeating the sequences down the entire length of a border. To create this effect, a large, deep border is needed. Alternatively, single plants can be dotted into a border but repeated throughout the planting scheme. In double borders, you can use symmetry so that the planting scheme is reflected on both sides of a path. This makes the border feel balanced, gives it structure and order, and avoids a messy, random or clumsy design scheme.

Getting started

Whatever pattern you are using, set out all your plants first in the bed before planting. If you have bought them when they are in flower, it helps to get a sense of how the colour schemes are going to work in the flower-bed. Do not feel you have to stick rigidly to your planting plan – even the top garden designers will do a lot of tweaking to their plans once they start to physically create the border and the design can be adapted.

Above, left Artichokes grow alongside the flowers at Powis Castle, adding texture and height to the borders. **Above, centre** The borders at Peckover House, Cambridgeshire, were designed by Graham Stuart Thomas. **Above, right** Viewing the borders at Nymans from above, means that you can see the intended design of the planting. **Opposite** Contrasting colour planting in the herbaceous borders at Polesden Lacey, designed by Graham Stuart Thomas.

Step-by-step:
How to plant herbaceous perennials

Many herbaceous species die a few weeks after being planted. This is partly a result of being planted in the incorrect soil or aspect (always read the plant label from the garden centre), and sometimes a lack of water during the summer. Planting them during a harsh cold winter when they are young and susceptible is another route to failure. However, very often they do not survive because they are planted incorrectly and rot in the soil. They may be planted too deeply or, more commonly, they are smothered in mulch. To avoid this happening:

1. Set the plants out in the place where you intend to position them.

2. Gently squeeze the plants out of their pots. Sometimes it may be necessary to carefully scrape away the top 2cm (¾in) of loose compost as this can contain weed seeds. If you are using environmentally friendly coir pots, they can be planted directly into the ground without removing the plants from their pots.

3. If the roots are pot-bound, gently unravel them to encourage them to grow outwards rather than continuing to go round and round.

4. For each plant, dig out a hole that is no deeper than the rootball, but twice the width of the diameter.

5. Put the rootball in the hole, making sure that the top is level with the soil.

6. Backfill the soil and use your hand, not feet, to firm the plant into the ground – your feet would compact the soil too much.

At Polesden Lacey we buy many of our plants in hairy coir pots as an environmentally better option than the problems associated with factories producing plastic ones. Hairy pots are handmade from the natural waste material from fibres from the coconut industry and mixed with latex to bond it together. The roots are naturally air-pruned when they stretch outside of their pot, which prevents them from becoming rootballed and compacted within the pot. The pots can be planted directly into the soil, where the coir material breaks down naturally, saving you the extra job afterwards of recycling your plastic pots.

7. Place the plastic pots upside down over each plant to protect them from the mulch. If the plants have too much growth, cut it back with secateurs.

8. Carefully cover the bare soil with mulch such as well-rotted manure or garden compost

9. Remove the flower-pots and check that the mulch is not smothering the plants, which would cause them to rot.

10. Water the plants in well. Even if it is raining, the plants will still benefit from a good soaking. The area left around each individual plant makes a natural water reservoir that helps to retain the water and prevent run-off.

11. Gather up all your pots and take them to a recycling area locally. Alternatively, save them for sowing your own plants in next year.

'Small plants establish and adapt to their environment much better than mature plants.'

Paul Gallivan
Head Gardener, Woolbeding Gardens, West Sussex

Planting bulbs

Bulbs are the most exciting little gems in the garden – they stay under your radar for most of the year, then suddenly erupt from the ground in an incredible, vibrant display of colour, as if to say 'Here I am, don't you forget about me', then disappear back under the ground to be forgotten about for a few more months.

These are the plants that, more than any others, punctuate the seasons of the year. Most people's fondest memories of spring flowers will be associated with bulbs – bluebell woods in springtime, or bright yellow daffodils when visiting a National Trust property for Mothering Sunday. And during a refreshing winter walk, seeing the snowdrops poking their heads up from the frosty ground reassures us that a new growing season is underway.

Versatility is the key for using bulbs in the garden. They disappear discreetly when they are out of season, yet can offer an extra blaze of interest in a bed when everything else has finished. For example, at Polesden Lacey we have used the beautiful *Galtonia candicans* to offer an added season of interest to the peony border after the peonies finish flowering in early summer. There are bulbs for every season and for every type of location, whether they are alliums basking in the open sun or snake's head fritillaries thriving in damp meadows.

Tulips are fantastic for using in formal flower-beds, bedding displays and mixed borders. Other bulbs such as gladioli, lilies, crocosmia and dahlias are perfect for cut flower borders and for adding a splash of colour in the flower-beds from mid- to late summer.

In wooded areas you can try natural drifts of snowdrops or winter aconites (*Eranthus hyemalis*) for a winter display, or wood anemones (*Anemone nemorosa*) and cyclamens for later in the year. For naturalising in lawns, nothing is better than crocuses and daffodils.

Generally, spring-flowering bulbs should be planted in autumn, and autumn-flowering bulbs in spring, although there are a few exceptions. Snowdrops prefer to be moved when they are 'in the green', which means still in leaf and just after flowering. It is possible to buy bulbs in containers and they can be planted out in the garden at any time of year.

Get the naturalised look

There is nothing worse than seeing bulbs growing in a lawn or under a tree in regimented rows. To make effect more natural and create drifts, simply scatter the bulbs over the surface of the lawn and plant them where they fall.

The easiest way to plant them is to use a bulb planter, which cuts out a core of turf and a section of soil underneath. You can get short-handled ones, but if you have a large number of bulbs it is best to get a long-handled planter that you can push into the ground with your foot to save you getting backache. It is of course possible to use a trowel or border fork, too. Place the bulb in the hole, generally at two or three times the depth of the bulb, and then replace the soil and core of turf. Remember to plant the bulb the right way up, with the pointy end facing upwards!

If you have a larger area, you can strip off areas of turf, place the bulbs in the soil with a trowel and then re-lay the turf. At some National Trust properties a tractor with a mounted bulb-planting machine has been used to plant thousands of bulbs *en masse*.

After the bulbs have finished flowering, do not be tempted to cut back the foliage to tidy the garden. Let the foliage die back naturally as the bulb needs this time to replenish itself.

Above, left Spring bulbs, ready to be planted. Above, left Tulips in deep purple, white and yellow fill the borders at Sizergh Castle, Cumbria. Below, left *Zinnia elegans* 'Early Wonder Mixed' add intriguing shapes to a herbaceous border. Below, right At Polesden Lacey, 30,000 bulbs were planted in a single border for a tulip festival to provide a stunning display in spring.

Fleeting beauty: sowing annuals directly

Annuals are plants that live for one year and then die. The group includes bedding plants, although some of these are really perennials but live for just one season in our temperate climate before getting zapped by our cold winter. This section is about hardy annuals, which can be sown directly outdoors and will die back naturally as soon as the frosts arrive.

If you do not have much money or time, annuals are the plants to go for. They are also invaluable if you cannot make up your mind what you want in your garden – sowing some annuals will give you plenty of time to think about what you want to do with your garden long term, and in the meantime you can enjoy the vibrant colours of your hardy annuals and also the bees and butterflies that will be attracted to your garden.

For the cost of a few packets of seeds, you can pack a border full of flowers that will bloom all summer long. The results are pretty quick – it is possible to have an impressive floral display only a few weeks after sowing. It is a great project to get children involved with as well, because they love the excitement of sowing seeds and seeing them flower so quickly – for them it is a bit like colouring-in, as you can make lots of swirly patterns in the soil, and then colour them in with the flowers of your choice. Depending on where you live, you should be able to sow from about April onwards. Remember to keep the plants well watered so that their swift growth is not checked. Some of the taller plants such as sunflowers may also need staking to prevent them flopping over.

Step-by-step: Sowing hardy annuals

1. Prepare the ground by lightly digging it over with a fork. There is no need to dig deep as annuals have only a minimal root run. If the soil is really impoverished, some compost can be added to give the plants an extra boost once they're established.
2. Remove any perennial weed roots you come across and then rake the soil level.
3. Trickle sand to create patterns into which you will sow the specific plant seeds.
4. Scatter the seeds loosely into each area and gently rake them in.

Below Cosmos can be an annual or a perennial, either are ideal for brightening the garden.

Mound planting

If you garden on really heavy, claggy soil, then you can try a technique, known as 'mound planting' to help improve the drainage around the plant.

In a bucket, mix up equal amounts of grit and garden soil. If you have mole hills nearby, scoop them up for garden soil, as the moles' strong paws tend to break up soil into a lovely friable texture. The mound should be around the same size as the rootball.

Dig a planting hole in the top of the mound and plant into it. Water the plant in thoroughly. The angle of the mound should ensure that the plant does not rot in excess water.

Above An *Acer palmatum* grows at Biddulph Grange Garden, Staffordshire. Planting a tree will leave a long-lasting legacy in your garden.

The long-term view

We gardeners like to think long term. We dream of the garden's future and how it will be enjoyed by generations to come – and dreams do not come much bigger than in the 'tree kingdom'. Planting a tree really is like leaving your legacy to the future. If the right tree and the right conditions are found, you can reasonably expect that your tree will outlive you to be enjoyed by future generations. Long after the memories of us mortals fade, a tree will remain, standing tall as silent evidence of our life on this planet.

We depend on the existence of trees for our survival, for without the woods, forests and rainforests we would not have the oxygen to breathe. They sustain the life of millions of animals around the world, creating habitats and food resources for them. Their root systems help to knit the earth together, without which the soil beneath our feet would erode at an alarming rate as it gets washed and blown away by the rain and wind. They give us shelter, filter out pollution and enable us to live healthy and sustainable lives. In other words, trees are really important! If you have room to grow them, that is fantastic. However, there are a few things to consider before planting them.

- The height of the tree. They are very variable in size and some will grow to 40m (131ft), so always check the label before buying. A fast-growing large tree could quickly block your light and annoy your neighbours. If you have a small garden, choose small or medium-sized trees such as birches, cherries and most cultivars of *Acer palmatum*.
- The width of the tree – oaks, for example, can almost be as wide as they are tall, so do not forget to factor that in before you start planting.
- If you do choose a large tree to plant in your garden, remember that you are responsible for the maintenance of it. If it becomes dangerous due to disease or wind damage it could cost you a lot of money to pay for a tree surgeon to sort it out for you.
- Planting a tree with extensive root systems too near your house can affect drains and the stability of your house, or that of your neighbour.

Above A mature tree throws dappled shade onto the grass at Shaw's Corner.

Planting a tree

If you are willing to wait for an impressive height, buy your trees small. Buying big trees will give you instant impact in the garden but they will probably not live as long; they will have been languishing in pots for much longer, and will find it much harder to adjust to their new environment once planted in the soil, as they will not have had time to adapt and strengthen their tree trunk against the prevailing wind. Another drawback is that the size of their rootball is often out of proportion to the size of their canopy; the root system should be big enough to anchor the plant and provide it with water and nutrients, but one glance at the plastic container they are sitting in at the garden centre will probably tell you that this is not the case.

   A young tree will settle into its new home much quicker, growing away vigorously. It will not have formed such a compacted rootball and so will be less prone to become strangled by its own root system. In fact, after a few years, there is a good chance that a 3m (10ft) tree and a 60cm (2ft) tree bought for a fraction of the price will have reached a similar height. In addition, the originally smaller tree will almost certainly be healthier and live for much longer.

Above Rows of newly planted trees in springtime at Sissinghurst Castle.

Above A young tree ready to be planted in an air pot.

Right An apple sapling labelled for easy identification at Avebury Manor which is part of the Plant Conservation Programme.

The label reads:
The Plant Conservation Programme
Knightshayes Court
Tiverton
Devon EX16 7RG
018 4 259 547

Advantages of bare-root trees over container-grown

- They establish better because they are young and vigorous (most bare-root trees are one or two years old).
- They are cheaper than trees in containers.
- They will not be root bound.
- There is more choice – particularly in fruit trees.

Fresh from the field

The best type of young tree to buy is a bare-root tree. These are exactly what they sound like – trees with their bare roots exposed. They are dug up fresh from the nursery fields and transported immediately to the garden centres and markets. Once they reach retail, they are bundled up and plunged into beds of soil until they are bought and taken home to plant. They are the equivalent of getting fresh ingredients from the market, and are what the connoisseur gardener will request. Bare-root trees are only available from late autumn until late winter. The retailer will usually wrap the roots for you in a piece of hessian or a bag, but it is important that the tree is then taken home immediately and placed in the soil as it will die if the roots are allowed to dry out. If you are not ready to plant the tree properly, you can heel it in. This is a gardening term for quickly digging a hole, sticking the roots into it and covering them with soil. It is just a temporary method of keeping the roots moist until you can plant the tree.

If you cannot obtain a bare-root tree, then you could consider those in air pots which are made of recycled and recyclable HDPE (High Density Polyethylene). These are root containers made up of a series of cones with small holes in each tip that overcome the root-spiralling problem of conventionally container-grown trees. The outward-growing root tips are funnelled towards the holes, where they eventually dehydrate upon exposure to the air. This stimulates the root system, encouraging it to send out lateral roots. Like containerised trees, they can be planted at any time of year, but produce a far healthier specimen without the spiralling or 'girdling' effect. As soon as the tree is planted in the ground it will produce numerous little fibrous feeding roots, which will help get it established quicker.

When and where to plant your tree

The best gardeners learn not from books, lectures or talks, but from studying nature. Not only is nature inspiring, it has been doing what it does for millions of years and plants have adapted and evolved to suit their growing conditions. By re-creating a plant's natural growing conditions in your garden, your plants should grow happily and healthily.

This is very much the case with planting a tree. A tree in nature has usually grown from a seed that has either fallen from the tree or been dropped from a bird contained in a healthy dollop of bird dropping, nature's version of adding manure. Either way, most seeds germinate on or very near the surface of the ground. If you look at trees that have grown naturally in woods and parkland you will often see their large surface roots above the ground. You will certainly see the root flare (sometimes called trunk flare) where the base of the trunk is significantly wider. This demonstrates how close the roots should be to the surface of the soil. Bear this in mind when planting your tree, and make sure you do not plant too deeply.

Tip

Planting shrubs and trees with mycorrhizal fungi is a relatively new concept, yet the fungi have been present for millions of years, occurring naturally in healthy soil. The fungi and the tree roots benefit from each other's presence as the fungi extract sugars from the plant in exchange for providing extra moisture and nutrients. They do this by attaching themselves to the plant's roots, extending their network of fine fibres, which in effect extends the root system and thus enables it to absorb more water and nutrients. It is particularly effective in helping the plant gather phosphorus from the soil, an essential element for root development that is very often in short supply. It also appears to give some protection against root diseases.

Large tubs of mycorrhizal fungi granules can easily be found in garden centres or online. When sprinkling the granules, ensure that they come into direct contact with the roots to stimulate them into growth.

The basics of planting a tree might seem simple: dig a hole, plonk the tree in it, cover it up with soil and leave it to grow. If only it were that straightforward. Sadly, thousands of trees die within their first year after planting because it was not done correctly. The usual problem is that the tree has been planted too deeply, causing the trunk to rot at the base. The most important aspects of planting a tree are to ensure that the hole is not too deep and that the soil in the bottom of the planting hole is not loosened too much, as this causes the tree to sink over the following months.

The best time to plant a tree is in autumn when the soil is warm. This gives the tree roots an opportunity to settle into their new home before the onset of winter, and before growth starts in the spring.

If you are uncertain of the pH of your soil, it is worth doing a test to establish whether it is acidic or alkaline (see page 21). Some trees prefer certain conditions – for example a lilac tree likes slightly alkaline soil, whereas most acers prefer it very slightly acidic. It is usually best to choose a tree suitable for the soil conditions rather than trying to change them, since over time the soil will eventually revert back to the original pH.

Step-by-step: Planting procedure

1. Remove the turf and any encroaching weeds from around the planting position of the tree to a distance of about 50cm (20in). This bare patch can be any shape. It is usually circular, but I prefer oval as it is easier to mow around.

2. Dig out the planting hole. Most modern research shows that square holes are better than round ones as they prevent the roots from going around in a circle and eventually girdling or strangling the tree. The hole should be about three times the diameter of the rootball but the same depth. Any deeper and the tree will start to sink – one of the most common causes of death for an ornamental tree.

3. Lightly fork the sides of the hole to encourage the roots to grow outwards, as this will help stabilise the tree.

4. Add mycorrhizal fungi to the bottom of the hole, following the manufacturer's guidelines with regards to quantity. It is important that the rootball comes into contact with the fungus to encourage healthy root growth.

5. If the tree is in a container, remove it and pull out roots that are circling the rootball. If this is not done, the roots will continue to go round and round and will eventually end up strangling the tree.

6. Lay a cane or straight stick across the hole to check the level of the top of the rootball. It should be level or even 1–2cm (½ – ¾in) higher than the stick to allow for any sinkage after planting; it is essential that the tree is not planted too deeply. If there is excess top soil sitting on top of the rootball then pull this away – it can be as much as 5cm (2in) deep. Place the tree into the hole. Remove enough soil to expose the root flare (swelling at base of trunk) where the trunk meets the first set of roots.

7. Backfill the hole around the rootball, ensuring that all the spoil goes back into the hole. Adding compost and manure to the hole should be avoided, except in

7

8

9

11

extremely poor conditions, as this encourages the roots not to grow outwards but instead remain within the comfort of the hole, eventually making it a weak and unstable tree. It can also cause the tree to sink after planting, if the added material is lighter than the original soil.

8. As the soil is added back into the hole, use the heel of your garden boot to firm the soil in around the tree, pointing the toes towards the trunk. This should help to reduce excess air pockets in the soil and ensure that tree is stable in the ground.

9. The tree may need staking for its first couple of years, particularly in windy locations. This will help to avoid wind rock while the tree establishes itself, which can take up to three years. Drive in a diagonal stake at 45 degrees to ensure that it does not

hit the rootball, positioning it on the side of the prevailing wind so the tree does not get blown onto the stake and damaged.

10. The tree should be tied to the stake low down on the trunk, usually about a third of the way up. This is to encourage the stem to flex slightly in the wind, which will help to strengthen it, a bit like a muscle. Use either a tree tie with a spacer between the trunk and stake, or flexible cable tied in a figure of eight. A recycled pair of old tights is a good alternative method. It is important to make sure that the trunk does not rub on the stake as this will cause long-term damage. Check the next year that the tie is not too tight. After the second year you should be able to remove the stake.

11. Spread an organic mulch over the area of the rootball, such as well-rotted manure or garden compost. This will help to suppress weeds and retain the moisture. Keep the mulch away from the trunk, though, as it can cause the trunk to rot. The gap created by the lack of organic matter close to the trunk helps to create a sump for retaining the water slightly longer after watering.

12. Finally, water the plant in thoroughly. During its first year of establishment this will need doing regularly throughout the summer, but as the tree becomes more established it should be weaned off to encourage it to send out roots seeking its own source of moisture, making it self-sustaining.

Methods of staking a tree

Although an angled stake is the most popular method of supporting a tree as it does not damage the rootball and the angle offers the strongest stability, there are other methods available.

Really large trees can be stabilised by three or four galvanised wire guy ropes, attached around the trunk and then secured to low stakes banged at 45 degrees into the ground a few metres away from the tree. This is a particularly useful method when a large tree has been transplanted and needs to establish itself again in the soil without rocking in the wind. The wire around the tree can be covered with sections of hose pipe to prevent it damaging the trunk. However, you will need a large space to do this, and it can become a trip hazard if children play in the garden.

Upright or vertical stakes can be used on bare-root trees as they can be placed near the rootball without damaging it. These look pleasanter in the garden than the angled stake, as their direction follows the upright trunk. The stake should be driven into the ground first, before the tree is planted. Upright stakes are useful for supporting tall trees with a long, thin trunk that needs supporting until it has thickened up.

Two stakes either side of the tree trunk just below the crown of the tree can also provide strong stability. However, I have seen the heads of standard trees snapped off just below the head after a strong gust of wind when they have been fixed too firmly in place.

H-stakes are basically two sturdy stakes banged into the ground on either side of the tree, and then a piece of wood is attached between them. The tree is attached to this crossbar with a stake. This offers extra stability and is often used on large trees that require extra support.

Moving a tree

Occasionally it may be necessary to move a tree or shrub, sometimes because it has outgrown its original planting position or because you wish to redesign the garden. It might also be that you are moving house and want to take a favourite tree or shrub with you.

Transplanting a tree is not ideal. It is like an operation, severing the roots from the ground it has lived in, and as with surgery, there are sadly sometimes casualties. However, by taking your time, it should be possible to transplant a tree successfully. Moving trees isn't a new concept – the eighteenth-century garden designer 'Capability' Brown was famous for shifting trees around his landscapes, and he even devised a machine for doing it.

The younger the tree, the easier it is to move. There are however some shrubs that really do not like to be moved whatever their age, including magnolias, cistus and roses. If a tree has been in position for more than five years then it may be worth getting a contractor to come in with a machinery to move the tree as this causes minimal disturbance to the roots.

The best time to move a deciduous tree is during the dormant season (between late autumn

Right Trees reflected in the lake at Croome, Worcestershire. This parkland was the first of 'Capability' Brown's magnificent landscape designs.

and late winter) when it does not have a leaf canopy to support. Evergreens are best moved in spring as the plant is ready to grow in the warm soil and so will more easily absorb water and nutrients and will establish better. Evergreens can lose water from their leaves in winter, so will not be able to replace lost moisture if moved at this time of year.

In an ideal world, the process for moving a tree takes place over two years. The first year, half the tree underground is cut around, at a distance equivalent to the tree canopy, slicing through the roots with a spade. This encourages new fibrous roots to grow underground which are the essential ones for sustaining the plant after transplanting. The second year, the tree is dug up and planted in a new hole. The fibrous roots formed from the previous year will immediately start to provide water and nutrients for the plant. However, the reality is that most people want to dig up and move the tree in one move, as shown right.

Tip

Painting your wooden stakes black will make them stand out less in the garden, ensuring that it is the tree itself that takes centre stage. Try to use round stakes rather than square as they are easier to attach with a tree tie. Also, the corners of a stake can damage the tree trunk.

Step-by-step: Transplanting a tree

1. Before digging up your tree, prepare the new planting hole (or large pot if moving home) and get it ready. It is important that once the tree is dug up it is kept out of the ground for as little time as possible.

2. Dig a circular trench around the tree. This should be as wide as you can manage as you want to retain as much of the root system as possible. As a rule of thumb, digging out as far the drip line (the edge) of the tree canopy is ideal.

3. Once the trench has been dug, start to undercut the roots with a spade, again trying to retain as much of the rootball as you can.

4. Lean the tree back and slide a sheet of damp hessian or old blanket underneath it.

5. Wrap the rootball up in the hessian or blanket and give it another spray with water to keep the rootball damp.

6. Carefully lift the rootball out of the ground. It could be very heavy, requiring at least two people to do the job.

7. Plant the tree as quickly as possible and water it immediately. It will also probably need staking as the existing roots will no longer anchor the tree.

Above Bright azaelia provide a colourful splash of colour in spring, while the evergreens give the garden structure and provide year-round interest at Plas yn Rhiw, Gwynedd.

Planting shrubs

Shrubs are plants that produce woody stems and provide a permanent structure all year round, as opposed to herbaceous plants that die back in winter. They can be either deciduous or evergreen and are generally smaller than trees, although not always. They are usually multi-stemmed, but again trees can also be multi-stemmed, and some shrubs have a single stem such as a standard rose or bay tree. As you can tell, there is not a clear botanical difference between a tree or a shrub, but think smaller and multi-stemmed and you are probably visualising a shrub. There are many common shrubs that you will easily recognise, including most roses (except the climbers and ramblers), box, lavenders, hydrangeas, rhododendrons and witch hazel. Soft fruit bushes such as gooseberries, blueberries and currants are also a form of shrub.

While manure and garden compost should not usually be added into the planting hole of a tree as that may cause the tree to sink, some shrubs such as roses and fruit trees do benefit from an enhanced, richer soil mix. It gives them the quick start needed to produce a profusion of flowers or a bumper crop of fruit in subsequent years. A traditional gardeners' trick was to add plenty of organic matter to the planting hole of a fruit tree, but to prevent it from sinking afterwards, they would place a large stone directly under the rootball.

As when planting a tree, you should ensure that the roots of most shrubs are not buried too deeply. However, most shrubs are not going to live as long as a tree, so the depth is not as critical, although getting it right will prolong their life.

There are a few plants that do thrive from a deeper planting hole. Generally, climbers, and particularly clematis, like to have a cool root run and will benefit from being planted slightly deeper than most other trees and shrubs.

Blackcurrant stool bush

Blackcurrant bushes also like to be planted deeply. They are grown as stool or multi-stemmed bushes, meaning that the rootball should be planted about 5–10cm (2–4in) below the surface to encourage it to throw out lots of suckers from below ground. It is this vigorous young growth that produces the fruit the following year. After planting, cut back all the growth to one or two buds above ground level to prompt the plant to generate plenty of growth. If the bush is planted in summer, wait until winter to do this.

Above Blackcurrants are ready for harvesting in mid-summer but due to their small size, picking them can be a time-consuming pursuit and requires patience.

Tip
Build up a ridge of mulch around the edge of the planting area so that water will collect within it when it rains or the plant is watered. However, if you live in a cool area you may wish to remove the ridge in winter to prevent puddles freezing on top of the rootball.

Step-by-step: Planting a clematis

1. Prior to planting the clematis, give the roots a good soaking in a bucket of water for about 10 minutes.

2. Dig a deep hole just in front of the support that it is going to climb up. The hole should be a few centimetres deeper than the rootball, around 8-10cm (3-4in).

3. Place the rootball in the hole and cover it up with a 50:50 mix of compost and soil, ensuring about 5cm (2in) of the stems are below the soil.

4. Use the water in the bucket that the clematis was soaking in to give it a really good drink of water.

5. Give the planting area a layer of mulch such as garden compost or well-rotted manure.

6. Cover the base of the plant with crocks or tiles. Clematis prefer a slightly cool rootball, although their stems and foliage prefer warmth and sun. Alternatively, if you plant an evergreen species near the roots of the clematis you will provide shade without the need for covering over the root area with other materials.

propagation

Nuturing your plants

'The love of gardening is a seed once sown that never dies.'
Gertrude Jekyll

The magic of growing and nurturing your own plants from seed or cuttings never loses its appeal. Propagating plants is easy, as you are just giving nature a helping hand in the ongoing process of reproduction. All you need to do is provide a suitable environment in which they can thrive.

Producing a lot of plants for free is a great way to save money and to make new friends with your neighbours, or down at the allotment. By swapping seeds or cuttings you will quickly build up a more diverse collection of plants that can be shared again the following year. If you still have spare plants, you might be able to sell them at local plant fairs or car boot sales.

Growing your own plants will also give you a far better choice than you can find in a garden centre. There is a good chance your plants will be healthier, too, as you will have given them more individual nurturing than a commercial grower dealing with thousands of plants would find time for.

You do not need any specialist propagation tools to get started; a few recycled pots or seed trays, a sharp knife, a pair of secateurs and some compost will suffice for most propagation techniques. If you want to take things further, a heated propagator is a useful addition as it helps you to control the environment that the seeds or cuttings are growing in.

If you are going to be doing a lot of propagation, or are lucky enough to have your own dedicated space such as a potting shed, it is worth making or buying a potting bench. This is simply a table or workbench that has been modified to make a convenient surface on which to do all your propagation tasks. It is important to have it at a comfortable height to prevent you from having to bend over and strain your back or neck. Most potting benches have raised backs and sides so that you can push all the compost to one end of the bench without it falling over the edges. More fancy designs will have a separate compartment or cavity to keep the compost in, and some will have shelving and cupboards above or below the bench.

Simple gadgets

In the Polesden Lacey glasshouse are some really simple homemade wooden tools to speed up propagation techniques. A wooden board made from marine ply that fits perfectly into a seed tray is simply pushed into the compost to firm the soil before sowing. Another simple gadget is similar in design, but has numerous nails banged through the wood to make columns and rows at 4cm (1¾in) spacing. This can simply be pressed into the compost, leaving multiple holes for sowing or pushing cuttings in. They are both fantastic labour-saving devices that can easily be made at home.

Opposite, clockwise from centre left A good selection of gardening tools can make tasks like propagation much easier; A homemade multiple dibber can save time on making individual holes; A packet of seeds ready to be planted; One of the key propagation tools is a good-quality knife, which is essential for cutting stems and removing foliage. Sharpen it regularly to ensure it will make clean cuts.

Collecting seed

The easiest way to propagate a plant is simply to collect its seed. Do not take it all, though, as seedheads can make attractive autumn and winter displays and supply birds with food. Letting some plants self-seed naturally into the surrounding area can give a pleasing natural effect, too.

Wait until the plants have finished flowering and their seeds have matured – if you pick the seedheads too early the seeds will not germinate. Sometimes shaking the plant to hear them rattle, such as with poppies, yellow rattle or love-in-a-mist, is a good indicator that they are ready. Put the seeds in paper bags or envelopes and keep them in a dark place such as a drawer or cupboard – they will sometimes keep for a few years if stored correctly. Do not forget to label them. Avoid storing seeds in plastic bags as they will start to rot.

Above Seed drawers in the Gardener's Bothy at Calke Abbey, Derbyshire.
Right *Nigella damascena*, or love-in-a-mist, is an attractive seedhead.

Sowing seed

This is a wonderfully cheap way to grow plants, and in many cases such as vegetables and hardy annuals it is the only method. Do remember, though, that while cuttings will produce exactly the same plants as the original, seedlings can vary from the mother plant. It is of course this natural selection process that enables life to adapt and evolve, but it can sometimes be frustrating when the apple seed you have collected from your favourite tree does not grow into the same type of tree with the same fruit. Of course, on the positive side, it may just be that you discover an improved variety of plant! Some of today's best plants were discovered either as chance seedlings found growing naturally or raised specifically by inquisitive horticulturists wanting to see the results when two of their favourite plants were crossed.

The easiest way to sow seed is directly into the ground. Some seed, such as hardy annuals or grass seed, can be scattered into the ground and lightly raked in. Carrots and parsnips are sown in

Paul Gallivan,
Head Gardener at
Woolbeding Gardens,
West Sussex

'Thoroughly clean the greenhouse when it is empty to get rid of pests and disease. A handheld steam cleaner is great to get into the nooks around benches.'

Below Sprinkle very small seeds over the soil as you would salt onto your chips. If you are right-handed, tip the seeds into your left hand and use the right to sprinkle the seeds.

Below, right Two or three medium-sized seeds can be sown into these pots. There is plenty of room for them to germinate and be split into individual pots once they have germinated and formed a strong enough root system.

shallow drills in the location where they are to grow for the year, covered back over with soil and watered in. To produce good-sized vegetables, the emerging seedlings are often thinned out to give the remaining ones more space to grow to their optimum size.

Seed can also be sown in pots or seed trays and kept indoors on either a windowsill or in a greenhouse until the seedlings are ready to be planted out. This is for plants such as chillies and tomatoes that need a long growing season but cannot be sown outdoors early in the season as the temperatures are too cold. Sowing seeds indoors in pots also enables you to look after them better and produce plants quicker, which can be useful if you are doing a late sowing.

Seed packets will give you guidance as to whether you should sow directly or in pots or containers. As a rule of thumb, plants producing roots such as carrots and parsnips should not be transplanted so are directly sown, large seeds get sown in individual containers and smaller ones are sprinkled in seed trays, but this is not always the case, so do check that you are going about things in the right way.

Tip

Tiny seeds such as begonias or carrots can be mixed with sand to help with the equal distribution of the seed.

Tip

Sow large seeds such as courgettes and pumpkins on their side to prevent water collecting on their surface and rotting them.

Sowing small seeds in a tray

Fill a seed tray with peat-free compost and firm it down using the palm of your hand or a piece of wood. Lightly water the tray prior to sowing so that the compost is moist.

If you are right-handed, tip some of the seeds into your left hand. Then take a pinch with your right hand and sprinkle them equally over the surface, a bit like lightly sprinkling salt over your food. Lightly water them in, using a watering can with a rose attached to the nozzle.

Pricking out

When the tiny seedlings have formed at least two true leaves (the leaves typical of the plant, not the first leaves produced from the seed, known as cotyledons) they can be pricked out into individual pots. Pricking out is a very delicate process of gently prising the seedling out of the compost using a tool (I like using a plant label). Hold the seedling by a leaf rather than by its stem as this can damage the baby plant. Make a small hole in a pot of compost with a dibber or a pencil and gently place the baby seedling in the hole, ensuring its leaves are above the compost. Gently push back the soil around the base of the seedling. Once the plant is more established it can either be planted outside or potted on – removed from its existing pot and transferred to a slightly bigger one. This enables the plant to continue growing and start to produce a strong root system before being planted outside.

Below, left Pricking out can be done with a speical tool, or with the end of a plant label. **Below, centre** It is a delicate operation so take care not to damage the young seedling. Try to hold it by a leaf rather than the stem if you can. **Below, right** Always remember to label your plants after sowing or pricking out. so they can be easily identified.

Taking a softwood cutting

It is very easy to take a softwood cutting – keeping it alive afterwards is the tricky part, as they easily succumb to fluctuations in sunlight, moisture and temperature. Spring is the best time to take softwood cuttings, so called because they are from shoots that have not yet ripened and formed into woody stems. The shoots are the soft flush of new growth that appears at this time of year.

Try to take the cuttings first thing in the morning as the shoots will be full of moisture from the cooler night temperatures. The trick is to get them into compost as quickly as possible. If you cannot do that immediately, they can be placed in a plastic bag in the fridge overnight.

Step-by-step: How to take softwood cuttings

1. Prepare the pots with compost first to minimise the time between taking the cuttings and putting them in the soil. Fill the pots with peat-free multi-purpose or cutting compost and lightly firm it down so that it is about 1cm (½in) below the top of the pots.

2. Using a pair of secateurs, remove healthy-looking stems that are about 10cm (4in) long. Place them in a plastic bag or a bucket of water until you can get them back to the greenhouse or potting bench. This will help them to retain their moisture.

3. Once you are ready to put them in the compost, strip back the lowest one-third of the leaves up the stem and remove the tip by pinching it out between your thumb and forefinger. Alternatively, use a garden knife to make a clean cut. The lower part can be dipped in hormone rooting powder to encourage it to send out roots, but this is often not necessary.

4. Use a dibber or even a pencil to create a hole and then insert the soft cutting into it up to its lowest leaves. Space the stems around the edge of the pot so that their leaves are not touching.

5. Cover the cuttings with a plastic bag sealed with an elastic band, or a homemade cloche made by cutting a plastic bottle in half. Alternatively, place them in a propagator. Monitor the conditions closely, as they will need good ventilation and moisture levels to prevent the plant from wilting. If the cuttings get too warm they will produce lush new shoots at the expense of producing roots.

Semi-ripe cuttings

The process for taking semi-ripe cuttings is almost exactly the same as for softwood cuttings, the main difference being the timing. These cuttings are taken from mid-summer through to late summer and the shoots selected are the ones that are just starting to ripen and become woody. I cut the leaves in half on the cuttings from this plant to reduce water loss through transpiration, which should improve the survival rate. These structural and attractive shrubs can be propagated by seed, but the easiest method is to take semi-ripe cuttings in mid-summer.

Step-by-step:
Taking semi-ripe cuttings

1. Select healthy semi-ripe shoots from the outside of the plant, checking first that the plant has no pests or disease.

2. The cuttings should be about 10-15cm (4-6in) long. Cut them just below a node.

3. Remove the leaves from the lower half of the cutting – you should be able to just pull them off.

4. Cut the remaining leaves in half to reduce water loss.

5. Place the cuttings into a plastic bag while collecting them to reduce water loss.

Chris Gaskin,
Senior Gardener at
Polesden Lacey, Surrey

'When taking any cutting, try using this simple method of preparing your compost. Buy a multi-purpose compost (preferably peat-free) and mix it with sharp horticultural grit in a 50:50 ratio as this will help your cuttings develop a healthy root system. The theory is that when the root tip touches the sharp edge of the grit it will divide into two roots and go either side, creating twice as many roots and in the end a much better plant.'

6. Mix potting compost or multipurpose compost with horticultural grit at a 50:50 ratio and fill plastic pots with the compost.

7. Use a dibber to make the initial holes and then push the cuttings to about half or two-thirds of their length in the compost. The cuttings can be dipped into hormone rooting powder prior to inserting them into the compost. This may encourage better rooting.

8. Continue to insert the cuttings into the compost, going around the sides of the pots. Finally, water the cuttings.

Dividing plants

One of the easiest ways to increase your stock of plants is to divide them. With most herbaceous perennials you can be as ruthless as you like and slice them up into smaller sections, removing the old central crowns and replacing them with sections of new growth. Some smaller plants can be divided by gently pulling them apart. Not only will division supply you with new healthy and vigorous plants, there are usually plenty spare to give to your friends and neighbours. The pleasurable thing about dividing plants is that the effect is instant – you have to wait for seeds to germinate or cuttings to produce roots, but dividing a plant immediately gives you free plants to fill up any spaces in your herbaceous border.

Dividing plants usually takes place in autumn or early spring. Robust herbaceous perennials which are commonly divided include *Aster*, *Bergenia* (elephant's ears), *Convallaria* (lily-of-the-valley) *Crocosmia*, *Delphinium*, *Eryngium* (sea holly), *Euphorbia*, *Geranium*, *Helianthus*, *Hemerocallis* (daylily), *Hosta*, *Iris*, *Lysimachia*, *Primula* (primrose), *Sedum*, *Verbena* and ornamental grasses. Herbaceous perennials from the vegetable patch such as rhubarb and sea kale will also benefit from being divided every few years. The plants may start to wilt after division because of shock to their system, but they should make a quick recovery. Water them regularly afterwards to keep them alive.

Martyn Pepper,
Senior Gardener at
Coleton Fishacre, Devon

'If you do a lot of propagation, make a list of roughly what numbers you require as this will help you to remember what needs to be propagated and should prevent you from finding you have too many plants of one type that you do not need. This should also save valuable greenhouse space and save on compost. The list can then be updated annually.'

Step-by-step: Dividing a herbaceous perennial

Shown here is a large clump of *Persicaria amplexicaulis* which is getting old and would benefit from being divided to reinvigorate it and keep it healthy.

1. Using a space or fork, gently prise clumps of the plant out of the ground and shake off some of the excess soil.

2. Using a sharp spade, slice down right through the clump to break the plant up into smaller pieces.

3. Discard some of the older or diseased material and select the healthiest and most vigorous plants.

4. Space the plants out equally, giving them plenty of room as they will grow quickly, and water them in

Opposite, far left *Hemerocallis* (daylily) is a robust herbaceous perennial. **Opposite, left** *Lysimachia punctata* (Garden loosestrife) and *Crocosmia* in bloom in the walled kitchen garden at Knightshayes Court, Devon.

Hardwood cuttings

For hardwood cuttings, stems are cut from the woody parts of trees and shrubs in late autumn or winter when the plant is dormant. They are selected from the young growth produced that year. The length of stem depends on the species, but for most plants such as ribes, vines, gooseberries, willow and privet, they are usually 15–30cm (6–12in) long.

Cut the young woody growth from healthy plants, ensuring that it has ripened into wood. If there is still some soft growth in the tip, remove it just above a bud. Make the lower cut just below a node. If a plant is thorny, such as a gooseberry, remove the lower thorns which are going to be under the soil. Evergreen plants such as privet should have their lower leaves stripped.

Hardwood cuttings can be planted directly into the ground, but if the weather conditions are wet or too cold they can be stored in the fridge until late winter. Plant them into pots of peat-free compost, or directly into the soil, spacing them at about 20cm (8in) apart. Simply make a slit in the ground with a spade and slot the cuttings in to about half to two-thirds of their length into the ground. If you want the plant to have a short stem or leg, such as redcurrants or gooseberries, then you can remove the lower buds above ground, leaving just a few at the top.

Root cuttings

Plants can also be propagated by removing part of their root system. In fact, gardeners try hard to avoid doing this when trying to weed out dandelions; if the root accidentally gets chopped up and left in the ground, it regenerates and produces lots more plants and therefore increases the weed problem, rather than reducing it.

There are various methods of propagating by root cuttings, depending on the type of plant and its root system – whether it has fibrous roots, bulbs, tubers, rhizomes and so forth. The Polesden Lacey gardener Christina Clowser has been propagating bearded irises from the historic Edwardian iris beds during mid-summer. Digging up the irises every two or three years helps to reduce a build-up of pests and diseases and also reinvigorates the new rhizomes once they are put back in the soil.

Right Cuttings taken from a fig tree. **Far right** The striking flowers of the bearded iris.

Step-by-step:
Propagating bearded irises

1. A few weeks after the bearded irises have finished flowering, gently lift the entire plant out of the ground with a fork.

2. Using a sharp knife, cut some of the rhizomes into sections about 6cm (2½in) long, ensuring that they feel firm and have strong foliage coming off them.

3. Cut back the foliage with the knife to leave the leaves about 10cm (4in) long. This reduces water loss in summer.

4. Once the root cuttings are prepared, they can be replanted, keeping the top of the rhizome proud of the soil. If they are planted too deeply they will not flower and may rot.

Layering

Some plants naturally reproduce themselves by laying stems on the ground which then produce roots. Anybody who has had brambles in their garden will be fully aware of their ability to almost 'walk' across the garden as they send out shoots and put down roots whenever they come into contact with the soil. Strawberries do it too by sending out runners which root into the ground. If these roots are then severed from the mother plant, they become a separate plant and can be dug up and planted elsewhere.

Gardeners can take advantage of a plant's tendency for layering by manipulating the process. There are many shrubs suitable for doing this, including rhododendrons, *Cotinus coggygria*, forsythia and winter jasmine. The process could not be simpler; just peg down a section of a young branch that is growing near the ground. If you do not have a wire peg, sometimes even laying a stone on a section of the stem will work, so long as the stem is in contact with the soil.

The soil can be prepared by digging it over and adding soil improvers, but of course in nature this does not occur and you may find the plant will root easily without your extra effort. Bending the shoot helps to stimulate root formation as it restricts the hormones and movement of food. Sometimes wounding the shoot at the point of contact with the soil can also promote roots.

Long shoots on vigorous plants can be pushed in and out of the soil in a serpentine effect to produce a number of shoots. Plants such as blackberries and hybrid berries vary slightly in that they produce their roots best at their tips, meaning that this part of the plant should be pushed into the ground to make more plants. Once the layered shoot has produced its own root system, it can be removed from the mother plant and potted up to plant out later. It is essential to keep it well watered.

Suckers

An even simpler way of propagating plants is to remove suckers with a root system attached. There are numerous plants suitable for this method, including hops, sarcococca, blackcurrants, hazels, aronia and bay. If you have grown raspberries at home, you will know their tendency to produce numerous shoots throughout the fruit and vegetable patch.

To generate new plants, simply dig back some of the soil around the base of the sucker and sever it from the main plant using secateurs. Pot up the sucker and keep it well watered until you are ready to plant it out. Remember though that some plants, particularly fruit trees and roses, are grafted on to rootstocks which differ from the main plant. Removing a sucker from the root system of these plants will not give you the desired variety.

Below, left *Corylus avellana* 'Contorta' (corkscrew hazel). Hazel readily produces suckers making propagation simple. **Below, right** The cloud-like *Cotinus* smokebush can be propagated by layering.

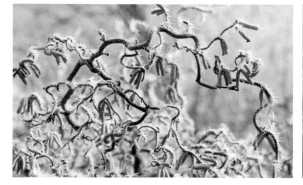

Case study: The National Trust Plant Conservation Centre

By Chris Trimmer, Nursery Manager at the Plant Conservation Centre

The Plant Conservation Centre (PCC) was set up to preserve the botanical diversity held within the National Trust's 271 gardens and parklands by propagating rare, unusual, threatened or historically significant plants and returning them to properties for free. Since 1982 over 32,000 plants have been grown and sent out to places across England, Wales and Northern Ireland. We are now also providing practical support to help achieve Target 13 of the Convention on Biological Diversity, an international agreement that aims to minimise genetic erosion and safeguard genetic diversity of the planets flora and fauna by 2020.

A major long-term project to propagate the National Trust's significant plants is now underway at the Plant Conservation Centre. We define a plant as 'significant' if it has become threatened or rare on an international, national or local level, or has cultural/historic links to our properties. Properties have been given their own Significant Plants List which is a working document of their significant plants. This list is intended to be a starting point for gardeners to document special plants, for example original introductions, champion trees or those planted in memoriam, in their collections. We are also working with Plant Heritage to identify plants which are threatened in cultivation. We intend to propagate as many of the plants identified in this way as possible over the next few years, thereby reducing the risk that they will be lost.

We are often asked for specialist propagation advice and anything plant-related, from sourcing the best kit for improving biosecurity to setting up quarantine areas. We use our Gardens and Parks Plant Database extensively to research the history of particular plants or collections in gardens, to source plants for restoration projects and to create reports on plants in Trust properties.

When we receive material on site it is processed in our clean room (or put into quarantine glasshouse if a whole plant) here it is checked for any obvious pests or diseases and tested for Phytophthora – thankfully we have never had a positive result. The material is then cleaned in a bleach solution, rinsed and prepared for propagation in our new, purpose-built propagation house. As plants grow they move through the various buildings on the nursery until they reach our large polytunnel, here they are looked after in air pots on an automatic irrigation system until they are returned to the property the material came from and often to other gardens.

pruning

The basics of pruning

The thought of wielding a pair of secateurs and saw for the benefit of a plant often fills an inexperienced gardener with dread. Pruning has a reputation for being tricky and rather mysterious and is regarded by many people as something only to be attempted by experienced horticulturists. In fact, pruning is really easy. It is very unlikely that you will kill a plant by pruning it and in most cases you will do it some good, even if you do not get things exactly right.

If you are just starting out it is best not to try to learn all the types of pruning at once, as that can seem overwhelming. Instead, focus on the existing plants in your garden, and once you have mastered these, you can then move on to some of the other basic groups such as fruit trees, roses and clematis. Once you get into the swing of things, you will find that pruning is really satisfying.

When to prune

There is a saying that goes 'the best time to prune a plant is when you remember'. This contains a fair bit of wisdom and indeed the reality is often that plants are pruned when you suddenly notice that they have got a bit unwieldy or just look in need of tidying up. There is usually no harm in this approach at all. However, with a bit of judicious and timely pruning, you can increase the flowering and fruiting of your plants and provide them with optimum strength to combat frost and drought.

Above Deadheading your roses will mean future blooms will be plentiful.

Above The regularly pruned box hedging and camellias at Plas yn Rhiw thrive in their coastal environment.

Basic rules to remember

- Avoid cutting trees and shrubs during the nesting season for birds. This is usually between the early spring and late summer.
- If you are doing tree work, or employing a gardener to do it, always check that you will not be disturbing bats. If you are unsure, seek professional advice.
- Pruning a shrub encourages it to grow back stronger, so by the same token hard-pruning a tree that is too vigorous will very often exacerbate the problem.
- Plants susceptible to the cold prefer to retain more growth during winter to give them some extra protection. Avoid pruning them hard in late summer and autumn.
- If you are going to be working on a tree, check that there are no legal restrictions on it, such as a Tree Preservation Order. If you are unsure, contact your local authority.

Reasons to prune

There are many reasons for making the time and effort to prune:

1. To keep your plant healthy. Usually gardeners refer to the three Ds when pruning – diseased, dying and dead! These are the essential branches to remove because otherwise the problem will rapidly spread.
2. To give your plant a good shape. Some plants such as topiary require regular clipping through the year while others look good with just an annual cut. Some plants, including magnolias, often do not need pruning at all.
3. To encourage more growth. When a branch is cut the terminal bud is removed, resulting in the production of more side shoots.
4. To get a tree off to a good start. Some require preliminary shaping after planting, known as formative pruning.
5. To crown lift a tree. If you wish to underplant a tree, it may be necessary to remove the lower branches to create space and let light in.
6. To make a tree safe. Limbs that could become dangerous, such as large limbs overhanging paths, need to be removed.
7. To create a specific effect, such as for foliage colours, winter stems or extra-large flowers.
8. To prevent a fruit tree from cropping biennially. Some fruit trees crop every other year but pruning your tree each year will encourage it to produce fruit annually.
9. To restrict the size of a tree or shrub. If one is taking over your garden you will need to prune it back to keep it under control.

Above Pruned and trained *Rosa* 'Constance Spry' underplanted with *Ipheion uniflorum* 'Wisley Blue' at Sissinghurst Castle.

Plants that bleed

Do not be concerned if you see your plant oozing sap from the cut areas after pruning. This rarely does the plant any harm, and it can even be beneficial on over-vigorous shrubs as it slows the growth. Modern pruning techniques tend to avoid the traditional methods of using wound paint such as Arbrex or binding up the wounds as this prevents the air circulating around the area and letting the plant heal itself naturally. Covering the wound tends to cause the area to go damp by hindering ventilation and makes an entry point for diseases.

Grape vines bleed copiously when pruned but birch is probably the worst bleeder of all – in fact people often draw off the sugary sap from their birch trunks in early spring, collecting demi-johns full to make it into wine, and the loss of sap does not seem to harm the trees at all. Other plants that are particularly susceptible to oozing sap include walnuts, Japanese maples, magnolias, limes, poplars and mulberries.

Sap is most commonly seen in spring, when the plants come into growth, and it starts to slow down from mid- to late summer onwards. If you really do have an aversion to the sight of sap, prune plants shortly before Christmas.

Below, left Silver birch tend to produce copious amounts of sap after pruning.
Below, right A mature mulberry bush at Chastleton House, Oxfordshire.

Choose your weapon

Getting the best results from pruning is all about having the right tool to do the job. Like a surgeon's knife, pruning implements should be kept sharp to ensure that cuts are made cleanly. Blunt instruments will crush the wood rather than cut it neatly, and will leave ragged or torn cuts on the remaining branches that will encourage infection.

'Always keep your secateurs sharp and clean to make the perfect pruning cut.'

Paul Gallivan
Head Gardener at Woolbeding
Gardens, West Sussex

Secateurs

A pair of secateurs is the essential bit of kit for pruning. There are two types: anvil and bypass. The former are generally cheaper and they cut through the wood by crushing down between a blade and an anvil, which can leave the remaining end of the branch damaged. Bypass secateurs have an action like a pair of scissors, making a clean cut. Pruning cuts should generally not be made with secateurs on anything larger than the diameter of a thick pencil because you will damage the plant and possibly strain your wrist and forearm.

There are different types of bypass secateurs to choose from, so take your time when buying them. A good-quality pair should last you a lifetime if they are regularly maintained. It is important to feel the weight and balance in your hand before buying as there can be substantial differences even between secateurs that look very similar. Secateurs with a rotating handle which is supposed to lessen the strain on the wrist are also available.

Pruning saw

These saws have a slim blade, enabling you to get into tight angles within the crown of the tree to make pruning cuts. They come in a variety of sizes, usually in a sheath which attaches to your pruning belt, and their blades are replaceable. There are also folding pruning saws which can be kept in your pocket and pulled out when needed.

Maintaining your secateurs

Secateurs suffer all sorts of abuse during pruning and regularly cleaning them after use will extend their life considerably. First, scrape all the sap and gunk off them immediately, otherwise it will dry and make the blades stiff to use. Use a piece of steel wool to give them a good cleaning down. Afterwards, add some lubricating oil to prevent them rusting and to make sure they are ready for action next time you need to use them.

Good-quality secateurs can also be stripped down completely to their bare components. This makes it easier to sharpen the blade on a stone and you can oil all the other parts before putting them back together again. When sharpening the blade, remember that it is only one side that should be sharpened, following the existing angle of the blade. This should be done once or twice a year. Damaged parts can usually be replaced, if the secateurs have been bought from a reputable supplier and are made by a good-quality brand.

Above These two pairs of secateurs have a
subtle difference in their handles, affecting
the amount of power that can be generated.
The angle of the blade differs slightly, too.
Right All the essential tools you need for
pruning in your garden.

Tool belt and holster

Some means of carrying your tools is useful to have, particularly if you need to keep your hands
free to climb stepladders or to hold a branch.

Loppers

While loppers can be used for pruning larger branches, a small pruning saw will give you a better
finish as the loppers tend to crush the wood. However, they are useful for chopping up your
prunings into smaller pieces. Loppers come in a range of sizes, some with telescopic handles; for
extra strength, choose one with ratchets. The longer the handle the better leverage you will get for
cutting through thicker branches.

Bow saw

Use a bow saw only for cutting up branches once they have been removed from the tree, as they
have large cutting teeth that make a jagged pruning cut. Their shape also makes them awkward to
get in close to the tree to make pruning cuts.

Long-arm loppers/saw

Tools with longer handles for removing branches high up on a tree are a much safer option than
climbing up a ladder. These have an extended pole, usually with interchangeable heads so that they
can be used as a either lopper or saw. Wear a safety hat if the branches are large.

Left Loppers in use at Ilam Park, Derbyshire. If you can reach the branch, do try to prune with a small pruning saw to avoid crushing the wood.

Tip
If you are doing a lot of pruning in the garden, keep an oily piece of wire wool handy with which to wipe the blades regularly, preventing the secateurs from getting jammed up. It will save you a few journeys back and forth to the shed.

Chainsaw

As a chainsaw is potentially dangerous, it should only be used by trained professionals. If you are employing a tree surgeon to carry out tree work in your garden, insist that you see their qualifications and insurance. They should be wearing protective clothing including chainsaw trousers, boots, gloves, ear defenders and a hard hat with visor.

Staying safe when pruning

- If you are sawing something above head height or on a windy day, wear goggles or other eye protection to avoid sawdust blowing into your eyes.
- Never lean a single upright ladder into a tree; ideally, use a stable platform to give you a sturdy work area. If you must use a ladder, make it a wide-based stepladder. Face the ladder into the tree so that you are not stretching to the side as this can cause it to topple over – it is much safer to lean forward. Avoid standing on the top rung and use a tool belt so that you have at least one hand free, enabling you to hold on. Never over-extend yourself as you may lose your balance.
- Wear gloves when pruning thorny plants. A thorn under your skin can lead to an infection.
- Be aware that some woody plants such as figs and smoke bushes have noxious sap and you need to be careful not to get it on your skin. Some people have specific reactions to certain plants; if you do get skin problems make a note of which plants you were handling that day so that you can discover the offender and take extra precautions in future.

Making use of your prunings

Large branches and felled tree trunks can be sawed up and made into log piles for wildlife. Alternatively, you can bring them indoors and use them on a real fire or wood-burning stove. If you do not have an indoor fireplace, you could consider a chiminea or fire pit in the garden.

Making firewood

Cut thick sections of wood into manageable lengths, then use an axe or log-splitter to chop them up into sections that will fit in your fireplace. Most logs will need seasoning for at least a year before burning; store them somewhere dry such as a shed or garage. Certain species of tree such as birch and ash can be burnt while 'green', but oak, beech and fruit wood will certainly need to be stored for a while. Apple wood is a favourite with many people as it has a beautiful aroma to it and provides good heat and a steady burn. Conifers, poplar and willow do not make good firewood as they tend to burn quickly and spit.

Making charcoal

In large woodland gardens, you can make charcoal that can then be used for barbecues. The ancient woodland craft of making charcoal goes back thousands of years, and the basic principles remain much the same today. Many National Trust properties make their own charcoal from the by-product of managing their gardens and it can usually be bought in their shops.

To make charcoal you will need a charcoal kiln, which can be bought from woodland stores or purchased online. This has vents at the bottom that will draw in oxygen to maintain the heat and chimneys at the top. Sand is often used to block any cracks or holes, such as around the lid. Stack the kiln with wood only when you are ready to use it to ensure that you do not kill wildlife that have made it their home. A 'burn' will usually take about 12 hours, depending on its size, and it is important to keep an eye to prevent fire spreading. Wait for the kiln to cool before opening it up to inspect your charcoal.

Above You can use your prunings for firewood. **Opposite** Bean supports have been made from prunings at Wordsworth House and Garden.

Other options for prunings

- Smaller prunings can be collected up, chopped up with loppers and secateurs, and used as kindling for fires once they have dried out.
- Lengths make good edgings for pathways, giving them a natural, rustic feel.
- You can hire a chipper or shredder and then recycle the prunings to make woodchip paths or a mulch under trees. Avoid spreading fresh wood chippings around herbaceous plants as the process of decomposition can deplete the soil of nitrogen.
- Wood chippings can also be added to your compost. The carbon helps to balance out excess nitrogen from green leafy plants and grass clippings.
- Prunings from twiggy plants can be used to provide climbing supports for pea plants. Longer branches can make wigwams for climbers such as sweet peas, runner beans and clematis to scramble up.
- A log pile will make a home for various wildlife.

Pruning Roses

When?

Early March is an excellent time to prune repeat-flowering roses such as Hybrid Teas (large-flowered), Floribundas (cluster-flowered) and most modern Shrub and Climber varieties. For comfort's sake, choose a mild, dry day if possible, simply to make the work more enjoyable.

Why?

Roses will survive with the minimum of attention, but if they are to thrive a certain amount of careful pruning needs to be undertaken. The aims of pruning are: to develop shape; control size; maintain vigour; encourage flowering; and produce a happy and healthy plant.

A well-shaped rose bush is an adornment to any garden, even out of the growing season. Maintain a balanced and open-branched structure by pruning main stems to an outward-facing bud and completely removing any dead or entangling stems at, or near to, ground level. Remember that a naturally tall-growing rose cannot be kept short by hard pruning. However, careful attention at the right time can help to contain strong-growing varieties within manageable proportions.

David Stone,
Head Gardener,
Mottisfont,
Hampshire

In March: complete all major pruning and mulch with manure or organic (peat-free) compost. Remember, prune lightly for quantity of bloom, prune hard for quality of bloom.
In July: remove the spent blooms from repeat-flowering varieties to encourage the development of a second crop.
In October: tie in new shoots of climbing roses to avoid damage by the autumn gales.

How?

Most repeat-flowering roses can be divided into the following pruning groups.

Bush (Hybrid Tea and Floribunda)

New plants should be pruned back hard to within 10–15cm (4–6in) of the ground to encourage the formation of new, strong branches from near the plant's base. In subsequent years, prune away all weak and ageing wood before reducing the remaining stems by approximately one-half to two-thirds of their length. Strong growers, such as the ever-popular 'Peace' (Hybrid Tea) and 'Iceberg' (Floribunda) can be pruned less severely. As a general rule, prune lightly for quantity of bloom or hard for quality of bloom.

Climbers

With new plants, the emphasis should be on training new shoots to cover the supporting wall or trellis. Shorter side shoots, which may have flowered the previous summer, are best pruned back to within a bud or two of the main branch. As the plants develop, they may become 'leggy', with flowers held above eye level. To encourage the formation of fresh young shoots from ground level, prune away the occasional older stem completely. If such stems are stouter than 12mm (½in), you will need long-handled pruners or a small, sharp saw to cut through the stems.

Above, left and right Early March is the ideal time of year to deadhead your roses. **Below, left** Pink Hybrid Tea rose 'Savoy Hotel'. **Below, right** *Rosa* Graham Thomas 'Ausmas' growing at Mottisfont in June.

Modern Shrub roses

This wide and varied group of mainly repeat-flowering varieties includes the English roses, such as 'Graham Thomas', and the older but ever-popular Hybrid Musk varieties 'Cornelia' and 'Buff Beauty'. In general, it may not be necessary to do more than tip back the leading shoots of established plants, but it never does any harm to reduce all new stems by approximately one-third of their length. According to the habit of growth, some thinning out of the stems may be required in order to avoid overcrowding and hard pruning of older stems may prove necessary from time to time in order to encourage further new growths. Most Shrub roses are best left to form largish specimens, although there are many excellent varieties available for the smaller garden.

Above, left Climbing roses frame a window at Sissinghurst Castle. **Above, right** In autumn, *Rosa moyesii* produces red rosehips.

Old-fashioned Shrub roses

Within this large group of mid-summer flowering roses are included rambling roses such as 'Albertine' and species roses such as *Rosa moyesii* as well as the ancient *R. gallica*, *R.* x *damascena* var. *semperflorens*, *R.* x *centifolia* and *R. alba*. Such roses flower best on the shoots that were produced the previous year, but will continue to bloom on older stems for several years. In general, they are best left to form naturally wide and branching shrubs, but in order to keep them within bounds some formative pruning may be required. Newly planted shrubs will need little in the way of pruning for their first year or two; thereafter selected thinning of older, already flowered stems can take place any time through July and August, when the flowering season is finished for the year. Pruning at this time will encourage the rose to produce those all-important new shoots, which will bear the best blooms in future summers. In order to maintain a robust shrub, new shoots of the previous summer should be reduced by approximately one-third in winter and any untidy branches lightly pruned to shape.

Plants for pruning-shy gardeners

No plant has to be pruned. In nature, animals such as deer and goats may graze on the lower shoots of trees and shrubs but most plants continue to grow unimpeded and often live to a ripe old age. However, we gardeners are fussy and want our plants to perform at their best, with an abundance of flowers and fruit, and look neat and tidy. Plants can be left unpruned but most will rapidly become overgrown and untidy – great for wildlife, but perhaps not for somebody with a small garden.

If you really do have an aversion to pruning, there are a few plants that are generally fairly happy if left to do their own thing. Most of these trees are slow-growing and do not send out vigorous new shoots: rock roses (*Cistus*), *Daphne cneorum*, bay (*Laurus*), *Edgeworthia*, Japanese maple (*Acer palmatum*), snowy mespilus (*Amelanchier lamarckii*), deciduous azalea (*Rhododendron* species), compact rhododendrons, flowering dogwood (*Cornus kousa*), magnolia, lilac (*Syringa*) and strawberry tree (*Arbutus unedo*).

Dealing with the basics

If you are not confident about when to prune, follow these basic principles.

Rubbing branches If two branches rub against each other, one of them should be removed to avoid them damaging each other and leaving a wound that could leave the tree susceptible to diseases.

Crossing branches Where one branch crosses over another this creates shade, which will reduce the plant's ability to produce flowers and fruit. Removing a branch will reduce the competition for sunlight.

Congested canopies Congestion caused by masses of branches reduces the air circulation, making the plant more susceptible to disease. Reducing the amount of branches should create a healthier tree.

Dead or dying branches Always remove these to prevent the problem spreading further, or to neighbouring plants.

Suckers These grow from the base of the plant, sometimes from underground. They should be removed to prevent them from sucking energy from the plant. Very often they will be suckers from rootstocks (the roots that the tree is grafted onto) and so not the desired variety of tree anyway. One theory is that a sucker should be ripped out by hand rather than cleanly removed by secateurs as this will prevent it from regrowing.

Twin leaders Sometimes trees have two competing main trunks. This is fine if you want a multi-stemmed tree, but if you want a single trunk the weaker of the two leading stems should be removed, otherwise there will be a weak join between the two leaders. Do this when the plant is young as the size of the wound will be smaller.

The big boys

If you have a tree in your garden that is past its best, think twice before getting it felled. There are many wildlife benefits to retaining a standing tree, and a professional contractor should be able to advise you on how to make it safe. If a tree becomes unstable it can be retained as a monolith to provide a rich habitat for wildlife such as birds and bats as well as food for invertebrates. Creating a monolith tree means retaining the trunk but removing the top and side branches for safety reasons. As a last resort, even if the tree is felled, it is worth leaving it *in situ* on the ground to decompose if room allows, encouraging an abundant range of biodiversity into your garden.

Above Pruning a step-over fruit tree (see page 161). **Opposite** Norway Maple (*Acer platanoides*) grow alongside oak trees (*Quercus ruber*) in the garden at Kingston Lacy, Dorset.

Pruning with secateurs

When pruning a stem, cut back to just past a bud. Never leave too much of a stub as this will die back and could make the plant susceptible to disease problems. Avoid cutting too closely to the bud and if you are using bypass secateurs ensure that the blade side is nearest the trunk, or section of wood that is to be retained. The beak side should be facing away. This is because the tiny space between the blade and beak crushes the section of wood, so it is important that this part of the branch does not remain on the tree as it is damaged. By cutting with the blade facing the trunk, you will ensure that the remaining branch is left with a clean cut.

Pruning with a saw

Never prune a branch by cutting it completely flush with the trunk as this causes the surrounding area to start decaying. It removes the natural defensive system of the branch which would enable it to start callusing over and recovering from the cut. Instead, trees should be left with a slight stub.

Step-by-step: Crown lifting

This beech tree needed to have its lower branches removed to make it easier to mow around. Also, allowing more light into the base of the tree would enable it to be underplanted with bulbs and other low-growing plants. The removal of lower branches is called crown lifting. Ideally, this process should be carried out while the tree is young to minimise the size of wounds created on the trunk.

1. The weight of the branch needs to be reduced before making the final cut to prevent it tearing down the length of the trunk. Using a pruning saw, make an undercut about halfway into the branch, about 20cm (8in) away from the trunk of the tree.

2. Now cut downwards from above, a few centimetres from the undercut, further away from the tree trunk. There should be a slight cracking sound and the branch should cleanly fall away. Thanks to the undercut, there should be no tearing underneath.

3. The final cut can now be made. As there is hardly any weight in the remaining branch it can be removed with one downward cut, leaving a very small stub which will enable the tree to callus over.

4. To continue crown lifting, remove the remaining lower branches to a height which makes the tree look balanced, with a healthy canopy above. Smaller branches can be cut with secateurs.

5. Remove the cut branches and recycle them in the garden, either by shredding them and adding them to the compost heap or spreading as mulch around the base of trees.

Left Apple trees respond well to pruning and will produce more fruit as a result.

Pruning fruit trees

Apple and pear trees are fantastically versatile and can be trained into all types of different shapes, although the most common are cordons, espaliers and step-overs. They are pruned twice in the year, first in late summer when they have finished growing. This is to allow the sunlight into the canopy at a critical time, because the plant is preparing either to produce fruit buds for next year or instead create vegetative (or non-fruiting) growth. Pruning now promotes fruit for next year. This method is called the Modified Lorette System. The second prune is in winter, when the tree is dormant.

The pruning for espaliers, step-overs and cordons is practically the same for each. In summer the new growth is pruned back to one or two buds past the base of the shoot. If you look carefully you should be able to recognise where the new growth begins and last year's growth ends. The older wood will be darker and thicker and there will be a swelling where the new growth begins. Work systematically along the plant. Anything shorter than the length of a pair of secateurs can be left. In winter, the shortened stems can be thinned out. This is a harder prune, cutting into the older wood. Thin out congested clusters of spurs and remove any shoots growing from underneath the main branches as these will be shaded and are therefore unlikely to be productive.

Most apple and pear trees are grown as open-centre trees, shaped a bit like a goblet, although centre-leader or spindle trees are also popular. The principle behind pruning any freestanding fruit tree is to ensure that as much as possible of the tree is bathed in sunlight, because this will maximise the crop.

The main time for pruning a freestanding tree is during winter; it is easier to see the branches without the leaves and the tree does not bleed sap. However, modern gardeners sometimes prune apple trees in spring and summer, as the bleeding sap does no harm to the tree and pruning at this time of year can slow down the growth of an over-vigorous tree.

Step-by-step:
Pruning a freestanding fruit tree

No two trees are the same, and an experienced gardener learns to read the tree and adapt this pruning regime accordingly. Some trees fruit on short spurs, known as spur-bearing varieties, while other trees produce their fruit in the tips, known as tip-bearers. Most trees are a mix of both, though. Using the basic pruning technique below should help to produce a regular crop of fruit each year regardless of how they fruit.

1. Remove any branches that are growing into the centre of the tree as they will cast shade over other branches.

2. Look for any crossing branches and reduce the weaker one of the two. This will ensure that the stronger branch receives the most amount of sunlight.

3. Remove shoots growing from lower down on the trunk, as these will sap energy from the tree and if left unpruned will develop into large branches where you do not want them.

Pruning stone fruits

The key thing to remember when pruning any of the stone fruits from the cherry family (plums, cherries, damsons, apricots and peaches) is that they must not be pruned when they are dormant. This is because they are susceptible to bacterial canker and silver leaf problems when wounds are left open. Instead they are usually pruned in spring, when the sap is rising and so they are able to recover quicker from their pruning wounds. Because of their susceptibility to problems, it is advisable to clean your secateurs thoroughly in between pruning trees so that no infections are transmitted on the blade. Using a standard household kitchen surface spray is usually sufficient.

4. Prune back the leaders (the shoots at the end of each branch) to outward-facing buds to prevent the branches from growing into the centre.

5. Remove strong, thick, vigorous upright shoots as they will not produce fruit and will quickly dominate the tree.

6. If some of the branches are bare, tip back some of the new growth to stimulate some lateral growth. Obviously, if the tree is a tip-bearer you should not do this to all the branches as you will have no fruit left.

7. The resulting tree should have an open centre, allowing the air and sunlight to penetrate into the canopy. There should be a clean trunk with no suckers and the leading branches should be left with outward-facing buds.

Pruning soft fruit

Gooseberries, redcurrants and pink/white currants are treated in almost exactly the same way; they are pruned once a year in winter by cutting their new growth back to a couple of buds. This is because they produce fruit on old wood and at the base of new wood. If they are being grown as a standard, or as a bush on a short leg, the leaders on each branch structure should be cut back by about a third to encourage fruiting further down the stem. The one difference between pruning the currants and a gooseberry is that the leaders of a gooseberry are usually pruned to an inward-facing bud to prevent them flopping outwards, whereas a redcurrant has a tendency to grow into the centre of the plant and should therefore be pruned to an outward-facing bud.

Cordons should be treated like bushes, with their new growth pruned back to two buds. The single leader can be left unpruned each year until it has reached its desired height, after which it can be tipped back to maintain it at that height. They also benefit from being pruned in summer, cutting back the new growth to five leaves. This lets in more light and allows the air to circulate around the canopy, which should prevent the build-up of pests and diseases.

Blackcurrants and blueberries are pruned in a similar way to each other. They produce fruit on younger wood, meaning that a system of replacing old branches with new ones is needed. Use a pair of loppers or a pruning saw and cut through some of the older stems at the base of the plant, removing about a third of the branches, retaining the younger growth and removing the older, thicker growth. Also remove any shoots that are lying horizontally or close to the ground as once

Above Hybrid berry boysenberries should be treated in the same way as summer-flowering raspberries.

Above It is important to clean your secateurs before pruning stone fruit such as damsons, so as to avoid infection.

they are laden with fruit they will be ruined as they lie on the ground. Blackcurrants are usually pruned in winter, when the plant is dormant. Blueberries can suffer from dieback, so gardeners often wait until early spring to prune them, as it is easier to spot the swollen buds and distinguish them from dead branches.

Summer-fruiting and autumn-fruiting raspberries are pruned in completely different ways, so it is important to know which type you have since if you get it wrong you will have no fruit at all the following year. The former fruit on the canes produced the previous year. After they have fruited, cut down the old canes to ground level with secateurs and tie the new canes on to the wires in their place. The tips of the canes should be bent over and not pruned at this stage because this will encourage laterals to form on the stems which will affect next year's crop. The tips are usually pruned in early spring, which then encourages the fruit stems to start producing a crop. The whole process is then repeated the following year, with the fruiting canes being removed after they have cropped and the new shoots tied in.

Autumn-fruiting raspberries fruit on canes produced in the same year. The pruning system for them is very simple. They are left over winter and then cut down to ground level in early spring with secateurs.

Hybrid berries such as Japanese wineberries, blackberries, tayberries, boysenberries, sunberries and loganberries should be treated like summer-fruiting raspberries and have their old canes removed after fruiting and their new canes tied in, to fruit the following year. To make it simpler to distinguish between the two, bundle the new growth up as it develops and keep it to one side of the plant. When the fruiting canes are removed, it is easy to transpose the new canes to their training position. Some of the more vigorous canes can be trained into elaborate shapes on a system of wires, which provides additional winter interest in the garden. The Japanese wineberry is particularly useful for creating a vibrant seasonal display with its bright red stems.

Pruning hydrangeas

Most people grow *Hydrangea macrophylla* cultivars, which produce mophead or lacecap flower heads during the summer months. The old flower heads help to protect the future flower buds from frost and winter damage, so pruning is usually left until late spring. Furthermore, the flower heads provide fantastic winter structure and interest in the garden, and look beautiful when the frost catches them. Pruning is simply a matter of removing the flower heads and cutting back to a healthy pair of buds. If the plant is old and congested, some of the older shoots can be cut back harder.

Hydrangea paniculata cultivars flower later than the mopheads and can be used to striking effect by pruning them hard in late winter. This encourages the plant to produce huge cone-like flowers that provide a stunning crescendo to late summer and early autumn and their flower heads provide winter interest too. To get the effect, prune back new growth to two buds to leave an open framework of branches. It may look a bit drastic, but this hard pruning promotes the extra vigour needed to produce the huge flowers that appear on the growth produced that year.

Other shrubs that flower on shoots developed in spring will benefit from this type of hard pruning. They include *Buddleja davidii* (butterfly bush), *Caryopteris*, *Ceratostigma*, *Fuchsia magellanica*, *Leycesteria*, *Romneya* and *Spiraea japonica*.

Above, left Wisteria climbs across an archway at Monk's House. **Above, right** Gorgeous purple-blue blooms of *Hydrangea macrophylla* 'Europa'.

Renewal pruning of deciduous shrubs

Most shrubs do not have to be pruned, but they will flower much more prolifically if they are. The earlier flowering shrubs of the season benefit from a form of renewal pruning after they have flowered, which involves removing older flowering stems and encouraging new young stems to grow. Shrubs that produce flowers on the older wood are suitable for this type of pruning. Plants suitable include *Buddleja alternifolia*, *Deutzia*, *Exochorda*, *Forsythia*, *Kerria*, *Kolkwitzia*, *Philadelphus*, *Ribes sanguineium* and *Weigela*.

Pruning wisteria

One of the most popular climbers on account of its attractive blue racemes of fragrant flowers, wisteria should be pruned twice a year to maximise the floral display. After it has flowered, cut back the new growth to about 15cm (6in) from the main framework. This helps to keep the plant tidy and will encourage more flowers for the following season. In winter prune it harder, cutting the growth back to a couple of buds from the main framework of branches.

Clematis

People tend to feel anxious about pruning clematis, yet it really is easy once you work out which of the three groups your plant belongs to.

Group one includes *Clematis alpina*, *C. armandii*, *C. cirrhosa*, *C. macropetala* and *C. montana*. These climbers are deciduous or evergreen clematis that flower during winter or spring on the previous year's growth. They do not really require much pruning, although *C. montana* can be particularly rampant if not kept in check. Give them a light prune after flowering in spring, just cutting back over-extended shoots and removing any dead wood. If you really want to have a tidy

Step-by-step: Renewal pruning a philadelphus

This philadelphus has finished flowering for the year and so needs to be pruned back to encourage more flowers for next year.

2. Prune back the flowering stems to stronger lateral branches further down the plant. This will encourage new growth. Remove weak growth to try to open up the plant slightly.

1. Remove some of the thicker, older stems with a saw to start new shoots into growth from further down the plant.

3. Finally, tip the highest shoots to a height you wish to retain the plant at and keep it under control. This tipping will also promote more flowering shoots further down the plant in subsequent years.

up they can be cut back to 15cm (6in) above ground level, but you will forgo flowers for that year and it must not be done again for a few more years.

Group two contains the large-flowering early summer types such as *C. florida* and its hybrids and *C. patens* and its hybrids such as 'Countess of Lovelace', 'The President', 'Nelly Moser' and 'Corona'. These produce flowers on the older previous year's wood, and sometimes produce a second flush of flowers on the current year's growth, later in the year. They are pruned on a renewal system, cutting about a fifth of the plant back to about 30cm (12in) above ground level in late winter. The remaining shoots can be trimmed back to a permanent framework of branches and shoots.

Group three clematis include *C. texensis* and its hybrids such as 'Etoile Violette', *C. viticella*, *C. orientalis*, *C. tangutica* including 'Bill Mackenzie' and *C. viticella*. These flower from mid-summer to autumn, producing their flowers on the current growth. Pruning could not be simpler – just cut the entire plant back to a pair of buds 15cm (6in) above ground level in late winter or early spring. Alternatively, they can be lightly pruned, trimming back any excess growth and lightly cutting back side stems. This type of pruning can be effective when they are trained over a wigwam, as it provides a permanent structure through winter and can encourage the clematis to flower slightly earlier in the year.

Pruning for foliage effect

Paulownia tomentosa is commonly known as the foxglove tree and produces impressive large leaves. If left unpruned it will grow into a handsome large tree, producing unusual foxglove-like flowers. However, if pruned hard each year, it can be used to create an impressive mass of foliage that makes a great feature in its own right or an eyecatching backdrop to a deep herbaceous border.

To get the effect, take your pruning saw or loppers and cut the branches down to about 20cm (8in) above ground level. Do this in late winter and watch those branches and leaves grow. The leaves will be even bigger than if the plant was grown as a tree.

Bear in mind that you will be foregoing the flowers for foliage, but once you have tried it, you will probably feel that the effect is worth it. Allow young plants to establish for a couple of years before pruning them back hard.

Other trees or shrubs to try for foliage effect include *Catalpa bignonioides* 'Aurea'; *Cotinus coggygria*; *Rhus chinesis*; *Sambucus nigra* 'Blacklace'; *Eucalyptus* species; *Cercis canadensis* and *Corylus maxima* 'Purpurea'.

Cutting plants back nearly to ground level as in the pruning technique above is known as coppicing and is an ancient technique used to promote the production of vigorous stems. Coppicing is practised in woodlands on hazel, ash and chestnuts to produce vigorous upright shoots that are used for stakes, beanpoles and woodcraft.

Instead of coppicing trees to near ground level, some trees are pollarded instead, which involves cutting back branches that are already on a framework of branches or an upright trunk. This encourages a mass of branches and foliage, but at a higher level.

Pruning for winter stem effect

Shrubs with attractive winter stems can provide a stunning visual display during the months when there is a lack of flowers in the garden, and if you plant them near your house you can enjoy them from the comfort of your armchair. Most are cut back to a framework 5–15cm (2–6in) above the ground, but plants such as ornamental brambles can be cut right back to ground level.

Plants suitable for coppicing for winter stems

Salix alba var. *vitellina* 'Britzensis' (willow)

Salix alba var. *vitellina* 'Chermesina' (willow)

Cornus sanguinea 'Midwinter Fire' (dogwood)

Cornus alba 'Kesselringii' (dogwood)

Cornus alba 'Sibirica' (dogwood)

Cornus sericea 'Flaviramea' (dogwood)

Rubus cockburnianus (ornamental bramble)

Rubus thibetanus (ghost bramble)

Above, left and right Prune *Cornus* (dogwood) in late winter/early spring to maximise the time during winter when the colourful stem can be enjoyed. Pruning them hard will ensure a plentiful supply of colourful stems for the next winter.

Pruning evergreen shrubs

Evergreen shrubs are perfect for providing all-year-round interest in the garden. The good news is that most of them require minimal pruning. If they do need reshaping or cutting back because they have outgrown their space, the best time to do this is in spring, after the risk of frosts. If they are pruned in summer or autumn they tend to make sappy, weak growth that then becomes susceptible to the winter conditions, while pruning when the plant is dormant can cause it to suffer from the cold. Pruning in spring encourages good strong growth and gives the plant time to recover during the growing season.

Many evergreens can tolerate hard pruning if necessary. However, avoid hard pruning conifer trees, with the exception of yew – most other conifers will not regrow if pruning cuts are made into old wood.

Evergreen shrubs that thrive on pruning

Lavenders are classed as evergreen shrubs, and they do benefit from regular pruning to keep them in shape and prevent them from becoming leggy. In spring their growth can be closely trimmed back using a pair of hand shears. Avoid cutting back into the old wood, though, as sometimes this does not regenerate. After flowering in late summer, trim off the flower heads with a pair of shears. This helps the plant to retain its shape and also encourages more flowers for next year. Collect up the lavender cuttings for dry flower displays or pot-pourri as the fragrance is delightful.

Heathers also benefit from an annual trim. Using scissors or hand shears, lightly trim back the dead flower spikes in mid-spring, following the natural contours of the plant. This applies for autumn-, winter- and summer-flowering heathers.

> 'When you are trimming hedges and shrubs, propagate a few of the prunings to get some extra free plants.'
>
> Colin Clark,
> Senior Gardener at Greenway,
> Devon

Above Prune lavender regularly to avoid them becoming too spindly. **Opposite** The Winter Walk at Anglesey Abbey is planted with *Prunus serrula*, *Rubus thibetanus* 'Silver Fern' and *Cornus sanguinea* 'Winter Beauty', meaning the garden has colour all year round.

Above *Philadelphus* flowering beside a track at The Weir, Herefordshire.

Rejuvenating shrubs: hit them hard!

There are a number of shrubs that are as hard as nails and will take a good clobbering with a pruning saw or loppers, tolerating being cut down to almost ground level to rejuvenate them. Evergreen and deciduous shrubs include azaleas, *Acuba japonica* (spotted laurel), *Berberis*, *Crataegus* (hawthorn), *Elaeagnus pungens*, *Forsythia*, *Philadelphus* (mock orange), *Prunus laurocerasus* (cherry laurel), *Prunus lusitanica* (Portuguese laurel, *Rhodendron ponticum* and *Viburnum tinus*.

Len Bernamont,
Head Gardener at Bateman's, Alfriston Clergy House and Monk's House, East Sussex

'When you are cutting the top of a hedge which might not be completely level, start on the section which is highest and cut it down to your desired height – this will then give you a guide for the rest of the hedge. If you start on a lower section you might not be able to get it all to the same height without struggling with woody material thicker than your hedge cutter can deal with.'

Hedge-cutting

Hedge-cutting must be the simplest form of pruning imaginable as it usually involves nothing more than cutting in a straight line. If you do not have a good eye for getting something level, stretch out a length of string between two posts as a guide and cut along it. Every garden has room for a hedge. They are a great alternative to a fence, because they attract wildlife and add seasonal interest throughout the year with berries, flowers and foliage. Always check for nesting birds before starting to trim a hedge.

Above, left The extensive hedging at Polesden Lacey can take quite some time to prune.
Above, right The blades can be replaced on pruning saws.

Tools of the trade

Hedge trimmer Petrol hedge trimmers are noisy and heavy, but they are effective, and probably the best tool to get your hedge cut in the quickest amount of time. Electric trimmers are much lighter but you will need a source of power nearby to use it, and you need to be careful not to cut through the cable. Solar-charged battery hedge trimmers are becoming more popular as they are light to use, cheaper to run and better for the environment.

Hand shears These are the traditional option for clipping a hedge, and nothing speaks more of summer than the gentle 'clip clip' sound of hand shears being used on a Sunday afternoon in the garden.

Secateurs This method will make the cutting of a hedge a lot slower, but some of the large-leaved evergreens such as laurel and aucuba look terrible when their foliage is shredded by hedge trimmers and hand shears. Using secateurs takes longer, but the result will look much neater.

'When you trim a hedge, round off the edges rather than cutting them square. The hedge looks better and the levels are less critical.'

Colin Clark,
Senior Gardener at
Greenway, Devon

Right This box pyramid is tightly shaped by placing a homemade structure over the top of it to outline where the plant should be clipped to. **Opposite, left** Using a pair of hand shears to trim the gold yew hedges at Polesden Lacey provides more control than a hedge trimmer, ensuring the plant retains its shape. **Opposite, right** Pruning a spiral box plant with hand shears with extended handles.

Tip

If you would like box hedging but your garden suffers from the fungal disease box blight, try *Lonicera nitida* instead. It looks similar (its common name is poor man's box), but is not susceptible to the disease.

When to prune a hedge

Some of the most common types of hedges are listed below. Slower-growing hedges such as yew, beech and hornbeam only need cutting once a year, but more vigorous ones such as leylandii may need cutting a few times annually if you like to keep everything neat and tidy. Formal hedges may need light clipping two or three times a week. Most hedges are clipped either in spring or late summer, but restoration of a hedge usually takes place in winter, when some of the older wood is pruned back to encourage growth from further down in an attempt to reinstate the hedge to a manageable height and width.

Box (*Buxus* species) – late spring after risk of frost

Beech (*Fagus sylvatica*) – late summer

Cherry laurel (*Prunus laurocerasus*) – spring and late summer

Holly (*Ilex* species) – late summer

Hornbeam (*Carpinus betulus*) – late summer

Leyland cypress (x *Cupressocyparis leylandii*) – spring and late summer

Poor Man's Box (*Lonicera nitida*) – spring and early summer

Portuguese laurel (*Prunus lusitanicus*) – spring and late summer

Privet (*Ligustrum ovalifolium*) – spring and late summer

Western red cedar (T*huja plicata*) – spring

Yew (*Taxus baccata*) – late summer

Cloud pruning and topiary clipping

If you want to be more imaginative with hedge pruning, evergreen hedges can be pruned into all sorts of shapes including 'cloud pruning' (curved or wavy lines) or into topiary such as golden yew balls as shown above, left.

Step-by-step:
Formative pruning of a box hedge

Prune box hedges after the risk of frosts is over. Newly planted hedges should have their young tips cut back to encourage the plants to thicken out and send out laterals. If newly planted hedges are left unpruned they can tend to go leggy and eventually bare towards the base of the hedge.

1. Stretch out a string between two canes pushed in the ground at either end of the hedge to be pruned.

2. Measure the desired height of the hedge using a tape measure and adjust the string accordingly. Make sure that the string is pulled tight.

3. Use a pair of secateurs to methodically work along the newly planted hedge, cutting back the tips to the level of the string. Removing the tips of each plant will create a thicker and denser hedge.

maintenance

Taking care of the garden

The words 'garden maintenance' always make gardening sound like a chore, which it should not be. 'Garden care' might be more appropriate, as gardening is about nurturing your outdoor space; it should be a labour of love. Of course, it can be physically taxing if you want it to be, and your biceps and stomach muscles might ache, but exercise in fresh air is something to be embraced and enjoyed.

Having your own garden places responsibility on your shoulders, but in a good way. You become custodian of an outdoor living and breathing environment. There are plants that need your help and support to enable them to thrive. Your soil needs to be nurtured and there is an entire

Below Regular weeding among the bearded iris beds at The Courts Garden, ensures the plants aren't competing for nutrients and water.

mini-ecosystem right on your doorstep, including an abundance of wildlife that depends on your gardening credentials for survival. If taking care of your garden feels like a chore with a list of maintenance jobs to do, then gardening probably is not for you. It should feel enlivening when you step outside, breathing the fresh air and feeling the soil on your hands.

As a gardener for the National Trust I wake up every morning excited to see what has happened in the garden – which plants are thriving, which are struggling. There is always a palpable buzz in the garden mess room each morning when the team pull on their gardening boots and chat about what they are going to do that day. Depending on the season, I can admire the frost on the seedheads in the herbaceous border or a new rose about to burst into flower, a frond fern that is newly unfurled and glistening in the early morning sun, or a spider's web that has been caught by the overnight dew. Every day is different, the garden moves at pace and it is important to adapt and change plans depending on the weather and how the plants are reacting. Like a lithe gymnast, the gardening mind has to be flexible, reading the evolving landscape like a book and prioritising a list of jobs that need to be done.

Andy Goodwin,
Senior Ranger at Polesden Lacey, Surrey

'Do think twice about ripping out some traditional weeds – ivy, for example. Although it can affect and compete with some trees, it provides a nesting habitat for birds and a roost site for bats. It's a great late-season nectar source for insects and its berries provide winter food for wildlife, including small mammals such as wood mice.'

Weeding

Weeding is one of the main jobs that needs to be done throughout the year. As the climate gets warmer, weeding is becoming a job to be done almost every day in the year, but the main season is from spring until mid-summer. From late summer until early spring the weeding lessens considerably and gardeners are able to turn their hand to other jobs, just occasionally doing a spot of weeding in the milder spells.

A weed is simply an unwanted plant, and in many cases you can enjoy them just as much as the plants that you have bought and grown. Many of the beautiful plants in wildflower meadows could be considered weeds – it just depends on your outlook as to whether you see them as friend or foe. Working for the National Trust with both rangers and gardeners always highlights these differing opinions; the list of weeds that gardeners give to trainees so that they learn how to identify them in the herbaceous border or rockery often contains the same plants as the list that rangers use as highlights for their wildflower walks.

However, there are good reasons for removing weeds in some areas of the garden:
• Weeds will compete with your existing plants for water, nutrients and light. Tall weeds will cast shadows or sometimes completely smother smaller plants, while the root systems will suck moisture and nutrients from the soil, depriving your vegetable and ornamental plants of much-needed sustenance if they are to perform at their best.
• Weeds often look unsightly and scruffy in your garden. Ornamental plants are selected for their aesthetic qualities, and while some weeds can be beautiful, nature's selection of plants focuses on their ability to survive and adapt to their environment.

- If ragwort is not controlled it will seed into nearby verges and grasslands. As it is toxic, this is a major concern if it spreads into fields being grazed by livestock, particularly horses. Although ragwort is host to the cinnabar moth, there is usually plenty of groundsel about that the larvae can feed on too.
- Most gardens have a design element to them, and weeds that encroach in your flower-beds will destroy carefully choreographed areas, including textures and colour combinations.
- Some of the most pernicious weeds such as ground elder, bindweed and perennial nettles can be a problem if their root systems intrude into the compost heap. The roots will make it impossible to use and if the compost is then spread onto beds, as the roots of the weed can take place there.
- Japanese knotweed is such an invasive 'garden escape' weed that it can destroy the foundations of the house. This weed is so serious and hard to eradicate that mortgage companies will often not lend to buyers if a surveyor reports that it is in the garden.
- Himalayan balsam loves moist conditions and smothers nearby wild flowers and ornamental plants. On riverbanks it causes erosion because it out-competes existing plants that have deeper root systems that would help to knit the soil together and prevent it washing away.

How to weed

There are numerous methods to control weeds and your choice of which to use is partly down to the type of weed.

Perennial weeds are the type that remain in the ground all year round, usually dying back in winter but then re-emerging in spring to wreak havoc in your garden. Removing the leaves and only part of the root system does not kill them – to properly eradicate them, their whole root system has to be destroyed. Some of the more persistent perennials require more than one attack, such as bamboo, bindweed, couch grass, ground elder, horsetail, oxalis and speedwell.

Annual weeds are easier to control and have a shallower root system, but it is important to catch them before they seed everywhere. Ephemeral weeds produce several generations in a year and are treated in the same way as annuals.

Tim Parker,
Garden and Countryside Manager at Chartwell, Kent

'Weeding is a time-consuming activity which is unpopular with most gardeners, so in our vegetable garden at Chartwell we have been experimenting with different techniques to offer us greater opportunities to concentrate on developing our crops and keeping our kitchen garden fully productive. We use green manures such as phacelia and red clover which will grow rapidly over exposed soil to suppress weeds. If dug in before flowering they will enrich the soil and improve its structure.

As well as green manure, we have been using companion planting as a repellent for unwanted pests around our vegetables depending on their specific requirement: herbs and strongly scented vegetables with our brassica family, marigolds and broad beans with our potatoes, sunflowers and tagetes with our roots, squash with our corn crop and calendula and nasturtiums with our legumes, which, in addition to repelling pests, provide a rich and vibrant spectacle within our walled garden.'

Tools for the job

Above, left to right A daisy grubber is useful tool for removing weeds with tap roots; Hand shears can be used to cut back weeds in awkward places such as beneath benches; A long-handled hoe will save you from having to bend too much.

Daisy grubber A long, narrow, two-pronged hand tool used to pull out long-rooted daisies and weeds, this tool has the advantage that it can dig deep and cause little or no disturbance to the surrounding soil. It proved invaluable in the quest to banish unsightly daisies and weeds from the pristine lawns of the Edwardian country houses.

Hand-held trowels and forks Small hand-held trowels can be used to prise out annual weeds, or perennial weeds that are just establishing themselves with a small root system. Hand-held forks are just as effective, and better for heavy ground as they are easier to work the soil with. They are also useful for lightly cultivating small areas of the ground if you have trodden on areas during weeding, and for breaking up a capped surface.

Hand shears These can be used to cut back weeds around tricky, tight areas where a mower or strimmer cannot reach. Repeatedly cutting back herbaceous perennial weeds can sometimes weaken the plant.

Hoe Used for scraping through the surface of the soil to remove annual weeds, this is one of the most traditional gardening tools. The most popular type is the Dutch hoe, which has a long handle and is pushed back and forth through the soil, severing the plant from its roots. There is also a draw hoe which is used with more of a chopping

action, bringing the hoe down behind the plant and drawing the blade towards the user.

Shorter-handled types such as the onion hoe are useful for scraping away weeds. This is best used on a dry day with a light wind to allow the weeds to desiccate on the surface in the sun. If used when the soil is slightly moist, the weeds should be picked up and removed to prevent them germinating again.

Knee protection If you are going to be spending a long time on your knees pulling out weeds, invest in a pair of knee pads. Alternatively, buy a kneeler, which is a cushioned pad to kneel on. The more elaborate ones have handles to help you get up and down and tool racks on which to hang your different weeding implements. Some can be inverted to double as a bench for working at a different height, such as when deadheading roses or collecting seed.

Pronged cultivators Used for loosening up the surface of the soil after it has been walked on when weeding, these usually have three prongs and may have either a long or short handle. They are good for breaking up capping on the surface of the soil, enabling water to penetrate to the roots of plants.

Clockwise from top left Pronged cultivators; Standard spade and smaller border shovel; Trug and strimmer.

Spade Deep-rooted weeds such as bindweed or ground elder will need digging out. Be warned though, roots of some perennials can go down as far as 1m (3¼ft) under the surface. Be careful not to slice through the roots as anything remaining will regrow. A border spade is slightly smaller than a standard spade, and is a useful tool for digging out smaller weeds or making lighter work of a job as it is not as heavy.

Strimmer A strimmer can be used to cut back invasive weeds but it will not kill them. It is possible to use battery-powered strimmers that are charged by solar panels if you want to avoid using fossil fuels.

Trugs and buckets These are indispensable for putting weeds or tools in. Plastic, colourful trugs can be bought cheaply and are light to carry.

Weed knife A tool that usually has a hooked edge, this is used to scrape between the gaps in paving slabs and in other narrow gaps to pull out weeds.

Wheelbarrow Where would gardeners be without their trusty wheelbarrows? They are ideal for shifting mulch, transporting tools or putting your weeds into. The standard traditional barrow has three wheels but there are other types available, such as the four-wheeled plastic barrows which are sturdier, very light and have a much bigger capacity. It is a good idea to ensure the barrow you prefer will fit down your garden paths before purchasing one.

'Buy good tools and look after them. You can never have enough buckets to hand – one for annual weeds, one for stones, one for pernicious weeds, one for plants that you've lifted and so on.'

Martyn Pepper,
Senior Gardener
at Coleton Fishacre, Devon.

Tip

Most people in the UK use a traditional short-handled spade with either a T-shaped or D-shaped handle. The reason for these short handles was so that people could work in confined spaces such as in the mines. However, the old-fashioned spade with a much longer handle and a pointed rather than square blade is far more effective. The long handle saves back-breaking work as the weight at the end of the spade can be counterbalanced by using your thigh to support it. It also means less strain on your back as there is no need to stretch into the trench. Finally, the sharp contour at the end of the blade means it slices into the soil far more effectively. It can be used as a shovel or spade.

Above National Trust gardeners enjoy using some of the more traditional skills, reviving what could otherwise be a dying countryside craft. This bill hook is being used to sharpen the ends of hazel rods for training runner beans up.

Tales from the Potting Shed

Garden tools by Tracey Parker, Assistant House Steward at Polesden Lacey

Garden tools are not a modern invention and some of the oldest ones date back to around 10,000 years ago, when the microlith was developed in the Neolithic period. This was basically a small, sharp, stone blade set into a handle made of wood, bone or antler – the first multi-tool!

The Romans first developed the basic pattern for tools such as the shovels and spades we use today when they harnessed the technology of the forge and discovered the process of heating iron to its malleable point. As a result various crude tools began to be developed, but it was not until the middle of the fourteenth century that the smelting of iron made it possible to create lighter, more precisely shaped tools. By the mid-eighteenth century, when popular interest in gardens exploded and gardeners had to be well equipped, catalogues of the time have illustrations of a wide range of unusual and conventional tools and accessories made for specific purposes in the garden. They included hedge shears, pruning shears, cultivating forks and trowels – in fact, almost every non-mechanical gardening tool available today. With the coming of the Industrial Revolution, steel and alloys were developed and this led to the manufacture of tools that were lighter, finer and far more durable. Tools provide us with a direct link to our heritage and when you look at the history of some of the common garden tools that the National Trust gardeners use today you will find that not much has changed in hundreds of years. However, there are some tools that you are unlikely to spot in a National Trust gardening tool shed.

FOLDING TROWEL This is an early twentieth-century trowel and fork that was spring-loaded and made of steel with a coil spring.

RINGBARKING TOOL An Edwardian tool used to remove a complete strip of bark from the entire circumference of a branch or trunk of a tree or woody plant. This technique, known as girdling, was employed to yield larger fruit in the orchards of the country houses, though it resulted in the death of the entire tree over time.

SARCLOIR An early twentieth-century French tool, used for weeding between stones and rocks as well as harvesting crops such as cabbages and lettuces.

Bare soil: much mulch!

No gardener likes to see bare soil left for long in the garden. Except for the vegetable garden prior to sowing, bare soil looks out of keeping, makes the existing planting seem sparse and lessens the potential for wildlife habitats. Although farmers often leave an area to go fallow, or 'rest', for a season, bare soil will rapidly be colonised by weeds. It will also be far more susceptible to wind and rain erosion, which can mean all the goodness in your soil being washed away. The one time of year when it can be beneficial is during winter; if the soil has been dug and turned over, the frosts can help to break down large clods in the soil and expose and kill some weed seeds.

Applying a mulch over bare soil has many benefits. Acting like a permeable blanket, it improves the soil, helping it to retain the moisture during dry periods, and suppresses many annual weeds. It will also increase the worm activity in the soil as they come closer to the surface and drag organic material into the root zone.

The best time to put an annual mulch on the border is in early spring. This is when the plants need the biggest boost as they are starting their growing cycle. It is also when the weeds start to grow. Mulching in autumn can be a waste if nothing is being planted until spring as very often the material gets washed away before it is needed. However, newly planted trees and shrubs will benefit from mulching at whatever time of year they are being planted.

Types of mulches

Gravel, slate, crushed shells or stones are perfect mulch for dry gardens or herb beds as they retain the moisture, suppress weeds and don't add excessive nutrients to the soil. They're unsuitable for vegetable gardens and traditional herbaceous borders which prefer a rich, organic supplement to the surface of the soil.

Manure and garden compost works well as a permeable cover allowing moisture and rain water to seep through, but at the same time, helping to retain it and slow down evaporation. Water the mulch after placing it down to encourage the worms to start taking material into the soil and to reduce having to irrigate later when the season gets drier.

Woodchip spread them around woodland plants but avoid using fresh material. Allow it to rot down a bit first. The chippings help to improve drainage.

Wool fleeces Wool is a natural by-product of the farming industry, and in some rural areas you can get hold of it very cheaply, or even for free. It is permeable yet thick enough to smother out weeds.

Right, top to bottom Ground-suppressing membranes are useful for smothering weeds in large areas at Sissinghurst, as is woodchip if not used fresh. Wool fleecing is used as a weed suppresent at Nunnington Hall, North Yorkshire.

Beating the weeds

- Cover up the soil – the best way is simply to get it planted. There is no mulch that can match the benefits of having garden plants in the soil. The foliage helps to shade the soil and cool the temperatures, which in turn will reduce water evaporation. The root systems should help to hold the soil structure together. Choose ground-cover plants to provide a dense, low canopy such as *Euonymus*, *Ballota*, *Pachysandra*, *Vinca* and *Waldsternia*.
- Hoe annual weeds or dig them out, ideally before they set seed and spread throughout the garden, otherwise your job will be much bigger next year. Some annual plants can be removed by hand, particularly on light soil – hold them at the base and pull. Groundsel and fat hen can be controlled effectively in this way.
- Dig out and remove the entire root system of perennial weeds to prevent them regenerating.
- Use fabric to cover up bare soil. You can buy black landscape fabrics, but old carpets will do the job. Avoid using carpet with a foam backing it can leach noxious chemicals that can later cause problems in the soil. Synthetic carpet is made of petroleum products that have been treated with chemicals and cleaners, so only use ones made of natural fibres such as wool, jute or cotton.
- A flame gun is a quick way of burning off annual weeds, but they are ineffective against perennials.
- You can use chemical weedkillers if you are not an organic gardener. The systemic chemical treatment containing glyphosate is a particularly effective treatment for herbaceous perennials as the plant absorbs it through the leaves and takes it down into its roots, killing the entire plant. It tends to be most successful on plants with big leaves and is not particularly effective on weeds such as horsetail (*Equisetum arvense*) which has a waxy surface and practically no leaf target to spray, although bruising or stamping on the stems prior to spraying helps. Do not use it on the lawn to kill weeds as it will wipe out the surrounding grass too. A ready-mixed spray or weed stick can be bought from garden centres. Always spray when there is no or little wind to prevent the weedkiller drifting onto your ornamental or edible plants.

Above *Echinops* and ornamental grasses growing in the borders at The Courts.

Above *Euonymus phellomanus* provides good ground cover.

Step-by-step: Making a slug trap

Slugs are the bane of a gardener's life as they can devour seedlings and even entire plants overnight, causing heartbreak for anyone who has worked hard to produce healthy plants only to see them destroyed. Beer traps are a simple and effective way to entice these slimy creatures away from your delicious vegetable patch and herbaceous border and into a cup of delicious beer buried in the soil. The slugs get one whiff of the heady brew, find it irresistible, slither into the container and never crawl out again.

1. Avoid containers with thin, sharp edges as slugs tend not to cross over them. You need a container that has a smooth lip to it, such as a pint glass. Alternatively, use a recycleable cardboard cup that can simply be covered over with soil and left to biodegrade *in situ*. It saves having to dispose of those slimy pests.

2. Fill the container with beer – it is said that slugs prefer darker stouts with a yeasty aroma, but in my experience cheap lager works just as well.

3. Bury the container in the soil near to the threatened plants. Leave the container just slightly proud of the ground level as this will prevent beneficial creatures such as ground beetles that love to devour slugs scurrying into it. If you are still worried about creatures falling in, put sticks into it as an escape route so that they can crawl out. Slugs will be too drunk to make the effort themselves.

4. Slugs tend to prefer damp moist conditions and will often be more persistent when it rains. To prevent your beer trap becoming diluted with rainwater, place a stone over it, leaving a gap for slugs to crawl under and plop into the beer.

Tip

Bindweed is one of the most invasive weeds in the garden. Because the roots are so difficult to dig out, sometimes the only effective method is to spray the plant with a systemic weedkiller containing glyphosate. However, it can be difficult if it is starting to scramble through your precious plants, as you risk spraying them too. To keep them separate, put bamboo canes in the ground and twist the bindweed on that. Let it grow for a week or two to maximise the amount of bindweed leaf canopy to treat. Spray on a dry day with no wind. This should prevent any of your plants getting hit by the chemical.

Increasing your stakes: support your plants

One of the essential tasks in the herbaceous border each spring is to prop up your plants to ensure that they do not flop over. The modern planting style often uses large herbaceous plants that will prop each other up, but traditional herbaceous perennials such as lupins and delphiniums will need support if they are not going to collapse, brought down by their profusion of flowers and foliage. Remember to put stakes in place early, otherwise you risk damaging the growing plant.

There are many different techniques to staking and which you choose partly depends on your personal preference but also on the type of plant you are trying to support. Here are a few of them.

Adam Cracknell,
Gardens and Estate Ranger at Ormesby Hall, North Yorkshire

'After delphiniums have finished flowering in mid-summer, cut them right down to ground level, mulch and water them, and you can then enjoy a second flush of flowers in mid-September. This secondary flush is not usually as dramatic or tall but they are more compact and sturdy and will not need staking.'

- Individual plants with large flower heads such as delphiniums or sunflowers will need individual staking with a bamboo cane or hazel stick. Use a figure-of-eight knot so that the stem does not get damaged against the stake. Tomatoes and peppers are also given a similar support system.
- Garden twine can be used to tie plants up. This is often done on soft fruit bushes such as redcurrants and gooseberries. Push in four canes or hazel rods at each corner of the plant to make a square. Thread string around the four stakes to keep the bush upright throughout summer and prevent the branches snapping under the weight of fruit.
- Natural woven structures, often made from birch brushwood, make a beautiful support. The wood should be harvested in winter, prior to buds and leaves forming on the plants and the onset of the nesting season for birds. Store the brushwood in a dry place until you are ready to use it in the garden.
- Dahlias are often kept upright by running a 10cm (4in) black or green pea net between dahlia stakes, enabling the emerging shoots to grow between the mesh and disguise the sight of the support once fully in flower.
- There are many types of ornamental stakes available to buy from garden centres. Most are made from metal which should last for a few years. Choose brown or green ones as they will not show up in the display.
- Pea sticks are rustic twiggy sticks put next to peas to enable them to scramble up with their tendrils.

Tim Parker,
Garden and Countryside
Manager at Chartwell,
Kent

'Rather than going to the garden centre and buying expensive canes that have been shipped around the world, you can harvest canes locally from overgrown bamboo plantings either in your own garden or from a friend's planting. This means you can save time and cash which you can use for other parts of your garden. At Emmetts Garden we have a huge bamboo planting so there is no shortage of supply and we use the canes at our sister sites Chartwell and Quebec. Bamboo is a vigorous grower so harvesting some canes won't leave you short in future years.'

Above, left and centre Lupins and dahlias both benefit from staking. **Above, right** Staking peas using hazel twigs. **Below** Staking emerging delphiniums using stout hazel sticks and garden twine.

'Stake herbaceous plants early, when they are around 15–30cm (6–12in) high, because the taller they get the more difficult they are to control.'

Martyn Pepper,
Senior Gardener
at Coleton Fishacre, Devon

Making more flowers

Throughout the growing year, you can prolong flowering by constantly deadheading blooms as soon as they start to fade. If you allow the flowers to go completely to seed the plant believes it has done its job for the year and stops producing more blooms, so regularly check your borders and remove spent flowerheads to extend the season of interest right into autumn. Plants not to deadhead include vegetable and fruit crops because that will destroy your future harvests, plants that have thousands of small flowers, simply because it is not worth the effort, and plants that provide an attractive autumn display of berries.

Bedding plants Most, such as busy lizzies, geraniums and petunias, should have their spent flowers simply pinched off between finger and thumb.

Bulbs Although you should not cut back the foliage until it has died back naturally, removing the flower head on large daffodils will ensure that the energy goes into the development of the bulb and not seed production. However, leave the flowerheads on smaller, naturalised bulbs as they will naturally spread their seed when ripe.

Delphiniums Cut back the flower stems to encourage new ones to grow.

Roses Cut back to a pair of healthy buds further down the stem.

Sweet peas Regularly cut the flowers when they are in full bloom to enjoy their heady scent in flower displays indoors.

Clockwise from top left Cutting back roses; Petunias should be pinched off; Sweet peas need to be cut regularly.

Cutting back plants

One of the most popular techniques for cutting back used by National Trust gardeners is the Chelsea Chop. This means partially cutting back large herbaceous plants during mid-spring with a pair of secateurs or hand shears. There are three reasons for this apparently rather brutal treatment. First, it extends the flowering season of the plant; if you cut back half of a large perennial plant, the section that has been cut back will flower later in the year, while the part that was left will flower during the earlier part of the season.

The second reason is to create a greater depth to the planting scheme. Cutting back half the clump makes the border feel bigger and deeper. The second flush will flower lower down than the plants' usual height, creating interesting tiers of floral displays.

The third reason is that it makes a much more compact, stouter plant. It is also worth trying this technique if you were plagued by a pest or disease the previous year, since tweaking the time of flowering could help to disrupt the life cycle of a fungus or aphid causing you problems.

The Chelsea Chop gained its name because it is usually carried out about the same time as the world-famous RHS Chelsea Flower Show in May. It is best suited to some of the larger herbaceous perennials such as *Echinacea, Eupatorium, Helenium, Monarda* and *Sedum*. Apply it only to healthy plants and avoid it in periods of drought.

Far left Applying the Chelsea Chop to the front section of this vigorous *Persicaria superba* will make it flower at a lower height than the other part of the plant at the back, creating a more three-dimensional effect to this section of the flower border. **Left** Pinching out a tomato plant.

Pinching out

Sometimes it is useful to pinch out the growing tip of a plant. This creates a bushier plant, which in turn should make it produce more laterals and therefore more flowers. This technique is usually carried out when a plant has reached about two-thirds of its intended natural height. It is often done with herbaceous plants such as asters, cosmos, cerinthe, penstemon, osteospermum, fuchsias and sweet peas. It is called pinching out because the shoots should be young and tender enough to pull them off just by squeezing them between your thumb and forefinger. Occasionally side shoots are pinched out too, such as on fuchsias, or on standard plants, like bay trees, to encourage them to bush out more.

Pest and disease control

A gardener has to keep a vigilant eye out for pests and diseases, which can strike at any moment and ruin a crop or floral display almost overnight. There is little that can be done with some of the more prevalent and virulent problems, but just as your body has built up a healthy immune system to deal with many common germs, a balanced garden can make your plants healthier and stronger, enabling them to combat some of the nastiest of attacks.

Regularly pruning shrubs will avoid congested canopies where the shrubs become susceptible to fungal diseases due to the restricted movement of air. It will also prevent wounds where branches have rubbed together, providing entry points for disease. Watering your plants will help to keep them strong and vigorous so that they can combat pest and disease attacks, while ensuring that plants are planted correctly in healthy soil will help to sustain them in the future.

The treatment of pests and diseases has turned almost full circle back to the practices of the eighteenth and nineteenth century before chemical pesticides and artificial fertilisers were used. Many National Trust gardeners avoid using commercial pesticides in the garden where possible and have returned to traditional, tried and tested natural methods of control.

The use of chemical controls developed apace during the mid-twentieth century, some of which were the results of laboratory testing during the two world wars. It was discovered that some of these deadly chemicals could also be used to kill garden pests, including DTT, nicotines and organophosphates. The treatment was indiscriminate, wiping out any creature that came into contact with the pesticides, including many of the beneficial insects. Thankfully horticultural practice has moved on. After all, destroying the environment and risking human health was hardly considered to be an enjoyable and sustainable outdoor experience.

Caring for the ecosystem

Most gardeners nowadays focus on creating a balanced ecosystem – instead of chemical warfare in the garden, we tend to work with nature rather than against it. Good plant hygiene and horticultural practice enable many plants to help themselves in combating pests and diseases.

Digging organic matter into the soil creates a healthy environment for plants to grow in. Keep them watered during dry periods so as they are not under stress and susceptible to problems. Also, ensure that there is a good variation of plants to encourage natural predators such as hedgehogs, frogs, toads, shrews, birds and ground beetles to prey upon slugs and snails. This should also encourage natural pest control, such as ladybirds and lacewings which will feed on aphids, and in larger gardens foxes help to control rabbit populations. In many cases, if you let nature take care of itself, it leaves you free to relax and enjoy your garden. Having many different creatures in your garden should help to ensure that not one creature dominates, which is when the problems occur.

Friend or foe

The wider the range of flowers that you grow, the wider diversity of habitats to provide insects with homes, food and of course a hunting ground. There will be a few pests in the mix, but they actually make up a tiny proportion of the overall population and number of species that are in the garden. Like a good film, a garden needs the baddies as well as the good guys; pests are an essential part of a balanced food chain and you get a better balance of predators and parasites, and less damage overall, than if you had just eradicated pests with a spray.

There will be times when the natural balance tips in one direction or the other, and when you

Left A green lacewing. **Above, top** Watch out for marks and discolouration on your plants, which can be signs of disease. **Above** Ladybirds feed on black-bean aphids.

do have to intervene there are plenty of gentle techniques to reduce the problems. Washing-up liquid can be sprayed to control aphid damage, while garlic sprays can be used for pest control, as a fungicide and to generally increase the health of a plant. Instead of using inorganic fertilisers which has led to the leaching of nitrates into the ground and the water supply, overstimulating algae growth in our rivers and lakes and choking aquatic plants, invertebrates and fish, many gardeners are using natural materials to feed their plants. These include compost tea, or homemade comfrey or nettle tea, supplemented with seaweed extracts, plant oils or plant invigorators. Extracts of

Above The Rose Garden at Polesden Lacey on a summer evening.

citrus can be used to clean the greenhouse, ridding it of lingering pests and diseases before moving plants in over winter.

At Polesden Lacey we apply a three-in-one natural plant invigorator to our plants which helps to combat insect pests such as aphids, mealy bugs and woolly aphids while at the same time reducing fungal diseases. It also contains a foliar feed and leaves no harmful chemical residues.

Traditional versus modern varieties

One of the difficulties in maintaining gardens with historic collections of plants is that many of the older types are not as resistant to modern-day pests and disease, which have evolved in time into more virulent strains. Choosing modern resistant varieties is a good solution, but it could be argued that this compromises the integrity of the historic collections, so it needs to be done with care.

At Polesden Lacey the rose garden is considered to be one of the finest examples of an Edwardian rose design, but there were many problems with the older varieties being susceptible to traditional rose problems, such as black spot and mildew. A compromise was reached whereby newer disease-resistant varieties very similar to the original forms were planted. An example is the classic Edwardian rambling rose 'Dorothy Perkins', introduced in 1901 and named by the famous rose breeder Charles Perkins for his granddaughter Dorothy, which had pride of place in this classic Edwardian garden. The National Trust gardeners wishing to maintain the importance of the rose collection have combined some of these beautiful original roses, which had been struggling to grow on the thin, chalky soil of the North Downs, with more modern varieties with better resistance, making the overall display look much better for the 300,000 visitors walking under the rose-adorned pergolas each year.

Natural predators

It is a dog-eat-dog world out there, or rather a bug-eat-bug. There are natural predators that you can buy online and let loose to do the pest control for you, based on the natural order and food chain of life. *Encarsia formosa* is a parasitic wasp that can be introduced into greenhouses to control whitefly, while tiny microscopic nematodes can be used to control vine weevil which can wreak havoc on the root system of plants, particularly those grown in containers. Nematodes can also be used to control slugs, while the cannibalistic mite *Phytoseiulus persimilis* can control red spider mite in the greenhouse.

Ladybirds can be bought and introduced to help control aphids, but it is far easier and cheaper to simply make a home for them and you will discover that they find their own way there.

Step-by-step: Making a ladybird and lacewing home

1. Recycle plastic bottles by cutting them in half with a pair of scissors.

2. Roll up corrugated cardboard and push it into the bottle halves.

3. Use a skewer to puncture two holes in the side and thread string through it.

4. Hang the bottles in trees from the string, so that the length of the bottle is parallel with the ground.

These days, fortunately, most of us have a more relaxed approach to plant pests and diseases. There are still some major sources of concern for the health of some of our most popular plants, such as the arrival of ash die-back and sudden oak death, and there will be many more in the future that will need controlling. However, we can have our own outdoor space rich in plantlife and wildlife and enjoy a healthy green environment in which to relax and and enjoy our gardening.

Seasonal chart planner

Spring

- Mulch around your plants to retain moisture.
- Plant out bulbs for an autumn display.
- Start to cut your lawn, keeping the blades high for the first few cuts.
- Divide herbaceous plants before they come into full growth.
- Cut back winter stems such as cornus or willow in early spring.
- Check your beehives to see how they have recovered from winter.
- Get your plant supports and stakes in place early to support herbaceous plants.
- Prune late-flowering shrubs.
- Sow vegetable seeds.
- Chelsea Chop some of the larger perennials to encourage flowering later in the year.
- Make bug 'hotels' for insects to nest in.
- Keep a vigilant eye out for pests and diseases.
- Cut hedges before the nesting season starts.

Summer

- Continue to mow the lawns, except for in periods of drought.
- Regularly deadhead flowers to encourage new blooms.
- Check if plants are drying out and water accordingly. New plantings, containers and hanging baskets most need an extra splash of water during dry periods.
- Stay on top of weeding. Try to catch annual weeds before they set seed and spread further.
- Pinch out young plants to encourage a bushier growth with more flowers.
- Feed plants with comfrey and nettle tea to encourage lush, green growth. Alternatively, use compost tea.
- Wherever you have bare soil, apply mulch to suppress the weeds.
- Put water out for birds and bugs – in mid-summer water supplies often dry out.
- If you are planning a redesign, label your herbaceous perennials now before they die back, so that you know what to save and what to get rid of.

Chickens

Just by following their natural habits, chickens do such useful work for the gardener that they can almost be regarded as a form of gardener's tool. I recommend anybody with enough space to acquire some. Put them in a weedy patch of garden with a bit of chicken wire around it to contain them and they will happily peck away at the soil and even scratch up some of the roots of weeds – in fact their feet are shaped like a three-pronged cultivar. Many of our common weeds gained names such as chickweed and fat hen because chickens like to eat them.

Not only will chickens help you weed, they will provide you with eggs and strong chicken manure as well. However, do not expect an immaculate plot afterwards – you will still need to tidy up. Of course, chickens do not discriminate between weeds and the plants you want to keep, so take care where you put them.

Autumn

- Scarify and aerate the lawn before the onset of winter.
- Divide herbaceous perennials to reinvigorate plants.
- Install a water butt in preparation for catching rainwater during winter.
- Sow winter green manures.
- Create homes for hedgehogs in your garden (see page 257).
- This is the best season of the year to plant a tree, giving it enough time to establish before winter.
- Cover slightly tender plants with horticultural fleece.
- Alternatively, move them into a greenhouse, a conservatory or even a shed.
- Plant out bulbs such as daffodils and tulips for a floral display in spring.
- Collect up fallen leaves on the lawn and add them to the compost heap.

Tip

Use stone, slate or wood to edge lawns that contain invasive weeds such as couch grass or speedwell to prevent them spreading into your flower borders. Ornamental plants that could potentially spread throughout your border quickly in a way you do not want should be planted in sturdy pots and plunged into the soil, leaving a slight lip above the surface of the ground to prevent surface roots spreading. Fast-spreading plants include non-clumping forming bamboos, mint and figs.

Winter

- Order vegetable seeds ready for the new growing year.
- Check tree stakes to make sure none have broken and ensure tree ties are not too tight on the trees.
- Plant bare-root fruit trees if the soil is not frozen or too wet.
- Install solar panels on your shed roof. They can be used for charging battery-operated hedge trimmers, mowers and strimmers.
- Put food out for birds to help sustain them during winter, and water bowls too in freezing conditions – even in winter they need to bathe.
- Take hardwood cuttings of fruit bushes.
- Prune soft fruit bushes and freestanding apple and pear trees.
- Mend things in the garden such as broken fences while the plants are dormant. Also consider laying paths, patios and decking or building a raised bed.
- Turn over the compost heap to encourage the material to break down.
- Move deciduous trees or shrubs while the plants are dormant.
- Restore hedges and overgrown trees.

grow your own

Growing fruit

The National Trust cares for thousands of orchards around the country and has walled kitchen gardens galore, replete with trees and bushes bearing luscious, ripe and juicy fruit. Anybody who has tasted fruit picked fresh from the plant will appreciate that the flavour surpasses anything found on the supermarket shelves. This is partly because much shop-bought fruit is harvested before fully ripe to allow time for storage and transportation. Picking ripe fruit from the garden ensures that the fruit has fully developed its sugary richness and flavour.

Many of the National Trust properties grow local and rare varieties that cannot be found in shops. As the Trust is a conservation charity it is important that it maintains as many of these varieties as possible, not only because they provide a vital gene bank for future generations but also because behind each fruit variety is usually a rich cultural heritage belonging to a specific local area. The reason some of those apples thrive in those areas is because they are suited to the climate and soil types of a region, so growing local varieties really is the best option. There are more than 2,000 varieties of apples in the UK, and if you taste some of the more unusual varieties such as the aniseed flavour of an Ellison's Orange apple or the exciting tang of a D'Arcy Spice you will never want to settle for a shop-bought apple again.

Below Vines trained along the walled garden at Barrington Court, Somerset.

Top fruit tree sizes

In the horticultural world, 'top fruit' refers to fruit grown on a tree. The four main types are apples, pears, plums and cherries.

You do not need an orchard to grow fruit trees; all of those four types come on rootstocks that restrict the size of the trees. The 30 Surrey and Sussex varieties of apple in the orchard at Polesden Lacey are all grown on M26 rootstocks as their height of about 2m (6½ft) makes the picking of fruit easier. When you buy trees from a plant centre or online, always check your chosen variety is available on the type of rootstock to suit your garden.

The sizes are as follows, although the height does vary slightly depending on variety.

Apples
M27 Very dwarfing – 1.2m (4ft)
M9 Dwarfing – 1.8m (6ft)
M26 Semi-dwarfing – 2.1m (7ft)
M106 Semi-vigorous – 2.5m (8¼ft)
MM111 Vigorous – 5m (16½ft)
M25 Very vigorous – 6m (19½ft)

Pears
These are usually grafted onto quince rootstocks to restrict their vigour and size.
Quince C – 3m (10ft)
Quince A – 4m (13ft)

Plums
Pixy – 2m (6½ft)
St Julien A – 2.5m (8¼ft)

Cherries
Colt – 4m (13ft)
Gisela 5 – 2.5m (8¼ft)

Right Apple trees can become enormous unless they are grown on a rootstock that will control their size.

Training fruit trees

The beauty of fruit trees is that they can be trained into a range of different shapes. This provides the most spectacular ornamental quality in any garden. Because fruit trees respond so well to pruning, it means their size can be restricted too (subject to the correct rootstocks). Here are some of the most common shapes for fruit trees.

Fan The branches are splayed out in a fan shape, usually against a wall but they can be trained on wires. Fruit suitable includes apples, pears, cherries, plums, gooseberries, figs, peaches, redcurrants and grape vines.

Cordon The tree or bush is trained as a single stem or trunk with short side shoots. Apples and pears are usually grown as 'oblique' cordons, at an angle of about 45 degrees to slow down the vigour. It is a great way of getting a lot of trees in your garden as they can be spaced as closely as 40cm (16in) apart. Fruit suitable for oblique cordons includes apples, pears, plums. Vertical cordons include gooseberries, redcurrants and grapevines.

Espalier This is probably the most attractive method of growing fruit in a garden. It is based on a single central trunk with horizontal, parallel tiers of branches trained out along a system of wires. Suitable fruit includes apples, pears, sweet cherries, plums, gooseberries, grapevines and redcurrants.

Step-overs As the name suggests, these fruit trees are so low to the ground that you can literally step over them. They are a wonderful method of lining a pathway or creating informal divisions

between areas of a kitchen garden. Fruit suitable includes apples (only on M27 or M9), pears (with low vigour), redcurrants and gooseberries. Take care, though, when stepping over a prickly gooseberry.

Spindle trees/pyramid trees These are shaped like Christmas trees. The theory is that pruning a tree narrower at the top and wider at the base enables the sunlight to reach the entire tree with minimal shading. Trees suitable include apples, pears, plums and cherries.

Bush trees This refers to the traditional tree or bush with a central stem holding aloft a goblet-shaped structure of four or five main branches. These open-centre trees allow the air to circulate around the canopy, reducing pest and disease problems. When the trunk is particularly long it is called a 'standard'. Fruit suitable includes apples, pears, plums, cherries, gooseberries and redcurrants.

Opposite, far left A fan-trained cherry tree at Tyntesfield, North Somerset. **Opposite, left** An espaliered tree grows against the wall at The Vyne, Hampshire. **Above, left** Summer pruning a step-over apple tree. **Above, right** A cordon of pear trees at BuscotPark, Oxfordshire.

Apples

Apples are one of the UK's most popular types of fruit and with such a wide variety to choose from, it is hardly surprising. They can be grown in containers if space is an issue and by careful selection of varieties and suitable storage conditions it is possible to have fruit from mid-July through to late winter.

Apple trees are usually pruned during the dormant season, which is late autumn through to late winter, although espaliers, cordons and step-overs can also be pruned in late summer. Pruning should be carried out every year to remove diseased and dying wood, retain the tree's vigour and encourage new fruit buds to develop. It also removes congestion, allowing sunlight into the canopy.

When buying fruit trees it is important to check the pollination group. Although some are self-fertile, usually at least two trees that will flower at the same time are required, so that pollinating insects such as honey bees can pass the pollen from flower to flower. Fruit is ready for picking when it can be removed easily from the tree without tugging. Fallen fruit on the ground is the best indication a tree is ready for harvesting.

Varieties to try

'Bramley's Seedling'
'Cornish Gilliflower'
'Discovery'
'Pitmaston Pineapple'
'Ribston Pippin'
'Worcester Pearmain'

Left, top A Discovery apple tree at Hardwick Hall.
Left, bottom Pitmaston Pineapple apples growing in the Orchard at Hanbury Hall, Worcestershire.

Pears

The soft, melting flesh of a freshly picked pear is irresistible, and the aroma and sweetness is unsurpassed by any other fruit. Pears have a reputation for being tricky to grow and it is true that their flowers can be susceptible to spring frosts, but if planted in a sunny, sheltered position they are just as easy to grow as apples.

Prune pear trees during the winter periods, removing congested branches and spurring back some of the new growth. Both apples and pears benefit from having their clusters of fruit thinned out, leaving two or three fruits to ripen fully. Pears are usually picked when slightly underripe and left to mature in storage. Check them over often as they can quickly deteriorate.

Varieties to try
'Beth'
'Beurre Hardy'
'Catillac'
'Conference'
'Doyenne du Comice'
'Louise Bonne of Jersey'
'Onward'

Tip
Most mid- to late apples and pears will store if kept in a cool, frost-free location such as a cellar, garage or shed.

Above An espaliered Conference pear tree at Buscot Park. **Left, top** Espaliered pears growing in the garden at Bateman's. **Left, bottom** Close up of unripe 'Beth' pears growing against a stone wall at Barrington Court.

Plums

The Victoria plum is a favourite variety with many people, but there are a whole range of other delicious varieties too. In addition there are the closely related golden and green types called gages and other family members that include damsons, bullaces, mirabelles and sloes. The plums and gages are delicious when eaten fresh, whereas the others are more suitable for cooking or making jams.

They usually ripen from July onwards, although damsons and bullaces can remain on the tree until autumn. They are usually grown as freestanding trees but are often seen as pyramids, cordons and fans.

Plums are easy to grow as they usually just look after themselves. They do not require much pruning – just the removal of a few crossing branches each year to reduce congestion. All stone fruit (including also cherries, apricots and peaches) should be pruned when in growth, avoiding winter, as they can be susceptible to the diseases bacterial canker and silver leaf.

Varieties to try

Plums
'Blue Tit'
'Opal'
'Victoria'

Gages
'Cambridge Gage'
'Oullins Golden Gage'

Damsons
'Merryweather Damson'
'Shropshire Prune Damson'

Bullaces
'Langley Bullace'

Cherry plums (mirabelles)
'Gypsy'

Below, left The orchard at Tatton Park contains varieties of fruit which are known to have been grown in Cheshire during the Edwardian period, including apples, pears, gages and cherries. **Below, above** Espaliered plums growing at Knightshayes Court, **Below, bottom** The distinctive blue fruit of 'Shropshire Prune'.

Tales from thePotting Shed

Kitchen Gardens by Tracey Parker, Assistant House Steward at Polesden Lacey

The kitchen garden represents a common feature of large country houses and estates from the mid-eighteenth century to the early twentieth century. The vegetable gardens would have been surrounded by high brick walls which prevented theft, but more importantly provided shelter and warmth. These walled gardens were expected to supply the country-house owners with a continuous and varied supply of fresh fruit, vegetables and flowers every day of the year. Gardeners were required to grow strawberries in winter and salads all year round in sufficient quantities to help the house cope with any number of unexpected house guests.

Perhaps the most extravagant era was that of the Edwardians, who ate well and frequently entertained on a lavish scale. As well as being tasty, the food had to look amazing and the dessert trays were filled with beautiful fancies, fruits and other delicacies. Virtually everything that happened in the great Edwardian houses was about displaying wealth and enhancing the social status of their owners, and the fruit and vegetable gardens of the day were no exception.

An example of how the wealthy owners of these houses dictated what was grown is shown at Polesden Lacey. The Edwardian society hostess Mrs Ronald Greville expected the very best food and wine to be served at her famous weekend house parties. When strawberries were to be served, Mrs Greville requested that they all be of equal size and shape and laid on a bed of strawberry leaves.

In order to achieve this constant supply of food all through the year, a sophisticated combination of forcing, retarding and storage was employed to extend the growing season. Forcing, which means encouraging the plant to develop far earlier in the season than it would do normally, was widely practised at this time. Hot walls were a method of forcing and the protection of the walls themselves brought fruit trees into production earlier. Pineapples, figs, peaches, grapes, soft fruit, pears and apples were all grown to perfection, polished, prepared and taken to the house to be served and discussed at the dinner table like a fine wine or cigar.

Cherries

In former times cherries were grown only in orchards on large estates and required huge ladders to pick the fruit, but thanks to dwarfing rootstocks they can now be enjoyed in the smallest of gardens. There are basically two different types; sweet cherries and sour cherries, of which morello is the most commonly known.

Sweet and sour cherries have different growing habits, which affect how they are pruned. Sweet varieties produce fruiting spurs on older wood, while sour cherries bear fruit on growth produced the previous year. Like plums and peaches, cherries should only be pruned when in growth to avoid contamination and diseases. In the past, gardeners used to apply an anti-fungus paint over the wounds, but this is no longer done as it is believed the sealing of the wounds actually caused more disease problems than it prevented.

Many cherry trees are self-fertile, which means you only need one tree to produce fruit – ideal if you have a small garden. Cherries come in a range of attractive colours, too, including black, red, yellow and orange. They are ready to pick when they feel soft to the touch.

Varieties to try
Sweet cherries
'Merton Glory'
'Lapins'
'Stella'
'Summer Sun'
'Sunburst'
'Sweetheart'

Sour cherries
'Morella'
'Nabella'

Left Cherry trees in blossom in April in Bohetherick orchard, near Cotehele Quay, Cornwall.

Figs

Figs are far easier to grow than most people think. Varieties such as the popular Brown Turkey are fairly hardy and will regularly produce bumper crops of sweet, succulent fruits from mid- to late summer. Having a Mediterranean origin, they do require a sunny, sheltered site, and are most commonly grown as fans on south-facing walls. In warmer countries the embryonic fruits are formed and ripen in the same year, but summers are not long enough in the UK. Therefore, baby figs over-winter in the tips of the shoots and become the ripe fruit for the following year. For this reason figs may need protection with a fleece or bracken during winter.

For figs to produce heavy crops of fruit they need to be treated mean – they should have their roots restricted by being grown in pots or surrounded by patio slabs. If the roots grow unimpeded the trees tend to make a lot of leafy growth at the expense of fruit. Restricting the roots makes them produce fruit as a defence mechanism to ensure they reproduce and survive.

Varieties to try

'Brown Turkey'
'Brunswick'
'Panaché'
'Rouge de Bordeax'
'Violetta'
'White Marseilles'

Above, right A fig tree trained against the kitchen garden wall at Barrington Court. **Right** Fig trees trained along a warm south facing wall in the walled garden at Stourhead, Wiltshire.

Tip

A fig fan is a traditional method of protecting the tree over winter. The fig is first pruned, then a net is placed over the fan-shaped structure. You can then cut bracken and stuff it between the net and the plant to ensure that the frost does not damage the over-wintering baby figs.

Peaches and nectarines

Surprisingly, peaches and nectarines are relatively easy to grow in the UK if they are given a warm and sheltered position. The best way to site them is as a fan on a south-facing wall where they can bask in the sun all day long. There are also compact patio varieties that are grown in a pot, kept on a sunny patio during the summer and then placed in the greenhouse over winter. Homegrown, they can be deliciously juicy.

Peaches and nectarines are essentially the same fruit, the main difference being that the former have a slightly fuzzy skin, whereas the latter are smooth. They produce fruit on growth produced the previous year and like their close cousins plums, apricots and cherries, should be pruned only between spring and late summer. Winter pruning makes them susceptible to disease.

Varieties to try

Peaches
'Bonanza' (patio)
'Duke of York'
'Garden Lady' (patio)
'Peregrine'
'Rochester'
'Saturn' (a flat 'doughnut' peach from China)

Nectarines
'Fantasia'
'Lord Napier'
'Nectarella'

Left Peaches growing in the garden in July at Chastleton House.

Apricots

Growing apricots outdoors is a relatively modern phenomenon in the world of fruit-growing, as traditional varieties such as 'Alfred' and 'Moorpark' struggle to ripen outside. Modern varieties such as 'Flavourcot' and 'Tomcot' are much hardier and more likely to ripen in the fickle climate of the UK. They are still usually seen as fans on south-facing walls, but they can also be grown as freestanding trees.

Tales from the Potting Shed

Glasshouses by Tracey Parker, Assistant House Steward at Polesden Lacey

A development of the sixteenth-century orangery, glasshouses played a crucial role in the intensive production of fruit and vegetables. By the nineteenth century they were common in almost all kitchen gardens, enabling the gardeners to grow every conceivable type of fruit, vegetable and flower. Forcing houses, vineries, peach houses, pineapple pits, cold frames and pits were all used in the quest to produce out-of-season food for the grand houses and could be found in the walled kitchen gardens in varying numbers, depending on the size of garden and household. The glasshouses were nearly always placed along the south-facing wall of the gardens, mostly as a lean-to in order to take advantage of the full sun and the brick wall warmed by it.

At Cragside in Northumberland, during the late nineteenth century, Sir William Armstrong devised a system of growing fruit in his greenhouses that used turntables. These enabled the trees to be rotated during the day to make full use of the sun and ensure an even distribution of heat. Sir William also developed a layout of railway tracks in the greenhouse to enable the fruit trees to be transported outdoors when necessary. He achieved this by making the floor of the greenhouse out of timber with wheels placed underneath. These wheels ran on tracks which extended far outside the greenhouse to allow the platform with its load to travel into the open air. The system was set in motion by turning a wooden handle. Both of these inventions used hydraulic pressure.

Soft fruit

The term 'soft fruit' refers to fruit grown on bushes, herbaceous plants and canes, as opposed to top fruit that is grown on trees. There are fruits to suit everybody's taste, from sweet and succulent strawberries to aromatic raspberries and sharp blackcurrants. Growing soft fruit is easy – it can be grown in small areas and you do not need to worry about pollination groups and rootstocks. In the garden, you can pick the fruit at its peak of ripeness. Soft fruit does not last long once picked, and this is why homegrown tastes so much better than the punnets found on shop shelves.

Most soft fruits are perennial plants, so it is important to give thought to their final planting hole as they will occupy that position for several years. The majority require a free-draining soil in full sun, but there are some exceptions – for example, gooseberries and redcurrants will tolerate shade and north-facing walls, and cranberries like damp conditions.

Growing fruit in containers

Most top and soft fruit are suitable for growing in containers. Mini-orchards can be made by planting three or four trees in terracotta pots on a sunny patio, while strawberries can be grown in planters or even in hanging baskets. Use a good-quality, peat-free potting compost and make sure there are drainage holes in the bottom of the container, with crocks covering them to prevent them becoming clogged up with soil.

Plants in containers will need watering each day during summer, so it is a good idea to install a water butt nearby. Check plants regularly for pests and diseases and give them a liquid feed every couple of weeks once they start to flower and produce fruitlets.

Slightly tender plants such as figs and citrus fruits can be grown in pots and then in winter moved back into a greenhouse, conservatory or even shed for winter protection.

Below, left Terracotta pots provide an attractive container to grow fruit in at Ham House. **Below, centre** Picking redcurrants in the kitchen garden at Calke Abbey. **Below, right** Citrus fruits growing in the glasshouse at Clumber Park, Nottinghamshire

Tales from the Potting Shed

Pineapple pits by Tracey Parker, Assistant House Steward at Polesden Lacey

By the eighteenth century Britain's gardeners were growing pineapples, and as this required considerable skill to achieve it was a signifier of status. The pineapples took about two years to mature and needed a high heat of 21–27°C (70–80°F).

The pineapple pit was essentially a development of the hot bed, but set into the ground for greater insulation, lined with brick and roofed in glass. It was filled with waste tanners' bark, which ferments to create a higher and more even temperature than manure. The pineapples were grown in pots plunged into the bark. The heat could then be augmented by heated flues or by fermenting horse manure laid outside the pit. With constant improvements in technology the later nineteenth century saw the introduction of hot water boilers which were used to heat the pits. In Georgian England the pineapple motif was used architecturally, especially on gate piers to depict a sign of wealth and welcome.

Strawberries

For the gardener, strawberries offer almost instant gratification; you can buy them from a garden centre in spring and by summer you can be gathering your first harvests of this delicious soft fruit.

There are two main types of strawberries: the traditional summer varieties that come into season in late spring and finish by mid-summer, and the perpetual strawberries that produce smaller crops throughout the season from summer right through to early autumn. The latter are excellent for extending the season so that you can enjoy strawberries from your garden for much longer.

In addition to these there are also the alpine types, which are more similar to the wild type of berry, with an incredible sweetness and aroma. They produce tiny berries, usually red but also yellow and white, and are often used as annual plants to edge pathways and the sides of vegetable beds. Strawberries are perennial plants that require full sun and a well-drained soil. They are usually grown in strawberry beds, but can also be cultivated in containers, planters and raised beds. Planting them in growing bags is another good option, but they will require regular watering.

If you are planting them directly in the soil, they should be given a distance of 45cm (18in) between each plant. Ensure that the crown is level with the surface of the soil – if it is too deep, the plants will rot. You will need to put netting over them to prevent birds pinching the berries before you harvest them and also lay straw beneath the berries to prevent them rotting on the ground. Alternatively, grow them through plastic mulch, which also suppresses weeds and retains moisture. Strawberries can be forced to crop about two weeks earlier by growing them under polythene cloches or placing them in the greenhouse.

Varieties to try

Summer-fruiting
'Alice'
'Cambridge Favourite'
'Elsanta'
'Florence'
'Pegasus'
'Pineberry' (white berry with a hint of pineapple flavour)
'Symphony'

Perpetuals
'Aromel'
'Flamenco'
'Mara des Bois'

Alpine
'Alexandria'
'Mignonette'

Left Strawberries grown at Fenton House and Garden, London.

> **Tip**
> The strawberries at Polesden Lacey are grown in bags of peat-free compost, raised on wooden planks to save the backbreaking work of weeding around these low-growing perennials. There is a trickle irrigation system rigged up to the water butts to ensure they do not dry out. Raising them also means there is no need to place straw under them to prevent them rotting on the ground.

Gooseberries

You could be forgiven for thinking that gooseberries are hard, hairy, acid fruits that make your eyes water just at the thought of eating one. If so, think again, because those gooseberries were the unripe fruits picked before they had developed their full flavour. A fully ripe gooseberry has one of the most delicious soft fruit flavours. They come in in a range of sizes and colours, ranging from the small, sweet, yellow Golden Drop to the huge red dessert variety London, which simply bursts in your mouth with amazing sweetness and flavour.

Gooseberries can be grown in sun or shade, as a bush, step-over, standard or a fan on a north-facing wall. There are many historic varieties to try, and a good number can be squeezed into a tiny space if they are grown as vertical cordons. Prune them in winter to encourage new growth, reinvigorate the plant and remove any diseased wood. They will need protection from birds with a net during summer and their roots will need watering regularly to prevent them suffering from American mildew. Some varieties, including Invicta, have some resistance to this disease.

Above The unusual white currant 'White Versailles' growing at Calke Abbey.

Varieties to try

'Captivator'
'Careless'
'Invicta'
'Lancashire Lad'
'Langley Gage'
Leveller
'Pax'
'Whinham's Industry'

Red, white and pink currants

All of these currants are basically the same plant, simply with different-coloured berries, and should be treated in the same way. Redcurrants are often overlooked in the kitchen garden as people think of the fruit as sharp and unpalatable. However, when cooked they can be made into delicious sauces and pies and of course they add that bit of acidity to summer pudding. These currants also contribute a fantastic ornamental quality to the kitchen garden, with their stunning long trusses of berries.

Currants have practically identical growth habit and requirements to a gooseberry. They can be grown as a bush, cordon, standard or step-over and because they tolerate shade, they can make an attractive feature as a fan on a north-facing wall. They should be pruned when dormant in winter but will also benefit from a summer prune to prevent the branches snapping and to allow the air to circulate, which will prevent the build-up of pests and diseases.

Varieties to try

Redcurrants
'Jonkheer van Tets'
'Junifer'
'Red Lake'
'Stanza'
White currants
'Blanka'
'White Versailles'
Pink currants
'Gloire de Sablon'

Blackcurrants

These plants are as tough as old boots and will constantly reward you with a bumper crop of shiny, black and aromatic fruits each year. They are famed, of course, for blackcurrant cordial, but they can also make delicious additions to pies, preserves and jams when cooked.

This member of the currant family has a completely different growth habit to red, pink and white currants. They are nearly always grown as stool bushes, meaning they are planted deep in the soil to encourage lots of whippy, young shoots to emerge directly from the ground. These young shoots are the ones that will produce the fruit in subsequent years. This growth habit makes them unsuitable for growing as cordons, step-overs or any other trained form.

Pruning is carried out each year in winter, although they also benefit from a quick trim in summer too. Harvesting the berries can be a laborious process, as they need to be picked individually, with the older varieties ripening at the top of the bunch (or strig) first, and developing further down later in the season. Currants need netting in summer to prevent the birds harvesting the fruit before you do. When the shoots are laden with currants in summer they will probably need supporting with string and canes to prevent the branches snapping or collapsing on the ground.

Varieties to try

'Baldwin'
'Ben Connan'
'Ben Lomond'
'Ben Sarek'
'Big Ben'
'Ebony'

Above, left Blackcurrants grow in abundance during the summer months. **Above** It is a good idea to grow blackcurrants under netting to prevent birds from stealing the fruit.

Blueberries and cranberries

Above, left and right Blueberries and cranberries will grow happily in an acidic soil.

Both blueberries and cranberries require an acidic soil to grow successfully. If you have rhododendrons and camellias in your garden, then you can grow these delicious berries too. In really alkaline and chalky soil it is very difficult to cultivate them, but neutral soil can be made more acidic with the addition of sulphur chips or plenty of mulched bracken and pine needles.

Cranberries have a further requirement in that they require a damp, almost boggy soil. This can be achieved by planting them with a pond liner below them to help retain moisture. However, it is worth puncturing the liner with a fork first so that the water can slowly drain away and does not turn stagnant.

Blueberries are grown as bushes and should be pruned once a year in winter time. Birds love them, so it is a good idea to put a net over them well before the berries turn blue. Cranberries produce their fruit later in the year, often cropping around Christmas time – the reason why their sauce is an accompaniment to the Christmas turkey. Cranberries require minimal pruning, just occasionally trimming about a quarter of the old straggly growth. Do this in late winter after it has fruited and prior to it flowering. Mulch both blueberries and cranberries at their base with rotted pine needles each year to help suppress the weeds and more importantly to keep the soil acidic and moist.

Varieties to try

Blueberries	Cranberries
'Bluecrop'	'Early Black'
'Bluetta'	'Pilgrim'
'Jersey'	
'Patriot'	
'Spartan'	
'Top Hat'	

Raspberries

The aroma of a bowl of freshly picked raspberries really does epitomise summer living. They are relatively easy to grow, and in fact almost too easy, as once they have been planted in the kitchen garden they tend to sucker everywhere. They are very hardy, and are happy growing in cooler climates of the UK such as Scotland. They like well-drained soil in full sun with plenty of organic matter in the soil. Ideally, they prefer it slightly acidic but will tolerate neural or moderate alkaline soil. Raspberries are usually grown in rows and require a support structure of sturdy posts with wires to train them on.

There are two types of raspberries – summer and autumn. It is important to know which type you have got as they have different fruiting habitats and getting them mixed up could result in removing all the potential fruit for the year. Summer-fruiting varieties produce fruit on canes that grew the previous year, whereas autumn types crop on growth made the same year. Autumn varieties are cut down to the ground each year in early spring, whereas summer types have their new canes tied in after fruiting and the old canes removed.

Varieties to try
Summer-fruiting
'Glen Ample'
'Malling Jewel'
'Octavia'
'Tulameen'

Autumn-fruiting
'Allgold'
'Autumn Bliss'
'Joan J'
'Polka'

Above, left Autumn-fruiting raspberries.
Left Yellow raspberries plants at Westbury Court Garden..

Blackberries and hybrid berries

There are very few of us who have not gone blackberrying among the hedgerows and tasted the wild fruits of our late summer labours. Blackberries from the wild can vary enormously in flavour and size, so it is worth growing some of the named varieties as the flavour is better and more reliable.

Blackberries are vigorous, thorny plants, so allow them plenty of space in the garden. Give them a sheltered position as their canes can be brittle; they will tolerate partial shade, while some of their hybrid relatives prefer full sun. They are far more manageable if trained onto a system of wires, and in fact their canes can be trained in attractive, swirly patterns that make a beautiful ornamental feature in the kitchen garden. Some of the other hybrid bramble-type berries such as Japanese wineberries produce beautiful red stems that look stunning in winter when tied up to the wires.

Blackberries should be pruned after fruiting. If the thorns deter you, choose Oregon Thornless, which, as its name suggests, is prickle-free.

Varieties to try

Blackberries
'Fantasia'
'Loch Ness'
'Oregon Thornless'
'Silvan'

Hybrid berries
Boysenberry
Japanese wineberry
Loganberry
Tayberry

Right, above Glossy fruit of blackberry 'Black Satin'.
Right Loganberries are among the soft fruit grown at Calke Abbey.

Grapevines

Vineyards have enjoyed a huge revival over the last few decades in the south of England, showing that grapes can successfully be grown in our cool climate.

Wine grapes are easy to grow and fully hardy, but they do require a warm, sunny and long season to ripen fully. Their climbing habit makes them extremely versatile. They can be trained up trellises, pergolas and arches, or grown as fans on south-facing walls and fences. Other options are to grow them as standards or cordons, train them on posts and wires or even plant them in a container. Prune them each winter, reducing some of the old growth and either tying in new shoots or reducing young growth down to short spurs.

Dessert grapes are less hardy and should be grown in a greenhouse, where they need plenty of space to develop fully. Many National Trust kitchen gardens have indoor vineries where they can be seen in their full glory.

Varieties to try

Wine grapes
'Bacchus'
'Chardonnay'
'Orion'
'Phoenix'
'Pinot Noir'
'Rondo'

Dessert grapes
'Black Hamburg'
'Buckland Sweetwater'
'Muscat of Alexandria'

Case study:
Ickworth vineyard, Suffolk

The only vineyard on National Trust land is in the walled garden at Ickworth in Suffolk, planted in 1995. The 1 hectare (2½ acre) site includes classic grape varieties such as Pinot Noir as well as less well-known varieties such as aromatic white Bacchus and Auxerrois and the red Rondo.

Roses were planted at the end of some of the rows to act as indicators for mildew; if the roses went down with this fungal disease, then the vines would also be susceptible. Lavender was also planted as a deterrent for wasps, although it would seem that this old wives' tale did not have too much truth behind it as the harvest of Rondo grapes in 2000 was devastated by wasps.

Tales from the Potting Shed

Grapes by Tracey Parker, Assistant House Steward at Polesden Lacey

Vines were historically cultivated outside for the production of wine, but the increasingly popular demand for dessert grapes meant that glasshouses had to be adapted to enable their cultivation indoors. It was not important to keep them heated all year, but the temperature had to stay above 10°C (50°F) during April and May when the vines were just starting new growth.

Grapes were an integral part of Victorian table displays and were often grown in pots, which were placed on the table so the guests could pick their grapes straight from the vine. For storage, the grapes were initially cut from the vine in bunches with a long stem attached and each bunch was then placed in a narrow-necked glass bottle filled with water. The bottle was placed at an angle on a custom-made rack and the grapes could then be kept for months in a cool dark room. Later in the nineteenth century, specially designed 'grape bottles' were used, with flat sides and a hole at the top for replenishing the water.

The Vinery at Greenway in Devon, the holiday home of the much-loved author Agatha Christie and her family, was built in the early nineteenth century and was also used to house exotic plants. It has now been replanted following its restoration in 2005.

Growing vegetables

There is a genuine earthy pleasure about growing your own vegetables. Not only can you enjoy the usual delights of gardening, you get to eat the fruits (and veg) of your labour. It's a double whammy. Growing your food will also appeal to your creative side. These days, vegetable plots are not just dull rows of cabbages, potatoes and leeks. Vegetables can be grown in among flower borders and in containers, and can be used to create elaborate patterns, shapes and textures. Many of them produce beautiful flower and seedheads as well as tasting good.

Above The thriving community kitchen garden 'Grace and Flavour' at Hatchlands Park, Surrey.

Six good reasons to grow your own

1. **Healthy lifestyle** Once you start growing your own vegetables, you will not need to visit the gym any more. Vigorous digging or pushing wheelbarrows laden with garden compost will keep you fitter and more toned than any gym subscription. In addition you will be outside, sucking in that healthy fresh air.

2. **Cheap food** You can supply yourself with enough food to eat throughout the year for just the cost of a few packets of seeds. Being realistic, it is unlikely you will be unable to avoid the shops completely, but you can certainly save yourself quite a lot on the household bills.

3. **More choice** Shops are certainly getting better at offering a wider choice of vegetables, but they still do not offer a huge range. Where are the exciting blue salad potatoes, or the purple carrots? Just flicking through the catalogues of some of the seed companies will show you how many exciting vegetables there are available. Growing your own ensures that you get a greater variety to eat.

4. **Reduced air miles** By growing your own vegetables in your back garden or down the road on an allotment, you are reducing your carbon footprint. The distance travelled from plot to plate becomes a matter of metres rather than air miles.

5. **Fresh produce** You cannot actually get fresher produce than by picking or digging it up from the garden or allotment, bringing it into the kitchen and cooking it. It is real fresh food that was still in growth until shortly before it went in the pot.

6. **Untainted food** Will eliminate concerns about the use of chemicals and fertilisers on commercial crops. By growing your own you will know exactly what has or has not been applied to your vegetables.

Food for everyone

Throughout history, growing food and particularly vegetables has appealed to people from all walks of life, from the aristocrats with their penchant for growing the finest gourmet vegetables to impress their dinner guests to families and pensioners growing their vegetables down at the local allotment.

Almost every grand house in Britain during the Georgian, Victorian and Edwardian period would have had a kitchen garden where produce was grown to feed the household and guests. Usually these were walled gardens which would have provided extra shelter from prevailing winds and created warm microclimates where vegetables could have been produced earlier in the season than if they had been grown in a field. The extra protection from the walls would have also extended the growing season well into autumn.

Recently, there has been a renewed interest in growing vegetables from people from every echelon of society, and it continues to be the largest growth area in the horticultural market. Not only do people enjoy 'growing their own', the historic walled kitchen gardens are still one of the most popular areas of a garden for visitors to historic properties.

Most people should be able to find some space to grow vegetables and enjoy the excitement of eating something they have cultivated themselves. If you do not have space in the garden you can grow vegetables such as radishes, carrots and lettuce leaves in window boxes. Alternatively, consider renting an allotment or getting involved with a community kitchen garden nearby. The growing of vegetables, as well as the eating of them, brings people together like nothing else.

There are many different styles of vegetable gardens, and modern-day urban living has encouraged people to become as creative as possible in finding growing spaces. Guerrilla gardening is now popular, with people growing vegetables in public spaces, waste land and basically any patch of soil they can find.

Almost all vegetables can be grown in containers – they will need more watering, but this means that crops can also be grown where there is no soil at all. Alternatively, raised beds can be built in urban areas and filled up with soil and compost, making instant gardens.

Above Rows of cabbages and runner beans in the kitchen vegetable garden at Sizergh Castle and Garden.

Above The raised beds are filled with crops at Trerice, Cornwall.

Improving the soil

The compost heap is the engine room of the vegetable garden. Kitchen waste can be recycled and mixed in with shredded newspaper and wood chippings to produce good-quality garden compost that can be used to enrich soil and mulch vegetable beds or be placed around the base of fruit trees. Every garden should have a compost heap; without one, the garden is unsustainable and soil-improving products will need to be bought in. Compost bins can easily be made out of recycled wooden pallets.

It is always worth having at least two compost bins on the go. This is because one needs to be in the process of composting down, while the other is ready for using on the garden. If you have space for more than two, that is even better. Compost bins should be 'turned' every few weeks, which basically means digging over the compost, enabling the garden waste to come into contact with the air, which speeds up the process of decomposition.

Liquid plant food

To provide a free source of liquid plant food, plant up a comfrey bed. Harvest the leaves two or three times a year and steep them in water for a few days to create a rich and nutritious feed for your plants. It is a wonderful method of making your garden more sustainable. Nettle leaves can be used in a similar way, and will attract numerous insects into the garden too.

Be aware that comfrey can spread quickly, so it will need to be kept in check. Although the flowers are beautiful and will attract wildlife, if you are concerned about comfrey seeding everywhere then choose a non-flowering or sterile type such as 'Bocking 14' to prevent the plant from taking over the entire area.

Step-by-step: Making a compost heap

1. Select three pallets of equal size. Measure the width and then knock in four posts to create a square of the same measurement.

2. Use long screws, nails, wire or even garden twine to attach the pallets to the posts, creating the back and two sides of the compost heap.

3. Fill up the compost bin with kitchen waste, lawn clippings and other organic material. You need to get the right balance: if there is too much nitrogen-based material such as grass clippings and kitchen waste the compost heap will go smelly and slimy. Add carbon-based material such as shredded newspaper and wood chippings too.

Recycling in the garden

There are many other items that can and should be recycled in the modern vegetable garden, such as:

• Old CDs make brilliant bird scarers and can be hung from string above vegetable beds. The reflecting light should scare off birds and prevent them dining on your vegetables before you do.

• Plastic bottles can be cut in half and placed over seedlings. They act as mini-greenhouses, bringing them into growth quickly and preventing them from being damaged by frosts.

• Panes of glass from old greenhouses can be recycled to make cold frames.

• Pallets and old timber can be used to make raised beds, pergolas, tables and benches.

• Old bricks and patio slabs can be laid to make paths and raised beds.

• Old shoes, kettles, sinks and so forth make excellent containers for growing vegetables. Look for them in skips

• Woodchip and recycled timber can be used for paths and raised beds respectively

• Old rubber tyres can make containers for growing potatoes.

• Cardboard tubes from toilet rolls are good for growing seedlings in and are more environmentally friendly than plastic containers.

• Old dustbins and similar watertight containers will serve as water butts to harvest rainwater.

Above Cold frames in the kitchen garden at Beningbrough Hall, North Yorkshire. **Below, clockwise from top** Everyday household items can often be put to use in the garden. Old boots make great planters, watering cans can be used to harvest rainwater and toilet rolls can be used to grow seedlings, and will decay naturally in the earth.

Tip

At Wimpole Hall in Cambridgeshire, composting and recycling was taken to new levels. They had a 'pee bale', which consisted of a 3m- (10ft) long series of straw bales alongside the compost heaps in the walled garden. The workers relieved themselves on the bale – out of visitor hours, of course! This was mainly for the male gardeners, but women were encouraged to fill a plastic container in the bathroom and empty it onto the straw. The urine-soaked pee bales were then added to the compost heaps. This saved water on toilet flushes, and urine is a brilliant compost accelerant because of its high nitrogen content.

Cheating the seasons

Historically, head gardeners would have been responsible for producing crops all year round to supply the household. Nowadays, individual householders love to try to cheat the seasons so that they can be eating certain crops earlier or later on in the year – and the seed manufacturers also come up with modifications, such as a new rhubarb called 'Livingstone' which crops in autumn rather than spring.

Forcing crops

Rhubarb is a good example of a popular crop that can be 'forced' early in the year so that the succulent pink stems can be enjoyed early in spring. To do this, a traditional rhubarb terracotta container is placed over the dormant crown of the plant in mid-winter. The container needs to block out the light, as this encourages the growth upwards early in the season. Nowadays, most gardeners can make do simply with a plastic bucket or even an upturned dustbin. Sea kale can also be forced for an early crop.

Grand gardens would have had 'frame yards' where many crops could have been grown in cold frames for early harvests in spring. They would have also extended the season into autumn. These days gardeners use cold frames which can easily be made from a recycled window frame and recycled timber.

Supplying veggies in winter
By Kate Nicoll, Senior Gardener at Attingham Park Walled Garden

In the past the walled garden at Attingham Park in Shropshire would have had to supply vegetables all year round to provide sumptuous dinners for the wealthy owners of the house and their guests. Nowadays, the gardening team need to supply their restaurants and kitchens with fresh produce to feed their hungry visitors.

We grow anything and everything – celeriac and squash are top of the list in autumn, then leeks and parsnips keep us going for soup in the winter. We keep winter leaves such as claytonia going through the winter in our greenhouses. It means that during the winter the chefs can cook delicious meals such as venison casserole with root vegetables (celeriac, parsnip, swede) and garden herbs. The starter might be leek and potato soup, and to finish, perhaps apple cake from our Bramley's Seedling and Newton Wonder apples.

Above, left Forced rhubarb in the garden at Knightshayes Court.
Above, right Green tomatoes grow at Clumber Park.

Tip

Modern breeding has led to slightly sweeter-tasting sprouts such as the variety 'Trafalgar'. Another alternative is Brassica Petit Posy, which is a cross between kale and Brussels sprouts, producing rosettes of loose, frilly-edged buttons that make very nutritious winter greens. The taste is more akin to spring greens than Brussels sprouts.

Heirloom varieties

If you love the idea of growing lemon-flowered peas or round and prickly cucumbers then heritage or heirloom varieties are for you. There is a huge revival of interest in some of our historic garden varieties, which is good news since if gardeners stop growing them, they will be lost forever. Many enchanting and deliciously flavoured vegetables are to be had, and a number of National Trust gardens are now growing these heirloom varieties for historic interest and integrity.

Some, but not all, of the old varieties have less resistance to pests and diseases and this is why many gardeners have forsaken them in exchange for modern varieties. They also do not always crop for as long and will often have lower yields. Modern breeding and developments have created a whole new world of possibilities. You can even grow tomatoes and potatoes on the same plant (called tomtato), if you are stuck for space. Other benefits include self-blanching celery that avoids having to dig out lots of trenches, carrots that are resistant to carrot fly and sweeter-tasting sprouts.

Storing vegetables

When you grow your own vegetables there will inevitably be periods of feast and famine at certain periods in the year. However, with careful planning you should be able to ensure that your crops are available when you want them. There will still be times when your garden is producing more than you can possibly eat, and this is when contingency plans for preserving your food are needed. This will allow you to enjoy the food later on in the year, particularly during winter when there is not much available to harvest.

It may sound obvious, but one way to avoid a glut is to grow only vegetables that you really like. If you do not particularly enjoy eating main crop potatoes then do not grow them, as they will take up a lot of space in the vegetable bed and you will end up throwing them away. Also, pick crops that are expensive in the shops but are relatively cheap to grow, such as mangetout or asparagus.

Freezing This invaluable method of storing vegetables is of course a major advantage we have over our predecessors – although in very grand houses they would have had ice houses. Some vegetables such as peas even taste better once they have been frozen as they tend to be sweeter.

Drying Crops such as chillies and most herbs benefit from being left out to dry and will then last for months or even years. Other crops such as onions and garlic should be left

to dry out before being plaited together and left in a cool, rodent-free place such as a shed or garage.

Preserving and pickling Most vegetables can be transformed into delicious chutneys and relishes, while some such as onions and beetroot can simply be pickled in vinegar.

Storage Most vegetables will last for longer if stored in a cool, dark place. Potatoes should be kept out of the light and can be stored in paper sacks in cupboards.

Carrots can be kept for up to six months if kept in suitable conditions. One traditional method of storing them is to make a carrot clamp. Parsnips can be left in the ground over winter, but they can then be hard to dig out of the ground if there is a big freeze. If you live in a very cold area they can also be stored in a version of the carrot clamp.

Step-by-step: Making a carrot clamp

1. Dig a hole about 30cm (12in) deep and cover the base of it with a thin layer of sharp sand.
2. Remove the soil from the carrots and trim off any foliage.
3. Stack the carrots on top of each other so that they are just below the top of the hole.
4. Cover with straw and then finally with another layer of soil. Remove the carrots as required.

Above The Mushroom House at Hanbury Hall. **Left** Beans left to dry at Lacock Abbey, Wiltshire.

Tales from the Potting Shed

Back sheds by Kate Nicoll, Senior Gardener at Attingham Park Walled Garden

Attingham's Walled Garden has a full set of 'back sheds' tucked in the shade of the North Wall. These are not a handy place for a sly cigarette, but a range of practical working spaces built in the early nineteenth century to perform very specific functions. There is a mushroom house, a fruit store and a root store – a dark and rather scary subterranean place lined with brick bays full of old sand. Now that we have most of the 0.8 hectare (2 acre) garden in full production this has really come into its own. During the summer it works as a brilliant walk-in fridge for storing leafy vegetables, salads and flowers for a day or so, but its true value is during the winter months. Once we have harvested our celeriac (500 or so), they are trimmed of leaves and roots and layered in sharp sand until required for the tea room soups. Safe from frost and slugs, they come out as good as new even as late as March the following year. The carrots, parsnips and swede work just as well, and given the hard frosts of rural Shropshire we are grateful to no longer have the task of prising a parsnip out of frozen ground.

While most people do not have access to a Georgian root store, a large storage box in a dark garage works just as well, with a sack of sharp sand from a builder's merchant. Come spring you might even get the bonus of a few succulent celeriac leaves to add to a salad as the plants emerge from suspended animation.

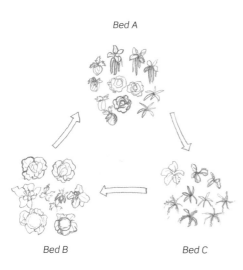

Bed A

Bed B *Bed C*

Crop rotation

For thousands of years, farmers and gardeners have known about the benefits of crop rotation. This basically means growing a different type of annual crop in a different area of the vegetable garden each year.

This has multiple benefits. First, it prevents a build-up of pests and diseases in the soil. It also means that certain crops will benefit by following others – for example the pea and bean family (legumes) fix nitrogen in the soil, and so are followed by the cabbage family (brassicas), which are nutrient hungry. Also, potatoes (and other root vegetables) break up the ground and are therefore followed by peas and beans as they like a deep root run. The onion family, pumpkin family, leaves and salads and stem and fruiting vegetables can be fitted in where there is space.

There are many variations and theories on the best way to practise crop rotation, but it is simple to do. Most people rotate three or four beds. A typical three-bed plan could work like this:

Crop rotation over four years

Year 1
Bed A Legumes plus onion family
Dig in plenty of manure or compost. Leave the nitrogen-rich roots in the soil to rot down for the brassicas.

Bed B Brassicas plus salads
Dig in leafmould or compost and lime the soil if it's acid to protect against clubroot. Mulch in autumn ready for root crops.

Bed C Root crops plus stem and fruiting vegetables
Dig in plenty of compost. You could sow green manure ready for the legumes next year.

Year 2
Bed A Brassicas plus salads
Bed B Root crops plus stem and fruiting vegetables
Bed C Legumes plus onion family

Year 3
Bed A Root crops plus stem and fruiting vegetables
Bed B Legumes plus onion family
Bed C Brassicas plus salads

Year 3
Bed A Legumes plus onion family
Bed B Brassicas plus salads
Bed C Root crops plus stem and fruiting vegetables

Opposite The community allotment at Felbrigg Hall.

Growing peas and beans

Peas and beans can be expensive to buy, particularly mangetout and sugar snaps, yet they are easy to grow and produce a bumper crop of tasty pods throughout most of summer. They belong to the legume family, meaning that during the growing season they fix nitrogen from the atmosphere and leave it in the soil for future crops to benefit from as part of the crop rotation system. They need a sunny, sheltered position, and plenty of goodness and moisture in the soil. If the soil is badly depleted of nutrients, a compost trench can be created to improve the growing conditions.

Step-by-step: Making a compost trench

1. During winter, dig out a trench at least 30cm (12in) deep where the beans are going to be sown later in the year if it is not too wet or freezing.
2. Put a layer of kitchen waste in the bottom of the trench and then cover it with a layer of soil.
3. Add another layer of kitchen waste and again cover it with soil. Repeat this process throughout the winter months.
4. When the trench is full, cover it with a final layer of soil. Do not worry if the ground is slightly raised as it will gradually sink.

Above, left Beans are grown on supports at Wordsworth House and Garden. **Above, right** A healthy crop of runner beans.

Supports

Peas and beans are climbing plants and require structures to scramble up. Peas will need twiggy sticks placed next to the seedlings to encourage them to climb, while the taller runner and French beans require taller structures such as netting or bamboo wigwams. It is best to get the structure in place before planting or sowing as it could otherwise damage the roots.

Step-by-step: Building a wigwam

1. Select bamboo canes or hazel rods that are approximately 2m (6½ft) high and push them into the ground in a circle at 15cm (6in) intervals.

2. Gather the tops of the canes into the centre and tie them tightly together, using garden twine.

3. When the risk of frosts is over, place two seeds in the ground at 3cm (1¼in) deep at the base of each cane or plant two seedlings. Water them in.

4. As the plants start to grow, twist or tie them around the canes to encourage them to grow upwards.

New technology
By Kate Nicoll, Senior Gardener at Attingham Park Walled Garden, Shropshire

'While plastic does not have pride of place in the walled kitchen garden at Attingham it does have its uses at certain times of the year. We struggle with mice in our glasshouses. Despite the efforts of our feral cat (and her frequent litters of kittens) we still lose many young seedlings to the mice and voles in the early spring. Last year we trapped 60 just in the melon house! But a humble clear plastic underbed storage box keeps the mice out perfectly. We turn the box upside down with the seed trays lined up on the upturned lid and then place the box over the top every evening, lifting it off in the morning to drain off the condensation and increase light levels. So far the mice have not managed to gnaw through the tough plastic (unlike netting which they seem to see as a challenge), and the extra warmth brings the young seedlings on a treat! Such tactics do not work outside in the garden for direct-sown seeds of course, so we resort to garlic powder for our peas, buying it in bulk from an Asian supermarket and rolling the pea seeds in it before sowing in a drill. Staking the row straight away with twiggy hazel pea sticks deters the pigeons which are the next foe likely to move in on the crop.'

Growing the cabbage family

Often referred to as brassicas, the cabbage family are the backbone of the vegetable garden, providing a wide range of delicious healthy veg. They require a heavy, rich soil to help them produce their leafy growth and are usually planted after the pea and bean family in crop rotation, which means they benefit from the additional nitrogen fix that legumes leave behind.

Kale and winter cabbages are particularly valuable in the vegetable garden as they provide much-needed crops in winter and early spring when there is a traditional harvest famine. For simplicity they are normally all grown together in the same bed. They can make attractive features in the plot, providing beautiful shades of foliage from the kale and the red, white and green of cabbages, with red and green sprouts providing additional structure and height during winter. Cauliflowers also can look beautiful with their fluffy-looking texture and a range of colours including orange, purple and yellow. This family is one of the toughest of the vegetable groups and can tolerate poorer growing conditions.

Growing cabbages can be confusing for new gardeners as there are spring, summer, autumn and winter types, named after the time they are harvested. The method for growing all types is basically the same, the time of sowing being the only main difference. Remember to dig over the soil and add plenty of organic matter before planting out any of the cabbage family, particularly if the soil is sandy and low in nutrients. Brassicas can be prone to pigeon damage, particularly during winter, and will need to be covered with a net.

One of the main pests of the cabbage family is the cabbage root fly. At Polesden Lacey, a collar made from recycled roofing felt is placed at the base of each of plant to prevent the adults from laying their eggs near the plant, which avoids having to resort to chemical control. A fine-meshed net is placed over the cabbages to prevent attacks from the cabbage white butterfly.

Clubroot is a fungal disease in the soil that causes the root to swell up and distort. The disease does not do well in alkaline conditions, so if you have problems with clubroot, applying lime to the soil should partially correct the problem.

Opposite As well as being good to eat, cabbages provide coolour and texture in the garden. **Above, left** Dig in plenty of manure prior to planting cabbages – they are hungry plants. **Above, right** Beautiful deep purple cabbages. **Below** Brassicas in the kitchen bed at Quebec House, Kent.

Growing root vegetables

Vegetables such as radishes, turnips, swedes, potatoes, carrots, parsnips and beetroot are grown for their edible delights that lie beneath the surface of the soil rather than above it. Carrots and parsnips like a fairly light but fertile soil and recently manured plots should be avoided. Their seed can go stale quickly, so it is worth buying new seed each year. Sow carrots, radishes, turnips and beetroot regularly from spring to late summer to harvest quick-growing young vegetables. Carrots will really struggle to grow on stony or compacted soil as their tap root cannot penetrate the ground properly. However there are modern small, round carrots called 'Parmex' that taste sweet and delicious, and will quite happily grow on thin soil.

Parsnips require a long growing season so are best sown in early spring. The beauty of these vegetables is that they then remain in the ground for most of the year, including winter, providing food when there are not many other crops available. Parsnips generally taste sweeter if they have been left in the ground to get hit by the frosts.

Potatoes are probably the nation's most popular vegetable – they are easy to grow and can be used in so many dishes. However, if you are short of space in the kitchen garden, consider carefully whether you want to grow them as they do take up a lot of space, particularly main crops.

At Polesden Lacey we grow only early potatoes or special varieties such as 'Pink Fir Apple' with its quirky, knobbly texture. We avoid most main crop potatoes as we are limited for space, they are cheap to buy from local vegetable growers, and it is harder to tell the difference in flavour once they have been cooked and added to a dish. Early potatoes have a more distinctive and identifiable flavour which is picked up from the minerals of the soil in Polesden Lacey's kitchen garden.

Above New potatoes freshly harvested from the ground taste delicious. **Opposite, left and right**
Beetroot foliage has a wonderful ornamental quality, and can be eaten fresh in salad.

To chit or not to chit

To get potatoes off to a flying start early in the year, gardeners have traditionally 'chitted' the
potatoes for a few weeks prior to planting. This involves placing the tubers with their 'rose end'
facing upwards in a frost-free place to encourage tiny shoots (called chits) to grow towards the
light. This saves valuable growing time before the potatoes are buried out in the cool, early spring
soil. However, the benefits of chitting are now controversial in the kitchen gardening world. Some
experts claim it causes premature ageing, meaning that it can reduce the potential yield as the
potato goes over quickly. Chitting some, but not all, is probably the safest way to guarantee a good
crop over the longest period – although it will probably be the weather rather than the chitting that
affects the earliness and success of the crop.

The blight of a potato grower's life

At Polesden Lacey we are affected by blight, a fungal disease that
can quickly wipe out the potato and tomato crops in a matter of
days. To overcome this we cut down the foliage on the potato
plants as soon as symptoms start to appear. This prevents
the disease from spreading down into the tubers. We also
grow blight-resistant varieties such as 'Sarpo' alongside
some of the older varieties to ensure we can always supply
the restaurant. Tomato plants are only now grown in the
greenhouse, as this prevents the blight spores travelling on
the wind and affecting the plants.

Carrot fly

One of the main problems when growing carrots is the dreaded
carrot fly. The fly lays its eggs near the base of the plant, and later
in the year the maggots hatch and infest the roots.

**Gardeners' tips on
how to avoid carrot fly**

• 'We erect a 70cm (27in) vertical barrier of fine mesh
around the carrots to create a fence, as carrot fly does not
fly far from the ground.'

• 'Carrot fly is attracted by the scent released from bruised
foliage, so harvest and thin out carrots on an evening with no
wind when the scent of the carrots will not travel.'

• 'At Greenway we use modern varieties such as 'Fly Away' and
'Resistafly' that have resistance to this pest.'

• 'We grow onions between the rows of carrots. The smell of
the carrots deter the onion fly, and the smell of the onion
confuses the carrot fly. Perfect.'

Know your onions

The allium family includes chives and the stunning ornamental alliums with impressive purple flower heads as well as shallots, garlic, elephant garlic, spring onions, leeks and of course the familiar everyday onion. This group of vegetables is a must for anybody interested in cooking.

Most onions and shallots are grown from sets, which are basically small, immature bulbs which are left to expand (and divide in the case of shallots) during the season and then harvested in mid- to late summer. Garlic is usually grown from cloves and left to form large bulbs. Leeks, one of the essential winter crops, are grown from seed and can be left in the ground throughout the colder months when there is not much else left to harvest.

Elephant garlic is now a very popular vegetable with chefs as it imparts a less overpowering garlic flavour to many dishes. It is actually a swollen stem rather than a bulb but is grown in a similar way to garlic cloves. Onions prefer a well-drained soil in plenty of sun.

Left, top Ornamenal alliums make a great visual impact in your vegetable garden. **Left** A superb onion harvest.

Step-by-step: Planting out leeks

Sow leek seeds early in spring as they need a long growing season. Plant out seedlings when they are about 15cm (6in) long and the thickness of a pencil.

1. Make holes with a thick dibber, 15cm (6in) deep and at spacings 15cm (6in) apart, keeping 30cm (12in) between the rows.

2. Trim the roots of the seedlings with scissors and place them in the holes so just the tips of the leaves are showing.

3. Do not firm the soil back around the plant – just water the plants in, allowing the soil to gently crumble back around the stems.

Case study:

Weaving vegetable supports

By Patrick Kelly, Garden and Countryside Manager for Ham House, Surrey

In about February each year the garden team travel to a local common to cut birch to use as plant supports around the seventeenth-century garden. Not only do they look authentic in our historic setting, we are also making a contribution to the heathland management of the common. Birch will rapidly encroach on the heathland unless kept in check, and this is a major task for the Surrey Wildlife Trust who manage the common.

We use stems of different sizes, from small shoots up to small trees of a height of about 3m (10ft), and weave domed baskets around individual plants such as the peonies in the south terrace border and rectangular cradles around the blocks of plants in the cut flower border.

To use this technique, you need to know the eventual height of the plant that you will be supporting and begin the process while it is still relatively small. Make sure the birch support structure finishes well below the eventual height of the plant so it will not overshadow the floral display. Choose a stem with a lot of twigs branching off it to give good options when weaving, clear the twigs away from the base of the stem and push it into the ground, making sure it is far enough into the ground to be sturdy. Depending on the size of the structure, use enough stems to create the basic form.

Do not leave the weaving process too long after cutting the birch, as the more sap that is left in the stem, the more pliable and workable it will be. To get a right-angle in the structure, use a pair of secateurs to nick the side of the stem facing into the structure and very carefully bend over. Wrap twigs together (do not try to do it with too big a bunch of them at once), then pull tight to draw the structure together. Fill gaps with smaller stems to add support or to prevent pigeons getting inside the structure with plants such as peas and brassicas in the vegetable garden – leave a few loose twigs to make the pigeons think twice about getting too close.

To make wigwams, we use sturdy stems of approximately 7.5cm (3in) diameter and 2.4–3m (8–10ft) length. When we harvest the birch we aim for straight-growing stems with good branching for weaving. The stems are laid on the ground and all cut to the same length. Using a crowbar, we make a pilot hole about 45cm (18in) deep in a square based on the width of the bed. The stems are then pushed as deep as possible into the earth and angled towards what would be the centre of the square, positioning the stems so that good weaving branches face in the right direction at this point. The four main stems are then tied at the top, after checking the apex is in the centre of the square. We then weave the branches in the same way as with the other plant supports.

The centre of a wigwam can be congested, so you may need to cut out any excess branching you have here. Fill any natural gaps at the base with thinner stems and weave them into the main structure. Plant seedlings or seed around the base of the stems. The dimensions of the wigwam can of course be changed to make a smaller version than the ones at the Ham House garden.

Growing cucurbits

This group of plants includes gourds, pumpkins, squashes, cucumbers, courgettes and marrows – hungry feeders that require a deep, rich soil to enable them to swell up. Add plenty of organic matter such as well-rotted manure or garden compost to the soil before planting. Some National Trust gardens grow their pumpkins and squashes on top of the compost heap, as the plants thrive in those conditions.

If you have room for just one type of plant from this group, then make it the courgette. Just one or two plants will provide you with enough food to feed a large family and plenty to spare. They are delicious fried with melted mozzarella cheese, tomato and basil, or they can even be dried out and made into crisps. Even their flowers can be fried up as delicious fritters. Do not forget to harvest them regularly, though, otherwise they swell up to the size of marrows and will then stop producing fruit.

Pumpkins, squashes and gourds love a sunny, sheltered spot where they can spread out their trailing habit. At Polesden Lacey, the head gardener during the Edwardian period would regularly enter the vegetables into local competitions, including those for the largest pumpkin. Here are the current kitchen gardener's tips on how to produce a huge pumpkin.

Above Harvesting a glut of courgettes. **Opposite** A young squash begins to take form.

Step-by-step: How to grow a champion pumpkin

1. Choose a seed type that produces large pumpkins such as 'Atlantic Giant' or 'Hundredweight'. Many varieties only produce small fruits.

2. Start growing the pumpkin seed early in the year. For successful germination, place the seed on its side to prevent it rotting.

3. As the plant develops, remove most of the flowers to leave just one or two on the plant.

4. Feed the plant regularly with a high-potash feed such as tomato feed.

5. Place the pumpkin on a patio slab or weed-suppressing membrane to prevent it rotting on the ground.

Making the most of salad vegetables

Lettuces are probably the most common type of salad vegetable, and these days they are just as useful for ornamental purposes as they are for culinary pleasures, as they come in such an incredible array of colours, textures and leaf shapes. Often they will be found adorning the edges of potagers and kitchen gardens and being used to create elaborate colour patterns. The Romans introduced them to Britain (although the original ones would have been fairly bitter by modern standards), and they are just as popular as they were 2,000 years ago.

There are numerous different types, including loose balls of soft leaves known as butterhead lettuces; firm leaves with a solid heart such as 'Iceberg', called crispheads; and upright, long crisp leaves with a tender heart, called cos or romaine lettuce.

Cut-and-come-again salad leaves are popular now and can be bought in packets of mixed seed. They include chicory, coriander, chard, dandelion, endive, komatsuma, cress, leaf celery, lettuce, mizuna, mustard, pak choi, parsley, radicchio, rocket, sorrel and spinach. They provide a whole range of flavours and textures depending on the seed mix, including ones that are hot and spicy, oriental, mild, crunchy and refreshing. As their name suggests, they can be regularly cut with scissors close to the base of the plant and allowed to resprout, meaning harvesting can take place about every fortnight.

To add a touch of the Mediterranean to the vegetable garden, tomatoes, chillies, peppers and aubergines are easy to grow and add an extra range of ingredients for the kitchen. Some of these need to be grown in a greenhouse, but most will thrive in warm sunny spots in the garden or on the patio during summer.

Using modern varieties makes growing celery much easier. In the past, gardeners would have spent days digging trenches for blanching the stems of their celery. Nowadays, by using varieties such as 'Lathom Self Blanching', long, stringless sticks of crisp celery are grown without the need for earthing up in trenches. Another benefit is that unlike some of the old varieties, this celery does not tend to bolt, meaning it can be sown early or grown under cloches to produce an early crop.

Below, left Homegrown green chillies can add a kick to your cooking. **Below, right** Lettuces growing at Trengwainton Garden, Cornwall, make a lovely feature in the garden.

Gourmet heaven

People's food preferences change over the years, and as society becomes more diverse and there is more variety of seed available in catalogues, gardeners are becoming more adventurous not just with their taste buds but with the type of crops they grow.

Jerusalem artichokes are closely related to sunflowers and bear beautiful large flower heads that can stand 3m (10ft) tall. They produce tubers underground which are harvested from late summer through to winter. Globe artichokes also produce attractive flower heads, but these are purple and thistle-like; it is the central 'choke' of the flower head that is eaten. Asparagus are grown for their succulent spears that emerge from the ground in spring and are harvested when they are about 20cm (8in) long. They are a perennial crop and should not be harvested for the first couple of years. Rhubarb and sea kale are also springtime treats, grown for their edible stems.

Planting sweetcorn

Sweetcorn is wind-pollinated and therefore seedlings should always be planted in a grid pattern instead of single rows, enabling pollen to blow across the plants. Growing squashes and beans among them is a modern, sustainable way of planting known as the 'three sisters method', the name originating from the Iroquois people of North America, who believed these three vegetables were inseparable sisters. This method saves space as three crops are planted in a single bed. The squashes sprawl on the ground and their large leaves smother out competing weeds, while the beans use the upright stems of the sweetcorn to scramble up. The beans also help to prevent the corn from flopping on to the ground and the roots from the beans fix nitrogen from the air, reducing the amount of fertiliser needed in the soil the following year.

Above, left Globe artichokes can create quite a striking display in the vegetable garden.
Above, right A summer harvest of sweetcorn and runner beans at Bateman's.

Harvest planner

Legend: I = In Season, P = Peak Season

	January	February	March	April	May	June	July	August	September	October	November	December
Artichokes, globe					I	I	P	P	P	I		
Artichokes, Jerusalem	P	P	I							I	P	P
Asparagus				I	P	P						
Aubergines							I	P	P	I		
Beans, borlotti							I	P	P	I		
Beans, broad					I	P	P	I				
Beans, French & green							P	P	I	I		
Beans, runner							P	P	P	I		
Beetroot	I	I					I	P	P	I	I	I
Broccoli, calabrese							I	I	P	P	I	
Broccoli, purple sprouting	I	I	P	P	I							I
Brussels sprouts	P	P	I							I	P	P
Brussels tops	P	P									P	P
Cabbage, green	P	P	P	P	P	I			P	P	P	P
Cabbage, red	P	I								I	P	P
Cabbage, white	P	P	I							I	P	P
Carrots	I	I	I	P	P	P	P	P	P	P	P	P
Cauliflower			I	P	P	P	P					
Celeriac	P	I								I	P	P
Celery	P	I						I	I	P	P	P
Chard	I	I	I	I	I	I	I		P	P	P	I
Chicory	P	P	P	I						I	P	P
Courgettes							P	P	P	P		
Cucumber							I	P	P			
Endive	P	P	I	I						I	P	P
Fennel							I	P	P	P		
Garlic							I	P	P	I		
Greens, spring & winter	P	P	P	P	I						P	P

	January	February	March	April	May	June	July	August	September	October	November	December
Kale	●	●	○	○					●	○	●	●
Leeks	●	●	●	○				○	●	●	●	●
Lettuce	●	●	○	●	○	○	○	○	○	○		●
Lettuce, lamb's					○	○	●	●	●	○	○	
Lovage						○	●	●	●	○		
Mushrooms, ceps							○	●	●	●	○	
Mushrooms, chanterelles							○	●	●	●	○	
Mushrooms, field								○	●	○		
Nettles		○	●	●	○							
Onions	●	●	○	○	○	○	○	●	●	●	●	●
Onions, spring	○	○	○	●	●	●	●	●	○	○	○	○
Parsnips	●	○	○						○	○	●	●
Peas, sugar snap & mangetout					○	●	●	●	○			
Peppers and chillies								○	●	●	○	
Potatoes	●	●	○	○	○	○	○	○	●	●	●	●
Potatoes, new				○	●	●	●	○				
Pumpkins & squashes								○	●	●	●	○
Radishes				○	●	●	●	●	○			
Rocket	○	○	○	○	○	○	●	●	●	○		○
Scorzonera & salsify	○	○						○	●	●	●	○
Shallots	●	●	○	○	○	○	○	○	●	●	●	●
Sorrel		○	○	●	●	●	●	●	○	○		
Spinach	○	○	○	○	○	●	●	●	●	●	○	○
Swede	●	●	○						○	○	●	●
Sweetcorn							○	●	●	○		
Tomatoes						○	●	●	●	○		
Turnips	○	○						○	○	○	●	●
Watercress	○	○	○	●	●	●	●	●	●	●	○	○

○ In Season   ● Peak Season

Creating a potager or a knot garden

Traditional knot gardens have always used tightly-clipped low box hedging, but sadly *Buxus sempervivens* is prone to box blight which is a fungal disease that can cause bare patches and dieback. Gardeners are now using evergreen plants that look similar and respond just as well to close clipping. They include:

Berberis × stenophylla 'Corallina Compacta'
Berberis × stenophylla 'Nana'
Berberis thunbergii 'Atropurpurea Nana'
Euonymus japonicus 'Microphyllus Albovariegatus'
Hebe cupressoides 'Boughton Dome'
Ilex crenata 'Convexa'
Lavandula angustifolia cultivars
Lonicera nitida
Osmanthus delavayi
Pittosporum tenuifolium 'Golf Ball'
Rosmarinus officinalis
Santolina chamaecyparissus
Taxus baccata 'Semperaurea'

A potager is a term used to describe an informal style of vegetable garden. The word originates from the French word for soup, a 'potage' implying that it is a mix or concoction of lots of different types of vegetables, and sometimes non-edible plants too. There are no hard and fast rules, but basically there is usually plenty of colour and an emphasis on the kitchen garden being just as ornamental as it is edible and practical.
You could try planting:

Box plants or step-over apple to line the edge of paths or vegetable beds.
Colourful vegetables such as squashes and pumpkins, rainbow chard, rhubarb and lots of foliage for textures such as lettuce, kale and cut-and-come-again plants.
A few upright structural plants such as sea kale, globe artichokes and Jerusalem artichokes.

Above The potager at Snowshill Manor and Garden, Gloucestershire. **Below** Lettuces planted around a topiary swan in the potager at Woolbeding House.

The herb garden

While herbs are generally grown for their medicinal or culinary uses, they do have ornamental qualities too. Many are evergreen, such as bay, rosemary and hyssop, offering all-year-round interest and structure in the garden.

Herbs must be some of the easiest plants to grow as most thrive in poor, arid soil conditions. Picture a traditional Mediterranean scene where many wild herbs thrive, basking in the heat in impoverished, rocky soil on a sun-drenched mountainside – those are the conditions that most of these plants love. Lavish too much care and attention on them, give them a fertile soil and lots of water and they will quickly perish. They are the perfect group of plants to grow if you have little time to spend gardening.

Planting

Plant herbs in well-drained soil in full sun. If you have a heavy clay soil, add grit or grow them in raised beds. The herbs can be planted through gravel or grit, which will prevent the leaves from being splashed when it rains.

Alternatively, lay recycled pallets on the ground and bolt them together to form a pathway or seating area. Fill the gaps between the slats with a gritty compost, and use them as planting pockets for herbs. As you walk among the herbs, your footfall will bruise the leaves and release their intoxicating fragrances.

Above A wide array of herbs growing in the walled garden at Hughenden, Buckinghamshire.

Grow herbs near the back door so that it is easy to dash outside and grab a few sprigs to chuck in the pot when required. Some herbs can be grown in pots on a kitchen windowsill, so that there are always some fragrant leaves close to hand.

Maintenance

Herbs need very little maintenance or watering. Most of the herbaceous herbs, such as mint and chives, benefit from being cut back hard, almost to ground level, a few times in the growing season. This will reinvigorate them and encourage new healthy growing shoots. It is usually this younger, fresh growth that has the best flavour. Avoid doing this with some of the shrubby plants, such as bay, rosemary or lavender, although they will benefit from a lighter trim after flowering.

Storing herbs

One of the best things about growing herbs is that they can be easily dried and stored for use in the kitchen all year round. Harvest leaves or stems on a warm day to capture the very best of their aromatic oils. Store them in a dry, airy place such as a garage or in the allotment shed. Once the leaves are dry and crispy they can be cut up and stored in airtight jars. Alternatively, fresh herbs can be chopped up and stored in the freezer. This method helps to preserve their natural leaf colour, making them look fresher on the plate.

Above, left The Herb Garden in the west walled garden at Llanerchaeron, Ceredigion. **Above, right** Rosemary grows in the foreground of the herb garden at Quebec House.

Clockwise from top left Borage; Fennel; Dill flower head and sweet pea 'Cupani' in the kitchen garden at Ham House.

Culinary herbs

Basil (*Ocimum basilicum*) A popular annual herb, usually with green foliage, although the purple-leafed variety is favoured too. The leaves are frequently used for flavouring Italian dishes. Bring inside before autumn frosts to extend the growing season.

Bay (*Laurus nobilis*) The aromatic leaves are often added to casseroles, stews and other meat dishes to improve flavour. This shrub is often grown as a standard in pots.

Borage (*Borago officinalis*) An annual herb that has a mild cucumber flavour. The attractive blue, star-shaped flowers are often frozen in ice cubes and served in Pimms. It is a prolific self-seeder and once established in the garden can be hard to eradicate.

Chives (*Allium schoenoprasum*) The fleshy stems impart a mild onion flavour to dishes such as potato salad and stir-fries. The purple flower heads are attractive in the garden.

Coriander (*Coriandrum sativum*) Add a taste of Asia by putting the leaves of this hot and spicy herb in your dishes. It is an annual and the leaves can be picked from early summer onwards.

Dill (*Anethum graveolens*) This culinary annual produces umbels of delicate yellow-green flowers that attract beneficial insects. Closely related to carrots and celery, it has attractive, feathery foliage, and the flavours are a good partner to fish and potatoes.

Fennel (*Foeniculum vulgare*) Closely related to Florence fennel of which the swollen stem is eaten, herbal fennel is a hardy perennial with feathery foliage. Its aniseed flavour is a perfect accompaniment to fish and seafood.

Lavender (*Lavandula officinalis*) This low-growing shrub has attractive silvery foliage and blue flower spikes from mid- to late summer. It is not commonly used for flavouring food, but very popular for distilling into an essential oil for capturing its beautiful scent.

Marjoram (*Origanum majorana*) Commonly found growing wild on chalk grassland, this tender perennial should be treated like an annual and sown each year. It has attractive pink-purple flowers that bees love. It is popular in Italian dishes, especially pasta.

Mint (*Mentha spicata*) There are several different flavours of mint including apple, spearmint and chocolate. Mint is a vigorous herbaceous perennial. Restrict its roots by growing it in a pot, otherwise it will swamp nearby plants.

Parsley (*Petroselinum crispum*) This hardy biennial is related to carrot and celery. Parsley has a versatile flavour that can be used to accompany pasta sauces, egg dishes, omelettes, poultry stuffing, soups and stews.

Rosemary (*Rosmarinus officinalis*) A popular herb in many dishes, rosemary is particularly good with lamb. It is an evergreen shrub which provides structure and an attractive foliage display during winter.

Sage (*Salvia officinalis*) There are many different sages, including a bi-coloured form and a purple form. It is a sub-shrub that can be harvested all year round. It is very versatile, particularly for meat dishes, but is most well known for sage and onion stuffing.

Tarragon (*Artemisia dracunculus*) This perennial has both Russian and French forms. The French form is considered to have the best flavour, but the Russian is a more vigorous and larger plant.

Thyme (*Thymus vulgaris*) A low-growing evergreen shrub with an aromatic flavour that is used in stews and roast meals. Prostrate forms can be grown *en masse* to create attractive thyme lawns.

Above, from left to right Lavender produces a wonderful scent; Mint is a vigorous plant best grown on its own in a bed to prevent it swamping other plants; Sage leaves can be dried and and used to flavour food such as poultry dishes.

Historic National Trust herb gardens

Acorn Bank, Cumbria (the largest collection of medicinal and culinary plants)
Buckland Abbey, Devon
Fountains Abbey and Studley Royal Water Garden, Yorkshire
Lytes Cary Manor, Somerset
Sissinghurst Castle, Kent
Woolbeding Gardens, West Sussex

Tales from the Potting Shed

Herbal history by Tracey Parker, Assistant House Steward at Polesden Lacey, Surrey

In Britain the Romans were the first to grow imported plants, particularly herbs for medicinal and culinary purposes. It was not until the medieval period that the monasteries became the main practitioners and chroniclers of gardening knowledge and, more importantly, herbal lore and medicine.

Very little documentary evidence remains about the content and design of these monastic gardens but they are likely to have consisted of a walled courtyard built around a central focal point such as an arbour or a well. Herbs such as parsley, sage, thyme, camomile and saffron, together with wild flowers, would have been grown here for medicinal and cooking purposes. Vegetables such as turnips, leeks, lettuce and garlic would also have been grown and used to feed the monks.

Although these gardens were largely for practical purposes for the monastic community, as opposed to creative display, colour was also very important and would have been provided by flowers such as lilies and roses, representing ecclesiastical symbols.

greener gardening

Treating the garden holistically

Although you may technically own your garden, there are plenty of other creatures out there that share your green space. As the Scottish-American conservationist John Muir said, 'When we try to pick out anything by itself, we find it hitched to everything else in the Universe.' There are millions, if not billions, of living organisms depending on your trees, lawn, compost heaps, ponds and flower-beds. Most of them are micro-organisms that you cannot see with the naked eye, but there are plenty of larger ones too. They all contribute to the ecosystem, and more than likely it will not just be your garden they use, but neighbouring gardens too. Bats, bees and butterflies depend on networks of plants over large areas when foraging for food or breeding. Without these wildlife corridors linking up gardens in towns and countryside, much of our wildlife would be lost.

Gardens should never attempt to replace natural habitats, but in many ways they are usually richer in biodiversity because of the range of different plants grown there and the amount of hedges, ponds and lawns condensed into small spaces. It is lovely to be able to think of yourself as saving millions of lives just by being a gardener.

Never work alone in the garden

That is not a health and safety message – it means that you should think about the bigger picture and garden along with the wild creatures, regarding them as your gardening buddies. Encourage

Below A pile of pallets made in the garden at Hidcote is intended to encourage insects to stay.

Above A colourful peacock butterfly feeds on a buddleia bush.

them into your garden, treat them well and and they will reward you in return. Your soil and compost will be rich in organisms that turn your soil, aerate it and speed up the decomposition of kitchen and garden waste. Aphids and other pests will be reduced effectively if birds, hoverflies and insects are encouraged to make your garden their home. Without the colour of butterflies' wings, the chirping of birds and the buzz of bees as they go about collecting their nectar and pollinating the plants, a garden feels sterile and false. Bring them into the garden and it immediately feels vibrant and exciting, embracing the natural rhythms and seasons of life.

There is a traditional image of wildlife-friendly gardens being messy, full of brambles, nettles, rotting wood and not much else. Although those are all very beneficial to a whole range of insects and bugs, a garden does not have to look untidy. Bees, butterflies and other pollinating insects will be just as attracted to your beautiful flower-beds or your vegetable garden as they will be to weeds. Log piles can be made neatly and will house many invertebrates, while a wildlife pond will attract small animals including newts, frogs, toads, birds and aquatic plant life.

Recent research has shown that many insects are just as attracted to non-native flowers as they are to native ones; so long as pollen and nectar are accessible to them, they are not picky. *Buddleja davidii* is commonly known as the butterfly bush because butterflies love it, yet it hails from China. So the message is that there is no need to worry about the derivation of your plants as they will all add to the variety of your garden's biodiversity.

Attracting wildlife to your garden

You do not have to put much effort into encouraging wildlife. In fact, by simply leaving your garden to mother nature you would quickly find it colonised by insects, birds and small mammals. However, there are plenty of things you can do that will enable you to have a beautiful garden and share it with your fellow creatures too.

Putting up bird and habitat boxes, creating a pond, having a range of different plants and creating log piles will all encourage wildlife into the garden. If you do not want to do all these things, there are probably existing features in the garden that wildlife has already colonised. Cracks in bricks and wooden posts may be home to bees, ladybirds and lacewings, while porches and sheds can be a sheltered haven for butterflies. Just leaving the grass longer will encourage a richer range of wildlife.

Tip

One of the best ways to enjoy nature is to set up a wildlife camera by a bird box. These are easier to install than you might think and will reward you with a real insight into the life of birds. Technology now even allows you to watch their comings and goings via your mobile when you are not at home. At Polesden Lacey, cameras have been set up to watch not just birds but also deer, foxes and the beehives.

Above Building the right kind of enviroment could encourage wildlife such as hedgehogs into your garden.

Step-by-step: Making a habitat

Habitat boxes can be bought from garden centres and online, and they come in a range of shapes, sizes and materials. These are great and make attractive features for the garden, but wild creatures are just as happy with a simple home that can easily be made from recycled material already in the garden.

Bumble bees make fantastic pollinators, and although there are different species with varying nesting requirements, many of them will simply create a home in a hole in the ground or at the foot of a tree. This habitat box replicates their needs and will probably be quickly occupied by one of your key garden buddies.

1. Take a 9cm (3½in) terracotta pot and fill it with dry material that can be found in your garden. This can include moss, dry grass and leaves.

2. Locate a sheltered spot in the garden, ideally at the foot of a fence or tree. Turn the pot upside down, pushing a thin piece of cane through the drainage hole and into the ground to prevent it being knocked over.

3. Rest the edge of the pot on a small stone so that bees can access the nest from below as well as through the drainage hole.

Encourage hedgehogs into the garden by making a larger version of the habitat box. Take a large pot or wooden box, fill it with dry material and and tuck it under a shrub or in a hedge, placed on its side. The best time to do this is in autumn when hedgehogs are looking for a place to hibernate for the winter.

Garden ponds for wildlife

Water is the essence of life. Not only do the plants in the garden depend on it, the wildlife also require it. Without water the range of wildlife will be limited, but if you create even a small pond in the garden the space becomes a paradise for the natural world. The diversity increases enormously as wildlife regularly visit the garden to drink; you may see dragonflies, damselflies, frogs, toads, hedgehogs, stoats, weasels and many other creatures.

In tiny gardens where there is no room for a pond consider a bird bath, or even a washing-up bowl or upside-down dustbin lid filled with water, as this helps to sustain the wildlife population.

Water will also increase the range of plant life available. Bog plants will thrive in the surrounding damp soil of the pond (if the pond is not made with a liner) while marginals will dwell on shelves

Crispin Scott
National Trust
Wildlife and
Countryside Adviser

'To attract dragonflies, it is helpful to have some floating pond plants as well as areas of open water. Native water lilies are ideal, and many damselfly species can be seen on the leaves of these for long periods when the sun is shining. It is also important to have emergent plants, such as flag iris, in your pond to enable larvae to climb out. Look out for the empty cases, or exuviate, once the adults have flown – identifying these is an interesting science in its own right! If you want to create a pond that is good for dragonflies it is best not to have fish, which will eat their eggs and larvae.'

Above As well as being an attractive feature, the ponds at Mount Stewart (left) and Monk's House (right) attract wildlife such as dragonflies and frogs to the garden.

Step-by-step: Making a wildlife pond

1. Dig out a hole in the garden. Use a spirit level to ensure the sides are level, because otherwise one side of the pond will be exposed. It can be as big as your garden will allow, but should ideally be at least 1m (3¼ft) deep in the middle so that the water maintains a more steady temperature throughout the year and will be less likely to freeze in winter. Create a shelf around the side of the pond for marginal plants, about 15cm (6in) below the surface and 20cm (8in) wide.

2. Remove any stones or sharp objects from the hole and then cover the base of the pond with sand or old newspaper to a depth of about 3cm (just over 1in) to prevent any punctures in the liner.

3. Cover the area with a butyl liner and then place heavy stones and a layer of soil over the top of the liner 'shelf' to hold it in place and to encourage plants to start getting a hold.

4. Fill the pond with water and then plant around the outsides of the pond to screen the edges. Use a mix of tall and shorter grasses to offer a safe environment for small mammals which need to be alert for predators.

around the perimeter of the pond. Aquatic or submerged plants, such as water lilies with their large, broad leaves, provide a dry resting place for frogs as well as dragonflies and other insects.

Ornamental fish, particularly koi carp, are beautiful additions to ornamental ponds but are not generally suitable for wildlife ponds. This is because they tend to devour many pond plants and bugs, leaving the water sterile and devoid of life. A few fish can be managed in a wildlife pond, but be careful that the pond does not become overstocked as the ecosystem balance will be lost.

Designing and siting your pond

When you are designing a wildlife pond it is a good idea to make it look both as natural as possible and in accord with the overall landscape. Avoid a perfectly symmetrical shape, which looks manmade, unless this fits in better with your garden design. Edging the pond with hard landscaping material such as bricks or patio slabs can also give a less natural feel to the garden.

Think carefully about where the pond is to be situated. If it is very near the house some wildlife species may be too cautious to approach it, although in a small garden this is the only option. A pond should ideally not be in full sun all day but in dappled shade to prevent the amount of algae and blanket weed that will start to grow. However, try to avoid siting the pond under a deciduous tree where the falling leaves in autumn will quickly add to the fertility of the pond and deplete it of oxygen. A wildlife pond should have a sloping section on at least one side as this will enable creatures to drink from the water's edge without falling in and drowning.

The traditional method for making a pond watertight is to use puddling clay, lining the bottom and sides of the pond, and tamping it down firmly. This is an expensive method and not always practical for small gardens. Alternatively, concrete can be used, but this is not a sustainable option and if it cracks – highly likely in cold weather – it can be very difficult to fix. The simplest option is to use a butyl liner, which is hardwearing and flexible and will mould to the shape of the pond.

Attracting birds to your garden

The best way to bring birds to your garden is to hang up bird seed, fat cakes and other food for them to eat. Bird baths regularly topped up with water (ideally rainwater) during summer will also encourage them. However, if you want to go the extra mile and encourage them to nest in the garden, you can create suitable habitats such as bird boxes. Birds usually start to look for a nesting site in early spring, requiring a dry, sheltered site away from strong winds and where they will feel safe from predators.

Making a bird box is easy, as it is just a matter of creating the type of hollow tree environment that they would inhabit in the wild. You can buy wooden kits with assembly instructions – look for ones made of timber from a sustainable source, ideally from a local woodland using surplus wood from tree management thinnings.

Of course, different birds have different requirements. For example, a barn owl requires a large box high in trees with good open ground below it where it can forage for small mammals and swoop easily back to safely. Other species of birds will be attracted to open-fronted nestboxes, particularly robins, wrens, wagtails and black redstarts. Most garden and woodland birds are not fussy, but as a rule of thumb, entrance holes of about 28mm (1in) diameter will provide a habitat for blue tits, great tits and tree sparrows. Larger holes of about 32mm (1¼in) in diameter will encourage house sparrows and nuthatches and, if you are lucky, the rare lesser spotted woodpecker.

Bird boxes can be screwed or nailed together and should ideally have a hinged opening so that they can be cleaned out easily. If you have a bird box kit that does not have any drainage holes in the floor, drill tiny holes to ensure that if rain water does penetrate the roof it will drain away. Wood can be made from hard or softwood and ideally will be about 20mm (¾in) thick.

Above, left
A moss-covered bird box in the woodland at Dinefwr Park and Castle, Wales.
Above, right
The garden can be a delight for budding ornithologists.

Making fat cakes

Fat cakes are packed full of protein, fat and carbohydrates, which help to sustain the bird population throughout winter. Hang them from trees or shrubs, safely out of the reach of cats, and you will help your garden birds to survive the harsh cold months. This is particularly important during snow and hard frosts, when birds cannot forage for worms and other food in the ground.

You will need:

Lard or suet
Ingredients such as wild bird seed, raisins, sultanas, oats, breadcrumbs, cake, grated cheese – avoid salty ingredients such as bacon or roasted peanuts
Mixing bowl
Saucepan
Spoon
String
Yoghurt pots or similar containers

Note: do not replace lard or suet with fat from cooking, polyunsaturated margarines or vegetable oils as these can smear birds' feathers.

1. Mix all the dry ingredients together in a mixing bowl.
2. Melt the suet or lard in a saucepan and add the dry ingredients. The ratio should be approximately one-third fat to two-thirds dry mix.
3. Make a hole in the bottom of each yoghurt pot and thread string through it, tying a knot at the bottom
4. Spoon the mix into the yoghurt pots, ensuring plenty of string remains above the top of the pot
5. Place in the fridge overnight to allow the ingredients to set. In the morning, cut through the pots and remove the cakes.

Right Bird feeders can make attractive features in the garden, as well as providing sustenance for feathered friends.

Keeping bees

Many National Trust properties have apiaries containing beehives and honey bees. Bees have been kept for hundreds of years in gardens and therefore have an important historic role. There is no more quintessentially rural scene than an orchard with attractive white beehives at the foot of majestic old fruit trees.

Keeping beehives has several benefits, the most important of which is that honey bees pollinate many flowers, increasing the amount of viable seed and contributing to the production of flowers, fruit and vegetables. Just one beehive may have more than 60,000 bees in summer. Of course honey bees also produce honey, which not only tastes wonderful but also has many health benefits. Finally, there is the simple pleasure of sitting in your garden on a warm sunny day and watching bees foraging for nectar and pollen from your plants. It is a truly relaxing way to spend

Above Beehives set back behind the apple trees in the orchard at Monk's House. **Opposite** Bees are drawn to plants such as chive flowers.

The sting in the tail

There is no getting away from the fact that a bee sting does hurt, although beekeepers become used to the pain. Bees sting to defend their colony and they die in the process. When they sting, they leave their barbed sting in the skin. This sting should be removed as quickly as possible to reduce the amount of poison pumping into your body.

Do not try to pull out the sting with your fingertips as this squeezes the venom sac in the tip of the sting, causing more poison to pump into the body. Instead, it can be quickly removed by scraping it away with your fingernail or a blunt instrument such as the end of ruler. There is often swelling and itchiness for a couple of days after being stung.

Occasionally people suffer from anaphylactic shock from an allergic reaction to a bee sting. In such cases, seek immediate medical assistance.

some time, making beekeeping one of the most rewarding and absorbing hobbies.

However, it is not just honey bees that will pollinate your plants – in fact solitary bees and bumble bees are possibly even better pollinators as they fly at lower temperatures. To encourage solitary bees to the garden, you can make a nest simply by drilling holes in a block of wood and attaching it to a warm sunny wall. Alternatively, cut hollow-stemmed plants such as bamboos into 25cm (10in) sections, tie them together and hang them in a warm, dry and sheltered spot in the garden.

Siting a beehive

Ideally, site a beehive where the sun falls on the entrance in the morning to entice bees to start foraging early on. Avoid frost pockets and damp areas. Place the hive on a stand or recycled wooden pallet to prevent the floor of the hive becoming wet.

If you have a large garden, pick a spot where there is a rich source of nectar and pollen, for although bees will fly as far as 4.8km (3 miles) they will be far more productive if they are foraging closer to their colonies. There should preferably be a range of plants that will flower for most of the year – even from late autumn to late winter, honey bees will forage on mild days. Plants popular with bees include mahonia, winter aconites, winter honeysuckle (*Lonicera fragrantissima* and *L.* x *purpusii*) and ivy.

In small gardens, place the entrance hole for the beehives away from where people will be walking or sitting. Erecting 2m (6½ft) high mesh or fencing around the site will ensure the bees'

Above, left
Mahonia will attract bees to your garden on mild winter days.
Above, right
The bright petals of winter aconites are also a draw for bees in cooler months.

Attingham Park Historic Bee House

Situated in the beautiful grounds of Attingham Park is a rare surviving example of an eighteenth-century wooden bee house. The honey bees are kept here in traditional straw skeps, which are baskets woven from straw or grass. Their design meant that the bees had to be destroyed when the honey was collected but now modern honeycomb frames are used to avoid this. In 2011 Attingham Park installed a transparent acrylic beehive in the walled garden close by which is an exact replica of an ordinary beehive but allows visitors to see the bees at work. This hive is home to more than 10,000 bees which enter and leave through a hole in the brick wall that forms the back of the hive, keeping the bees away from the visitors.

flight is above head height. The barrier should be at least 3m (10ft) distance from the hive and ideally suround it entirely. You could diguise the barrier with some creepers.

Above The beekeepers at Felbrigg Hall in protective attire

Essential kit for a beekeeper

Smoker Smoke is putted into the beehive to calm the bees before lifting the lid on the hives.
Hive tool This implement is used to prise apart the boxes and lift out the frames.
Protective clothing A beekeeper's outfit usually includes a veil with hat and suit. Gloves are also recommended for beginners.

Types of hives

National hives are the most commonly used hives in the UK. They are practical, can be stacked up easily and only have one layer around the outside. Other hives such as WBC have an extra box over the top and sides, which provides extra insulation but makes an inspection of the hive slower as you have more boxes to lift away in order to inspect the hive.
WBC hives are the attractive traditional beehive shape. As they have two layers they are slower to inspect, but this does provide extra insulation in winter.
Polystyrene hives are increasing in popularity as they are less expensive than the red cedar that is normally used and they have good insulation qualities.

Combinations of plants

Grow a wide range of plants in the garden to encourage a greater variety of wildlife. As well as typical wildflower mixes, plant as many trees and shrubs as you can, depending on the size of your garden. These act as habitats for nesting birds and many will bear berries throughout the winter. A bushy shrub will usually provide a far greater amount of flowers for pollinating insects than a herbaceous wild flower. Their height also encourages birds into the garden as they feel safer off the ground, away from predators. If you are really lucky you may attract dormice, which prefer to dwell in trees, particularly hazel.

Where possible, avoid using fences as boundaries and instead go for hedges as these provide wildlife habitats. Consider a mix of different plants in a hedge and try to use some evergreens as this will provide all-year-round cover.Hedging plants that are great for wildlife include elder for its berries and flowers, hazel for its nuts and crab apples, hawthorn and blackthorn for an abundant source of fruit.

Above, left and right Growing plants with a high fruit yield, such as hawthorn or blackberries, will encourage a wide range of creatures – maybe even a dormouse – into your garden.

Tip

In a small garden, the range of plants and the amount of time they flower for can be increased by training climbing plants into trees. For example, a crab apple such as 'Golden Hornet' or 'John Downie' could have a rambling rose such as 'Rambling Rector' trained up it so that after the apple tree finishes flowering in spring there is a secondary flowering period in summer from the rose.

Step-by-step: Planting a hedge

Hedges are best planted in two rows for a denser and richer habitat for wildlife. Use a string to mark out where the double rows of trees are to be planted, with about 30cm (12in) beween the rows.

1. Buy bare root hedging plants between late autumn and late winter. These are cheaper to buy than containerised plants, better for the environment as they are not grown in pots of compost and easier to transport.

2. To plant them, dig a spade into the ground, push the handle away from you to open up the ground and slot a hedging plant along the back of the space and into the ground. Continue this process along both rows, staggering the plants so that they are in a zigzag pattern and mixing the different types together rather than planting them in separate blocks. They should be 30cm (12in) apart within the row.

Step-by-step: Making a dead hedge

At Polesden Lacey community kitchen garden, the site was cleared and all the brushwood from the trees was used to make a dead hedge around the site to provide a habitat for wildlife. Sections of trunk were recycled into a structure for raised beds, while the remaining branches were chipped to make paths.

Making a dead hedge is easy to do. Not only does it make a useful screen between sections of the garden, it is a great way to use up surplus materials that would otherwise be disposed of in less environmentally friendly ways such as on the bonfire or in petrol-fed chipping machinery.

1. Straight 1.5m (5ft) branches were removed from the brushwood and set into the ground at a distance of 1.5m (5ft) apart, using a crowbar to make the pilot hole and a lump hammer to bang them in.

2. Two rows were made, 50cm (20in) apart, and the stakes on either side were staggered.

3. Brushwood was simply placed between the two rows of stakes. Branches that would not fit were chopped up into smaller sections with saws or loppers and added back in.

4. Eventually the kitchen garden was surrounded by an attractive natural-looking hedge that cost nothing. Any surplus brushwood in the following years can be added to the dead hedge.

Encouraging bats to your garden

Growing a wide range of flowering plants will encourage insects and bats. All of the UK's bat species eat insects such as moths, spiders, beetles and flies. Gardens can be very good for insects and most plants need them for pollination, so whether you have a tiny urban oasis or acres in the countryside your garden could be good for bats and bats could be good for your garden. (A tiny pipistrelle bat can eat up to 3,000 insects in a night.)

Plants that produce good quantities of nectar and pollen, whether they are native or exotic, are of most value for insects. Avoid hybrids and double-flowered varieties as these tend to produce very little or nectar and pollen. Pale flowers and night-scented species are good for attracting insects (and bats) at dusk and after dark.

Trees and shrubs, including non-flowering varieties are good for bats. As any gardener knows, many insects also eat leaves and bats will forage for insects around trees and shrubs, gleaning moths off leaves and scooping spiders out of webs. Trees also provide shelter for bats – bats roost in cavities, splits and holes in trees, as well as making use of buildings. If you don't have trees with such features, you could put up a bat box. Not all bats use bat boxes, but those that tend to visit gardens can use them. Water features are also good for bats, a small pond or lake will provide somewhere for bats to drink, slurping up water on the wing as well as attracting insects.

Lighting is not so good for bats as it generally discourages many species. If you have lighting in your garden think about keeping this low down, at knee level, or angling lights away from trees and shrubs, ensuring light doesn't spill too far into vegetation, and not leaving them on all night.

Jo Hodgkins, National Trust Wildlife and Countryside Adviser

Above Bechstein's bat, a species of vesper bat native to Europe. **Below** Log piles and log pile benches look even more appealing when bluebells begin to grow around them.

Making log piles

Log piles are another way to increase biodiversity, boost the numbers of beneficial insects and reduce waste. They are simply a pile of logs left to decompose in a corner of the garden. To start, to dig a hole in the ground and place a length of log into it, with about two-thirds of it above ground. Drill small holes into the wood and it will quickly be colonised. Add logs to the pile.

On a larger scale, you can create log stacks in a pyramid shape with five logs at the bottom, four above it, then three, two and one on the top.

Even the smallest of gardens can have a little path lined with lengths of timber that not only look attractive and rustic but also provide a home for a range of insects. Always make sure that the lengths of wood are in contact with the soil as this speeds up the process of decomposition.

Step-by-step: Making a log pile bench in the community kitchen

We always have plenty of surplus wood at Polesden Lacey as we regularly thin out our trees to enable sunlight to reach the woodland floor, which encourages a wider range of plant life than a thick canopy of trees. When the lime trees were removed from the community kitchen garden, we reused some of the material to create this log pile bench. If you do not have access to woodland, contact a local tree surgeon or timber yard. At Polesden Lacey we sometimes allow volunteers to take away timber in exchange for helping us with our conservation work in the garden or countryside, so it may also be worth contacting your local National Trust property to see whether they do the same.

1. Level the ground where the bench is going to be made and then start to stack timber lengths about 1.2m (4ft) long on top of each other, starting with the largest logs at the bottom

2. When it has reached knee height, place chicken wire tightly over the pile to hold it secure. Use staples to hold the chicken wire in place.

3. Add logs to the back and sides to make the back and side supports, building them up to about waist height, again using chicken wire to hold it in place.

4. Place batons over the top of the seating area for extra support if necessary and then attach a rustic plank of wood to the pile to form the seat.

5. Attach another plank to the back to form the back rest, using screws. Back rests are usually more comfortable if they are angled back slightly, but this can be trickier to achieve.

6. Make mounds of soil around the back and side of the bench and then sow grass seed or a wildflower mix into it to create an attractive, rustic and flowery seating area. In woodland, log piles and log pile benches look particularly beautiful when bluebells grow alongside them.

Rooftop gardening

Gardens can be created in the most unlikely of places, but if you really are short of space you could consider a 'green roof' on top of your garage, shed or house.

These roofs are becoming popular, particularly in the towns and cities where outdoor space is hard to come by. In addition to creating an open growing space, they also create a habitat for wildlife and provide extra insulation in winter. And when viewed from upstairs' windows, it enhances the landscape – much more attractive than looking out on dull shed roofing felt.

Any plants can be used to grow on a roof, but the most popular types are sedums and sempervirens as they have small root runs and are drought tolerant. Sedums are particularly useful where their succulent foliage knits together to form an attractive tapestry of texture and colour.

Always check that your building structure can take the weight of the green roof.

To create the roof, cut a piece of marine plywood to the size of the roof and cover it with a waterproof membrane such as butyl liner. Nail the wood to the roof and then create a 5cm (2in) deep edge around the outside of the marine ply, using planks of wood. Pallets are often useful for finding external pieces of wood. Fill the planting space with a mix of rock wool, perlite and non-peat compost. Drill drainage holes in the lower sections of the wooden frame to allow excess moisture to seep away. Plug the holes with rock wool to ensure the compost doesn't slide into it and clog it up. Finally plant the sedums at a spacing of about 10cm (4in) apart.

Alternatively, it is possible to buy rolls or mats of sedum plants which are simply stretched out over the roof and nailed down.

Below, left A red admiral butterfly pauses on sedum flower. **Below, right** A bee feeds on a yelow flag iris flower.

Case study: Green roofs

By Ed Ikin, General Manager at Morden Hall Park and Rainham Hall, London, and former Head Gardener at Nymans, West Sussex

A traditional form of roofing in Scandinavia for many centuries, green roofs are a growing trend in many European countries and in the USA, Canada and Australia. Germany in particular has embraced their benefits for decades, often on a grand scale on industrial buildings. The green roof revolution is now slowly gaining ground in the UK, too.

The presence of vegetation rather than tiles or roofing felt allows heavy rain to soak in then slowly percolate into guttering, reducing the risk of flooding; some plants, for example *Iris pseudacorus*, can even filter industrial pollutants out of rainwater, a boon if it is being collected. Another advantage is that a layer of vegetation does wonders for the thermal performance of a building, regulating the loss and penetration of heat so that interior temperatures are more consistent and require less heating and cooling that relies on fossil fuels.

A green roof can echo a wild vegetation system, such as a prairie (known as an extensive system) or a designed garden (intensive system). Well-chosen extensive systems need virtually no maintenance once they are established but tend to be most successful grown on a large scale rather than on a domestic roof. Intensive systems can include plants of any type but may require frequent watering and weeding, depending on the depth and type of growing medium on your roof.

The obvious consideration when planning a green roof is its weight. It is essential to work with a structural engineer when you are creating a green roof as part of a house extension as it will be much heavier than any conventional roofing material. Sheds look rather handsome with a well-chosen green roof, connecting seamlessly to their surrounding garden. A builder can advise on how to brace the interior of the shed and install simple aggregate retaining frames that will make a good base for establishing plants. *Sedum* is the green roof plant of choice, thanks to its compact habit and willingness to grow without water or fertiliser, but *Allium*, *Stipa*, *Crocus*, *Alternathera* and *Dianthus* are all worth exploring.

Watering wisely

Future weather conditions are increasingly hard to predict worldwide as the climate warms year by year and it is becoming increasingly important to garden sustainably. One way of doing this is to catch the rain when it falls and use it to water the plants during the summer months.

   The best method of doing this is to install water butts in the garden. These can be as simple as dustbins or other watertight vessels left without their lids on to catch the rainfall. However, the best types are those that are designed to catch the run-off from the roof of a building such as a house, shed or greenhouse. In addition to collecting rain water, it is possible to recycle grey water. This is the water used in showers, baths, sinks and even the dishwasher. There are various methods of doing this, from very high-tech plumbing to simply scooping out the bath water with a bucket and emptying it on a flower-bed. However, it is best to avoid using grey water on food crops as the effect that the detergents and bacteria in the water may have on the food chain is not known.

The best way to water

- Water your plants either in the evening or early morning, not in the middle of the day as the water tends to evaporate before the plants have had a chance to take up the moisture.
- Choose plants that do not require much watering. Plants adapted to dry climates tend to have less moisture requirements than most plants. Avoid plants with large leaves as these are often the plants needing the most amount of water to sustain them. Bedding plants also tend to be very thirsty.

Above, left
A rainwater harvesting tank is assembled at Nymans.
Above, right
The harvested rainwater is then used to water potted plants.

Below Making a sump around a plant will mean that water will not run off elsewhere.

Step-by-step: Connecting a water butt to a shed

1. The gutter should have a slight fall (10mm every 6m (20ft) of gutter) to help the water drain away down the downpipe. Identify where the downpipe is going to end (this should be be directly above the water butt) and screw the gutter outlet section in place to the roof of the shed. This should be the lowest part of the guttering section. To help work this out use a string to mark out the fall, from the highest to the lowest point of the guttering.

2. Following the line of the string, screw wall brackets in place about every 75cm (29½in) –1m (3ft) apart. Clip the guttering into the brackets and insert gutter stops on both ends of the entire length to prevent water spillage..

3. Cut the downpipe to length using a saw. Insert one end into the gutter outlet. When working out the length of the downpipe, bear in mind that it is useful for the butt to be raised off the ground so that is is easy to fit the watering can beneath the tap.

4. Secure the downpipe in place by using a wall bracket to hold it firmly in place about halfway down. Push the other end of the downpipe into the top of the water butt.

4 An overflow water butt can be attached so that when the original water butt is full, it continues to fill up another. Also, a divertor can be fitted to the downpipe, which senses when the water butt is full and directs excess water into a mains drain or soak away. Read the instructions on the label before fitting.

- Use a watering can to water plants as this helps to regulate the amount of water being used.
- Avoid spinning or overhead sprinklers, particularly in the middle of the day. They disperse water over a large area and much of it is lost before it has even hit the ground. Instead, use drip or seep hoses that slowly drip water onto the soil next to plants.
- Make sumps around individual plants by pushing the soil up into a doughnut shape, taking care not to expose the roots. This helps to concentrate the watering around the root system without it trickling away elsewhere.
- Mulch flower-beds with garden compost as this will help to maintain moisture levels. Prior to planting, dig in organic matter.
- Keep plants weed-free, as weeds will compete for nutrients as well as water.
- Do not grow a lot of plants in containers as they will need watering almost every day during the summer. In extremely dry and hot periods it might be worth moving plants in containers to slightly shadier areas to save on watering.

All-year-round gardens

At the National Trust we are very conscious that our gardens should reward visitors with stunning displays throughout the year. It is no longer enough to put on a display just through the peak season – expectations from visitors have increased, and so have the standards in our gardens. Many National Trust properties now have winter gardens that attract millions of people to visit them, whereas in the past it would have been deemed the 'closed season'. Wildlife too depends on there being plenty of winter vegetation for food and to provide material for their homes.

There are plenty of plants with winter interest in the garden, but summer plants too can provide a rich habitat for wildlife. Instead of cutting herbaceous plants down to near ground level after flowering, consider leaving them standing throughout the winter months. They can look majestic when standing there with their rich tapestry of seedheads, creating silhouettes and shadows against the low winter sun, and when the frost catches them they take on a magical, translucent appearance. If you encourage birds and small mammals to stay in your garden it will still feel alive in winter as they come out of their homes to feed and collect more nesting materials in mild weather.

Plants to grow for wildlife in winter

Seedheads Plants with winter seedheads include *Echinacea*, *Eryngium* (sea holly), *Rudbeckia*, *Echinops ritro*, *Veronicastrum* 'Fascination', *Cynara cardunculus* (ornamental artichoke), *Anethum graveolens* (dill) and *Phlomis fructicosa*.

Flowers and nectar *Prunus subhirtella* (winter-flowering cherry) and *Erica carnea* (winter-flowering heather) are among the many plants that will flower in winter to provide nectar for insects.

Berries Birds love to feed on berries and there are plenty to choose from, including cotoneaster, sorbus, ivy, hawthorns and blackthorn. Even fallen apples can be left on the ground to provide an additional food source.

Foliage Evergreen plants such as holly, ivy and yew will provide a sheltered and safe haven for birds

Above, left Cotoneaster berries provide winter food for birds. **Above, right** The seedheads of *Cornus sanguinea* 'Winter Beauty' will feed wildlife, while the stems bring welcome colour.

to hide in. Do not be too tidy in your garden; remove some fallen leaves if they are going to smother the lawn or you need some to make leaf mould, but leave some for the wildlife to take back for nesting material. Plant ornamental grasses too, such as *Calamagrostis* x *acutiflora* 'Karl Foerster', *Cortaderia selloana* 'Pumila', *Miscanthus sinensis* 'Morning Light' and *Stipa tenuissima*.

The Polesden Lacey winter garden

Winter gardens are a relatively new concept in the horticultural world. The National Trust advisor Graham Stuart Thomas was one of the first people to expound on the virtues of a winter garden, and in the 1970s he wrote one of the key horticultural books of the twentieth century – *Colour in the Winter Garden*. Polesden Lacey is lucky to have the only remaining example designed by Graham Stuart Thomas, which marks it out as one of the key heritage areas of the property. It is packed with scented winter-flowering plants such as *Viburnum* x *bodnantense*, *Chimonanthus praecox*, (wintersweet), *Sarcococca humilis* (Christmas box) and *Mahonia japonica*. It also features rare shrubs such as *Shepherdia argentea* and *Parrotiopsis jacquemontiana* and the floor is carpeted with yellow winter aconites and more than 20 varieties of snowdrops. Three *Parrotia persica* trees (Persian ironwood) that provide a nesting habitat for a host of different birds are the central focal point of the garden.

The garden is very sheltered and the scent is held in the small space. Very often in winter there are honey bees foraging on the flowers and the sound of bird song among the trees and shrubs. Even on the darkest of days it really is a flame of life for visitor interest and wildlife survival.

Above
Snowdrops, with their dainty, nodding white heads, are one of the first flowers to appear at the start of a new gardening season

Above Dawn seen from the east terrace at Cotehele. Plants such as magnolia thrive in the garden, which is maintained without the use of peat.

For peat's sake

The use of peat in the horticultural world still remains controversial. However, one aspect of it which is unequivocal is that the extraction of this finite material from peat bogs is unsustainable and of a serious environmental concern.

In 1991, the National Trust took the decision to stop using peat for mulching or improving soil. In 1999 they extended this to end the use of peat completely in their gardens, encouraging amateur gardeners also to use alternatives to peat. Alternatives such as green garden waste, leaf mould, composted bracken and forestry byproducts can all be added to the soil to help maintain healthy plants and beds.

In 2001 the National Trust began to phase out the use of peat in potting composts and from 2003 onwards the majority of plants grown, bought or sold at National Trust properties were in peat-free composts. The National Trust is now a peat-free organisation in all aspects of horticulture.

Peat is a finite fossil resource with deposits laid down over thousands of years which can be lost in tens of years. It is industrially extracted from peat bogs, causing irreversible damage to one

Nick Fraser

Gardener-in-Charge at
Nunnington Hall and
Rievaulx Terrace, North
Yorkshire

'Here at Nunnington Hall, we have had a problem with soil sickness in
our rose borders – this is because roses have grown in the same beds for
100 years. We try to add as much organic matter back into the rose beds
to help build up the diversity of bacteria and micro-organisms in the soil
which will stop the monoculture pathogens (allelopaths) from attacking
the young rose bushes. A healthy soil will also help the plants become
stronger and improve their resistance to disease.'

of the UK's most vulnerable nature conservation habitats and historic environments. Almost 90 per cent of the UK's peat bog habitats have been lost over the last century. UK peatlands store approximately 3 billion tonnes of carbon. If this was lost as CO_2 to the atmosphere, it would be the equivalent of more than 20 years of UK industrial emissions. Peat also develops very slowly, so it can take up to hundreds of years to replace each metre that is extracted for use in private gardens.

When peat is dug up for use in the garden industry it releases almost half a million tonnes of carbon dioxide a year into the atmosphere. Peat is therefore essential for the locking in of carbon into the ground and preventing it from entering the atmosphere, where it forms CO_2, the main greenhouse gas.

The National Trust cares for some of the most important gardens and cultivated plant collections in Europe, and it is hoped that demonstrating the high horticultural standards that can be maintained without using peat will inspire other horticultural organisations and individuals to do the same.

The National Trust and the horticultural commercial world have developed a number of alternatives to peat:

• Leaf mould, well-rotted farmyard manure and garden compost as a soil improver.
• Bark, composted garden waste and leaf mould as a mulch to conserve moisture and suppress weeds.
• Wood-fibre waste compost as a growing medium for pricking out and potting up.

Green-waste propagation compost is best used for growing on tougher plants, particularly herbaceous perennials and non-ericaceous shrubs. Its tendency to be slightly alkaline and salty precludes it from seed-sowing applications.

Below A nettle 'tea' can be made from weed clippings and makes an excellent natural plant food. To make the tea, chop nettles in a bucket and cover in water. Cover with a weight and leave to soak for a few weeks. Drain off the liquid. The resulting 'tea' can be diluted (at a ratio of one part tea to ten parts water) and used to feed plants.

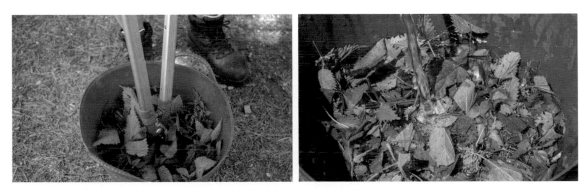

Above Composting bins lined up in the community kitchen garden at Hatchlands Park.

Making your garden sustainable

In an ideal world our gardens would be completely self-sufficient. We would propagate our own plants by collecting seeds and taking cuttings, never once driving to the garden centre. We would compost our own kitchen and garden waste and harvest enough rain water from our water butts to sustain our plants throughout the driest of summers. However, no matter how much we would like to achieve this, the reality is that this is very unlikely to be achieved. Yet there are always opportunities for us to cut down on consumption, recycle materials, and reduce carbon footprint and air miles that our purchases have had to travel.

When you buy products either online or from the garden centre, try to source ones made locally. That does not just mean the final product in the factory, but also where the parts for the final product have been imported from. If buying timber, look for the FSC mark that ensures that the product has been sourced from a sustainable woodland. Check bags of charcoal for barbecues for this too.

If possible, use gardening equipment that is not driven by petrol. There are very good battery-powered mowers, hedge trimmers and strimmers, and the batteries can easily be charged up from solar-panelled units. Alternatively, consider not using any machines at all. There is nothing wrong with using hedging shears – in fact you will probably get a far better cut and your arms will get a good healthy workout too. There is something very relaxing about the quiet clipping noise they make, as opposed to the roar of a hedge trimmer, and they are becoming increasingly popular.

Nick Fraser
Gardener-in-Charge at
Nunnington Hall and
Rievaulx Terrace,
North Yorkshire

'The ideal method of cutting back and tidying up under an organic regime would be to leave the herbaceous plants and some of the leaves down during the winter to allow birds to feed on the seeds and to pick though some of the leaf litter to feed on the overwintering insects. This also provides an overwintering habitat for various insects and mammals, including hedgehogs. You can then cut back and tidy up throughout February, adding all clipping and organic matter to the compost heap.'

Above, left Go green – use battery-powered devices to maintain your garden.
Above, right Compost bay in the cutting garden at Nunnington Hall.

Tip

'Use regular cheap chicken pellets as an accelerant on your compost heap. It works just as well as any commercial compost maker but much cheaper.'

Colin Clark, Senior Gardener at Greenway, Devon

Things to recycle

Almost anything can be recycled, and with a bit of imagination on your part can even take pride of place in your garden.

- Add kitchen waste to the compost heap rather than the rubbish bin.
- Recycle pallets to hold compost heaps. These can easily be sourced from local businesses, but always check first with the proprietors
- Old bins and other watertight containers can be used as water butts.
- Certain food waste can be made into bird feed.
- Use old CDs as bird scarers.
- Add wrapping paper to the compost heap rather than throwing it away
- Wrap old pairs of tights around bunches of grapes to protect them from birds.
- Cardboard can be used to suppress weeds and added to the compost heap too.
- Transform old window frames into cold frames.
- Cardboard toilet rolls can be used as flowerpots. Plastic pots can be re-used.
- Many things can be made into plant containers. Even an old wellington boot, given a drainage hole in the bottom, can be used to grow a tomato or strawberry plant.
- Trees that have to be felled for safety reasons can be chopped up to make seats, benches or tables, or chipped to make surfaces for pathways or as a mulch.
- You don't have to buy a new shed and greenhouse – look on Freecycle websites, as you will often find people offering secondhand structures for free in exchange for dismantling them.
- Constantly check in skips in the road as there is often material in there that can be used in the garden, such as timber for raised beds, wooden posts to support fruit trees and old patio slabs. Old bricks can be used to make garden walls, patios and a base for a barbecue.

Map of National Trust Gardens

Lindisfarne Castle

Cragside

Wallington
Seaton Delaval
NEWCASTLE
Gibside ▲ UPON TYNE
Washington
Old Hall

PENRITH
Acorn Bank
Wordsworth MIDDLESBROUGH
House
Townend
Ormesby
Hill Top ▲ Stagshaw Hall
Sizergh Castle
Rievaulx ▲ Nunnington
Hall
Fountains Abbey
& Studley Royal ▲ Beningbrough Hall
Treasurer's House ▲▲ Goddards
Gawthorpe YORK
Hall ▲ East Riddlesden Hall
LEEDS
Rufford Old Hall Nostell Priory

MANCHESTER
LIVERPOOL Dunham
Massey ▲ Quarry Bank SHEFFIELD
Tatton ▲ Lyme Park Clumber
Speke Hall Park Hare Hill Park
LLANDUDNO LINCOLN
Penrhyn Little Moreton ▲ Biddulph
Castle Hall Grange Hardwick Hall ▲ Gunby Hall
Plas Erddig ▲ STOKE-ON-
Newydd Bodnant TRENT Kedleston Hall
Chirk Castle Calke NOTTINGHAM
Abbey ▲ Belton Sheringham Park
Plas-yn-Rhiw Attingham Sunnycroft Shugborough House Felbrigg Hall
Park Moseley Old Hall KING'S LYNN Blickling Hall
Powis ▲ Wightwick Manor LEICESTER PETERBOROUGH Peckover NORWICH
Castle Benthall Hall BIRMINGHAM House Oxburgh
Dudmaston Lyveden Hall
Packwood House Baddesley Clinton New Bield
Croft Castle Hanbury ▲ Coughton Court NORTHAMPTON Anglesey BURY ST EDMUNDS
Berrington ▲ Charlecote Farnborough Hall Abbey ▲ Ickworth
Llanerchaeron Hall Park CAMBRIDGE Lavenham
The Weir Croome Hidcote Canons Ashby Wimpole Guildhall
Park Snowshill Upton Stowe Landscape Hall Melford
Colby Woodland Chastleton House Gardens Hall
Garden Dinefwr Manor Waddesdon ▲ Ascott
GLOUCESTER Westbury Manor
Court Buscot Park OXFORD
Clevedon West Wycombe Hughenden
Court ▲ Manor Fenton House
BRISTOL Dyrham Great Chalfield Greys Court ▲ Cliveden
Tyntesfield Park Manor Basildon ▲ Osterley Park Red House
Prior ▲ Lacock Abbey Park READING Ham House CANTERBURY
Park The Claremont
Dunster Courts The Vyne ▲ Hatchlands The Homewood Emmets Ightham Mote
Castle West Green Polesden Knole
Arlington Lytes Cary Stourhead House Clandon Lacey Chartwell
Court Manor Mompesson Mottisfont Winkworth Standen Scotney Sissinghurst
Knightshayes Barrington House Abbey Arboretum Nymans Wakehurst Place Smallhythe Place
Court Tintinhull Hinton Petworth Sheffield Bateman's Lamb House
Killerton Montacute Ampner Uppark Park Alfriston Clergy House
House SOUTHAMPTON Woolbeding Monk's House
EXETER Kingston Lacy PORTSMOUTH BRIGHTON EASTBOURNE
Castle ▲ Lanhydrock Hardy's
Drogo Cottage Mottistone
Buckland Compton Castle Manor
Lanhydrock Abbey
Godolphin Trerice Antony Greenway
TRURO Saltram
Trengwainton Trelissick PLYMOUTH Coleton Fishacre
St Michael's Overbeck's
Mount Glendurgan

Index

Page numbers in *italic* refer to illustrations

Acer palmatum 24
achillea *26*
acidity 20, 21
aconitum *25*
Acorn Bank, Cumbria 250
aeration 91, 197
Agrostemma githago 98
Agrostis capillaris 87, *87*
Alfriston Clergy House, East Sussex *68*, 92, 172
alkalinity 20, 21
alliums *26*, 238, *238*
Anglesey Abbey, Cambridgeshire *17*, 45, 72, *170*
annuals 44, 98, 112
Anthemis arvensis 98
aphids 192, *193*, 194
apples 201, 204, 205, 266, 274
    pruning 161–2
    thinning *8*
    training 202, 203, *203*
apricots 210
arches 52
Armstrong, Sir William 211
artichokes *243*, 244, 246
asparagus 243, 244
aspect 15, 54–5
astilbe 24
Attingham Park, Shropshire 226, 229, 233, 264
autumn 73, 74, 197
Avebury Manor, Wiltshire *41*, *116*

back sheds 229
balsam, Himalayan 180
bamboos 49, 189
bare-root trees 116, 267
Barrington Court, Somerset 70, *200*, *205*, 209
basil 249
Bateman's, East Sussex *41*, 92, 172, *205*, 243
bats 268
bay 249
beans 232–3, 243, 244
bedding plants 44, 56, 190, 272

beds: lasagne beds 104
    turf-raised beds 82
beer traps 187
bees 254, 255, 256, 257, 262–5, *270*
beetroot 236, *236*, 244
Beningbrough Hall, North Yorkshire 225
Bernamont, Len 92, 172
berries 164–5, 214, 217–19, 274
Biddulph Grange Garden, Staffordshire *113*
bindweed 180, 187
biodiversity 7–8, 268
birch 148, 152, 239
birds 256, 258, 260–1, 266, 274
blackberries 219
blackcurrants 124, 142, 164, 165, 216
bleeding plants 148
blight 237
blueberries 217
boardwalks 32, 46
Bodnant Garden, Conwy 8
Bohetherick orchard, Cornwall *208*
borage 249, *249*
borders, planting 105
boundaries 36–41, 52, 266
box 41, 61, 60, *174*, *175*, 246
brassicas 234–5
brick paths 46
Brown, Lancelot Capability 8, *38*, 120, *121*
Brussels sprouts 227, 244
buckets 183
Buckland Abbey, Devon 19, 250
Buffin, Mike 64
bulbs 72, 110–11, 190, 196, 197
Buscot Park, Oxfordshire *203*, *205*
bush trees 203
buttercups, creeping 15
butterflies 254, 255, *270*

cabbage root fly 234
cabbages 234–5, 244
Calke Abbey, Derbyshire *130*, 212, *215*, *219*
carrot fly 237
carrots 228, 236, 244

Castle Drogo, Devon 70
cauliflowers 234, 244
Centaurea cyanus 98
chainsaws 151
chalk 22
charcoal 152
Chartwell, Kent *95*, 180, 189
Chastleton House, Oxfordshire 148, 210
Chelsea Chop 191, *191*, 196
cherries 163, 201, 202, *202*, 203, 208
chickens 196
chives 249
chocolate vine *54*
Christie, Agatha 221
Chrysanthemum segetum 98
Chusan palm 32, *33*
citrus fruits 212
Clark, Colin 68, 83, 171, 173, 279
clay soil 20–1, 24–5
clematis 124, 125, 166, 168
climate 14
climbers 40, 54, 73, 124, 152, 166, 169
closeboard fencing 36
cloud pruning 174
clovers, micro 83, 89
Clowser, Christina 140
clubroot 234
Clumber Park, Nottinghamshire 212, 227
coir pots 109
Colby Woodland Garden, Pembrokeshire *65*, *66*
cold frames 225, 226, 279
Coleton Fishacre, Devon 19, 42, 183, 189
    lawns 80, *80*
    propagation 138
    tropical planting 70
    water features 60, *60*
colour 56–8, 69, 70, 72–3
Columbine *34*
comfrey 196, 224
companion planting 180
compost 137, 152, 185, 197, 276–7, 279
compost heaps 224
compost tea 196
Compton Castle, Devon 63

concrete paths 46
conservation 11
containers 44, 212, 223, 225, 273, 279
coppicing 168, 169
cordons 161, 164, 202
coriander 249
corn cockles 98, *98*
corn marigolds 98, *99*
cornflowers 98, *98*
Cornus sanguinea 74
Corylus avellana 'Contota' *74*
cosmos 112
Cotehele, Cornwall *276*
cotoneaster *26*
cottage gardens 68, *68*
courgettes 240, *240*, 244
The Courts Garden, Wiltshire *78*, *178*, *186*
crab apples *25*, 266
Cracknell, Adam 188
Cragside, Northumberland 211
cranberries 217
Croome, Worcestershire *121*
crop rotation 230
crown lifting 160
cucurbits 240
cutting back 191
cuttings 135, 136-7, 140-1, 197
cylinder mowers 86, *86*

dahlias *74*, 188, *189*
daisy grubbers 181, *181*
daphne bhlou *74*
dead hedges 267
deadheading *146*, 154, *155*, 190, 196
decking 32, 33, 46
delphiniums 188, 190
designing gardens 9, 28-75
digging 102-3
dill 249, *249*
Dinefwr Park and Castle, Wales *260*
diseases 132, 163, 192-6, 234, 237, 246
dividing plants 138-9
dormice 266, *266*
dragonflies 258, *258*, 259
drifts 105-6
drying vegetables 228
Dunham Massey, Cheshire *46*, 69

ecosystem, caring for the 192-3
edging shears 92, 94, *94*
edgings, lawn 92, 152
elder *25*

Emmetts Garden, Kent 20, 71, 189
Encarsia formosa 195
environment, gardening with the 18, 22
Erddig, Wrexham *89*
Erica carnea *26*
espaliers 161, 202, *202*, *205*, *206*
eucalyptus *26*
evergreens 49, 61-2, 123, 171, 274
exotic gardens 69-70

Farnell, Paul 56
Felbrigg Hall, Norfolk 32, *265*
fences 33, 36-40, 44
fennel 249, *250*
Fenton House and Garden, London *214*
fertilisers 23, 193
Festuca rubra 87, *87*
feverfew *35*
figs 209, 212, *202*
filipendula *25*
firewood 152, *152*
fish 259
fleece 185, *185*, 197
flowers 190, 196, 274
focal points 51
foliage 59, 168, 274
forcing crops 226
forks 181, 184
formal gardens 67
Fountains Abbey & Studley Royal Water Garden, Yorkshire *48*, 250
foxgloves *14*, *75*
Fraser, Nick 277, *278*
freezing vegetables 228
frost 15, 17, 104, 185
fruit 11, 200-21
    frost 17
    growing in containers 212
    planting fruit trees 197
    pruning 161-5, 197
    training fruit trees 202-3
    see also apples; pears, *etc*
fungal diseases 192
fungi 23, 117

gaiilardia *27*
Gallivan, Paul 109, 132, 149
garlic 238, 244
Gaskin, Chris 85, 88, 137
Gilbert, Sir Humphrey 63
glasshouses 211, 225, 233
Godolphin House, Cornwall *8*
Goodwin, Andy 179

gooseberries 202, 203, 212, 215
grapevines 148, 202, 220-1
grasses 49
    ornamental 59, 275
    paths and lawns 46, 76-99
    wildflower meadows 96-9
gravel paths 46, *46*
Great Chalfield Manor, Wiltshire *33*
green manure 23, 180, 197
greener gardening 11, 252-79
Greenway, Devon 59, 68, 83, 171, 173, 221, 279
Greville, Mrs Ronald 207
Gunby Hall, Lincolnshire *20*
Gunnera manicata 32

ha-has 38, 39
habitat boxes 256, 257
half moons 92, 94
Ham House, Surrey 59, *212*, 239
Hanbury Hall, Worcestershire *204*, *228*
hand shears 173, *175*, 181, *181*
Hardwick Hall, Derbyshire *17*, *204*
hardwood cuttings 140-1, 197
hardy annuals, sowing 112
Hardy's Cottage, Dorset *69*
harvest planner 244-5
Hatchlands Park, Surrey 70, *222*
hazel 142, *142*, 168
heather 171
hedge trimmers 173
hedgehogs 256
hedges 16, 18, 41, 44, 197, 266
    box 246
    clipping 62
    framing views 50
    planting 267
    pruning 173, 174-5, 196
    topiary gardens 61-2
height, creating 52
heirloom varieties 227
hellebore, stinking *34*
herbaceous perennials 105-9, 196, 197, 274
    dividing 139
    herbaceous borders 70, 73, 188, 189
    planting 108-9
herbicides 23
herbs 44, 63
    culinary 249-50
    herb garden 73, 247-51
    herb lawns 89
    storage 248

Hidcote Manor Garden, Gloucestershire 8, 30, *31*, 61, *99*, 254
Hill, Octavia 8, 11, 30
Hill Top, Cumbria *68*
Hinton Ampner, Hampshire *52*
Hodgkins, Jo 268
hoes 181, *181*
Holcus lanatus 88
holistic gardening 254-5
hostas 25, *75*
Hughenden, Buckinghamshire *247*
Hunter, Sir Robert 8
hydrangeas 20, *20*, 25, *55*, 165

Ickworth, Suffolk 220, *220*
Ikin, Ed 23, 271
Ilam Park, Derbyshire *151*
informal gardens 68
insects 254, *254*, 255, 256, 260
irises, bearded 140, *140*, *141*
ivy 39, 40, *179*, 274

Japanese gardens 69
Japanese knotweed 180
Japanese maple 24
jasmine 55
Jekyll, Gertrude 8, *47*, 70, 105, 128
Jerusalem artichokes 243, *246*

Kelly, Patrick 239
Killerton, Devon *56*, *105*
Kip, Johannes 71
kitchen gardens 68-9, 207, 223, 248
knee protection 181
Knightshayes Court, Devon 70, *138*, 206, *227*
kniphophia *27*
knives, weed 183
knot gardens 63, 67, 246
knotweed, Japanese 180

lacewings 192, *193*, 195, 256
Lacock Abbey, Wiltshire *228*
ladybirds 192, *193*, 195, 256
lakes 50, 60
landscape, working with the 32-5
lasagne beds 104
lavender *27*, 171, *171*, 220, 250, *250*
lawn mowers 85-6
lawns 9, 33, 44, 51, 196, 197
  care of 76-99
  edging 197
layering 142

leeks 238, 245
lettuces 242, *242*, 245, 246
Lewis, Andy 96
leylandii 18, 49
light 15, 50
lilac 25
Lindisfarne Castle, Northumberland *47*, 70
liquid plant food 224
Llanerchaeron, Ceredigion *248*
location 14
log piles 268-9
Lolium perenne 87
Londonderry, Lady Edith 61
loppers 150, *151*, 164
Lutyens, Edwin *47*
Lytes Cary Manor, Somerset 250

McNamara, Emma 71
magnolia *24*
mahonia *24*
maintenance 11, 176-97, 248
manure 23, 185
marjoram 250
meadows 44, *44*, 89, 96-9
Mediterranean plants 44
mice 233
microclimates 14-17
mint 250, *250*
mirrors 50
Modified Lorette System 161
Monk's House, East Sussex 14, *92*, *179*, 258, 262
mood, and colour 58
Morden Hall Park, London 23, 71, 271
Mottisfont, Hampshire *53*, 154, *155*
mount planting 112
Mount Stewart, County Down 61, 62, 258
mowers and mowing 79, 85-6, 88
Muir, John 254
mulch mowers 85-6
mulching 23, 44, 124, 152, 185, 196, 273
mycorrhizal fungi 117

nectarines 210
nematodes 195
nettle tea 196, *277*
nettles 15, 224, 245
Nicholson, Harold 57
Nicoll, Kate 226, 229, 233
Nôtre, André le 45-6

Nunnington Hall, Yorkshire 277, 278, *279*
Nymans, West Sussex 8, *16*, 23, *37*, *46*, *106*, 272

oak 7-8
onions 237, 238, 245
organic matter 20, *21*, 23, 103, 123-4, 192
Ormesby Hall, North Yorkshire 188
ornamental plants 197, 275
osteospermum *27*
Osterley Park, Middlesex *31*
Oudoulf, Piet 106
Overbecks, Devon 69, 70
Oxburgh Hall, Norfolk *67*

Papaver rhoeas 98
Parker, Tim 180, 188
Parker, Tracey 63, 184, 207, 211, 213, 221, 251
parsley 250, 251
parsnips 236, 245
parterres 61, 67
passion flowers 55
paths 45-6, 51, 152, 225
patios 33, 44, 279
patterns, planting 105-6
paving 46
pea sticks 188
peaches 202, 210
pears 201-2, 201, 202, 203, 205
peas 232-3, 245
peat 276-7
Peckover House, Cambridgeshire *106*
peony *24*
Pepper, Martyn 42, 80, 138, *183*, *189*
perennials, herbaceous 105-9, 139, 197
pergolas 52
perovskia *27*
perspective 51
pesticides 192
pests 132, 196, 233, 234, 237
  control 192-5
  slug traps 187
pH of soil 21, 66, 117
Philadelphus 75, 167
pickling vegetables 228
pinching out 191, *191*, 196
pineapples 213
pink currants 215
Plant Conservation Centre (PCC) 143
plant food 224, *277*

Plant Heritage 143
plants and planting 9, 100-25
  combinations 266
  dividing 138-9
  seasonal interest 74-5
  for texture 59
  to suit your soil 24-7
Plas yn Rhiw, Gwynedd *146*
plums 201, 202, 203, 206
Poa annua 88
  P. pratensis 88
Polesden Lacey, Surrey 6, *6, 19*, 22,
  22, 43
  bulbs 110, *111*
  colour 58
  framing views *51*
  fruit and vegetables 213, 214, 207,
  221, 234, 236, 237, 240, 251, 267
  garden tools 184
  glasshouses 211
  herbaceous borders *107*, 109
  knot gardens 63
  lawns 79, *79*, 85, 86, 88, 91
  maintenance 179
  pest control 194-5
  propagation 128, 137, 140
  pruning *173, 175*
  restoring 71
  winter garden 275
ponds 50, 60, 258-9
poppies *27, 32*
potagers 246
potatoes 228, 236-7, 245
pots, hairy coir 109
Potter, Beatrix *68*
Powis Castle, Powys *10, 106*
prairie-style planting 70
preserving vegetables 228
pricking out 134
pronged cultivators 181, *182*
propagation 9, 126-43, 171
  collecting seed 130
  dividing plants 138-9
  layering 142
  pricking out 134
  sowing seeds 132-4
  suckers 142
  taking cuttings 135-7, 140-1
propagators 128
prostrate plants 44
pruning 9, 144-75, 184, 196, 197
  fruit trees 204, 205, 206, 208
  soft fruit 164-5, 215, 216, 220

Prunus serrula 75
pumpkins 240, 245, 246
pyracantha 25
pyramid trees 203

Quebec House, Kent *235, 248*

ragwort 180
Rainham Hall, Essex 23, 271
raised beds 223, 225, 279
raspberries 218
Rawnsley, Canon Hardwicke 8
recycling 46, 225, 279
red valerian *34*
redcurrants 202, 203, 212, *212*, 215
Repton, Humphrey 8
rhododendron 27
rhubarb 226, *227*, 246
Rievaulx Terrace, North Yorkshire 277,
  278
ringbarking tool 184
Rodgersia 24
  R. aesculifolia 32
Rollinson, Phil 61, 62
rooftop gardening 270-1
root cuttings 140
root vegetables 236-7
rosemary 250
roses 73, 195, 220
  deadheading *146, 154, 155*
  pruning *147*, 154-6, 190
  types of 54, *54*, 154-6
rotary mowers 85, *85*
rotovators 103, *103*
rudbeckia *25, 74*

Sackville-West, Vita 8, *57*
saffron 251
sage 250, *250*, 251
salad vegetables 242
Saltram, Devon *6*
salvia 27
sandy soil 20, 26-7
sap 148, 151
sarcloir 184
Sarcococca humilis 6
Saunders, Cat 69
saws 149, 150, 159, 164
scarifying 90, 197
Scott, Crispin 258
screening, plants for 48-9
scythes 79
sea holly 75

seasons: cheating the seasons 226
  seasonal chart planner 196-7
  seasonal interest 72-5
secateurs 149, *150*, 159, 163, *164*, 173
sedum 270, *270*, 271
seedlings 134, 225, *225*
seeds: collecting 130
  seedheads 274, *274*
  self-seeders 34-5
  sowing 83-4, 87-8, 132-4, 196
Sellick *6*
semi-ripe cuttings 136-7
shade 15, 52, 66, 74
Shaw's Corner, Hertfordshire *87, 114*
shears 92, 94, *94*, 184
shovels *182*
shrubs 44, 266, 268
  moving 120, 122, 197
  planting 117, 123-4
  pruning *147*, 165-6, 168, 171, 172,
  192
  shrub roses 155-6
  woodland gardens 64
silt soil 20, 24-5
Sissinghurst Castle, Kent 8, *51, 57, 147,
  156*, 250
  maintenance 185
  trees *115*
  the White Garden *30*
Sizergh Castle and Garden, Cumbria
  111, 223
Skimmia japonica 75
slate fencing *39*
slug traps 187
snowdrops *35*, 275
soft fruit 212-21
softwood cuttings 135
soil 20-1, 23, 66
  improving 224
  mulching 185
  pH 21, 66, 117
  preparing 102-3
space, making the most of 50-3
spades *182*, 183
spindle trees 203
spring 72-3, 196
squashes 240, *241*, 243, 245, 246
stakes 120, 188-9, 196
step-overs 202-3, *203*
stipa 27
Stone, David 154
stone paths 46
storage: herbs 248

vegetables 228-9
Stourhead, Wiltshire 8, 209
Stowe Landscape Gardens,
    Buckinghamshire 38
strawberries 212, 214
strimmers 182, 183
subsoil 21
succulents 44, 59, 270
suckers 142, 158
summer 73, 196
sun 15, 17, 72, 74
sunflowers 75, 112
supports 188-9, 196, 232-3, 239
sustainability 7-8, 11, 18, 278-9
swedes 236, 245
sweet gum 74
sweet peas 190
sweetcorn 243, 243, 245
switches 92, 94

tarragon 250
Tatton Park, Cheshire 69, 206
texture 59, 69, 70
Thomas, Graham Stuart 9, 58, 71,
    105-6, 107, 275
Thompson, Mr Arthur 86
thyme 250, 251
Tintinhull Garden, Somerset 58
tobacco plant 35
Todd, Richard 72
tomatoes 237, 245
tools 150, 197, 278, 279
    for lawn repairs 92, 93, 94
    propagation 128, 129
    pruning 149-51, 159, 173
    weeding 181-4
topiary gardens 61-2, 174
topsoil 21
training fruit trees 202-3
transplanting trees 120, 122, 197
Tredegar House, Newport 58
trees 16, 54, 157, 266, 268, 279
    bare-root 116
    fast-growing 44
    fruit trees 201-3
    moving 120, 122
    planting 113-22, 197
    pruning 147, 158-63, 168
    slow-growing 44
    staking 120
    transplanting 197
    woodland gardens 64-6
trellis 16

Trengwainton Garden, Cornwall 242
Trerice, Cornwall 223
Trimmer, Chris 143
tropical planting 69-70
trowels 181, 184
true lutes 84, 92, 94
trugs 182, 183
turf 80, 82
twine 188
Tyntesfield, North Somerset 202

Uppark, West Sussex 96

valerian, red 34
Vaux-le-Vicomte, France 45-6
vegetables 7, 11, 44, 73, 196, 197
    crop rotation 230
    forcing 226
    frost 17
    growing 222-46
    heirloom varieties 227
    kitchen gardens 68-9, 207
    preparing soil for 103
    sowing seeds 132-3
    storing 228-9
    see also cabbages; potatoes etc
Verbena bonariensis 35, 75
vernacular style 38-9
Vibunum bodnantense 75
views, framing 50-1
Virginia creeper 55
The Vyne, Hampshire 82, 202

Waddesdon Manor, Buckinghamshire 56
Walker, Simon 20
walls 16, 39, 40, 50, 52
water butts 225, 272-3
water features 50, 60, 258-9, 268
water table 21
watering 192, 197, 272-3
weed knives 183
weedkiller 186, 187
weeds and weeding 178, 179-87, 196,
    273
Westbury Court Garden, Gloucestershire
    8, 50, 71, 83, 218
wheelbarrows 183
white currants 215
wigwams 233, 239
wildflower meadows 44, 44, 79, 89,
    96-9
wildlife 254-70, 274
willow fencing 36

Wilson, Chris 82
Wimpole Hall, Cambridgeshire 225
wind 16, 66
winter 72, 74, 197, 226, 274
winter cabbage 234
winter stem effect, pruning for 168
wisteria 54, 166
witch hazel 26
woodchip 46, 152, 185, 225, 279
woodland gardens 64-6, 73, 152
wool fleece 185, 185
Woolbeding Gardens, West Sussex 14,
    60, 109, 132, 149, 250
Woolf, Leonard 14
Woolf, Virginia 14
Wordsworth House and Garden, Cumbria
    42, 152, 232
woven fences 36, 38, 40

yellow rattle 96, 96
yellow-eyed grass 35
yew 16, 41, 41, 171, 274
    pruning 175
    topiary 61, 62

Recommended Reading

Akeroyd, Simon, *A Little Course in Growing Veg and Fruit* (Dorling Kindersley, 2013)

Akeroyd, Simon, *The Allotment Handbook* (Dorling Kindersley, 2013)

Akeroyd, Simon, *Lawns and Groundcover* (Dorling Kindersley, 2012)

Akeroyd, Simon, *Shrubs and Small Trees* (Dorling Kindersley, 2008)

Akeroyd, Simon, Geoff Hodge, Sara Draycott and Guy Barter, *Allotment Handbook* (Mitchell Beazley in association with The Royal Horticultural Society, 2010)

Akeroyd, Simon, Zia Allaway, Helena Caldon, Martyn Cox and Jenny Hendy, *RHS Complete Gardener's Manual* (Dorling Kindersley, 2011)

Allaway, Zia and Lia Leendertz, *How to Grow Practically Everything* (Dorling Kindersley, 2010)

Barber, Jacq, *Design Ideas For Your Garden* (National Trust Books, 2013)

Bean, W.J., *Trees and Shrubs Hardy in the British Isles (Vol 1 to 3)* (John Murray, 1950)

Boff, Charles, *How to Grow and Produce Your Own Food* (Odhams Press Ltd, 1946)

Brickell, Christopher, *RHS A-Z Encyclopedia of Garden Plants* (Dorling Kindersley, third revised edition, 2008)

Brickell, Christopher, *RHS Encyclopedia of Gardening* (Dorling Kindersley, fourth revised edition, 2012)

Crosbie, Colin, *Easy Pruning* (Dorling Kindersley, 2007)

Davies, Jennifer, *The Victorian Kitchen Garden* (BBC Books, 1987)

Gammack, Helene, *Inspirational Gardens Through the Seasons* (National Trust Books, 2014)

Gammack, Helene, *Kitchen Garden Estate* (National Trust Books, 2012)

Gardiner, Jim, *Encyclopedia of Flowering Shrubs* (Timber Press, 2012)

Hessayon, Dr. D.G., *The Vegetable and Herb Expert* (Expert Books, second revised edition, 1997)

Hillier, John G., and Roy Lancaster, *The Hillier Manual of Trees and Shrubs* (Royal Horticultural Society, eighth revised edition, 2014)

Ikin, Ed *Thoughtful Gardening* (National Trust Books, 2010)

Kapoor, Sybil *The Great British Vegetable Cookbook* (National Trust Books, 2013)

Klein, Carol, *Grow Your Own Vegetables* (Mitchell Beazley in association with The Royal Horticultural Society, TV tie-in edition, 2007)

Lacey, Stephen, *Gardens of the National Trust* (National Trust Books, 2011)

Larkcom, Joy, *Creative Vegetable Gardening* (Mitchell Beazley, 2008)

Laws, Bill, *Spade, Skirret and Parsnip, The Curious History of Vegetables* (The History Press Ltd, 2004)

Pavord, Anna, *The New Kitchen Garden* (Dorling Kindersley, 1996)

Pollock, Mike, *RHS Fruit and Vegetable Garden* (Dorling Kindersley in association with The Royal Horticultural Society, 2002)

National Trust, *Gardening Secrets: from National Trust Head Gardeners* (National Trust Books, 2014)

Royal Horticultural Society, *New Encyclopaedia of Gardening Techniques* (Mitchell Beazley in association with The Royal Horticultural Society, 2008)

Shepherd, Allan, *The Organic Garden* (Collins, 2007)

Stickland, Sue, *Heritage Vegetables* (Gaia Books Limited, 1998)

Thomas, Graham Stuart, *Colour in the Winter Garden* (J.M. Dent and Sons Ltd, 1957)

Welland, Frances, *Place that Plant* (Paragon Book Service Ltd, 1998)

Wilson, Matthew, *RHS New Gardening: How to Garden in a Changing Climate* (Mitchell Beazley in association with The Royal Horticultural Society, 2007)

Recommended websites

The National Garden scheme
www.ngs.org.uk

National Trust
www.nationaltrust.org.uk

Royal Horticultural Society
www.rhs.org.uk

www.simonakeroyd.co.uk

Picture Credits

© National Trust Images/Caroline Arber: pages 2, 14 (left), 27 (middle right and top right), 73 (middle and right), 100 (top), 111 (top left), 125, 126 (top), 144 (top), 161, 166 (left), 201, 250 (left), 258 (right), 262; NTI/David Armstrong 258 (left); NTI/Rosie Barnett 225 (bottom left), 241; NTI/Andrew Baskott 267; NTI/Mark Bolton 10, 24 (middle left), 25 (bottom middle), 27 (bottom middle and bottom right), 35 (bottom left), 73 (left), 100 (bottom), 106 (left), 140 (right), 158, 200, 202 (left), 209 (top), 233 (bottom right), 249 (left); NTI/Jonathan Buckley 3, 26 (bottom right), 27 (middle left), 31 (top left and bottom), 51 (left), 53, 55 (top left), 75 (top left), 76 (bottom), 98 (top), 99 (top), 147, 155 (bottom right), 156 (right), 180, 189 (top left), 246 (top), 252 (bottom), 254, 273; NTI/Andrew Butler 4–5, 8 (bottom right), 12 (top), 15, 17 (top), 19 (top right), 25 (middle left and bottom left), 26 (top right), 27 (top middle), 33 (right), 34 (top left), 41 (left), 46 (top), 52, 55 (bottom right), 58 (left), 59 (right), 66, 112, 113, 176 (top), 204 (top), 223 (right), 225 (bottom right), 231, 235 (bottom), 238 (top), 242 (right), 247, 248 (right); NTI/Neil Campbell-Sharp 27 (top left), 130, 142 (right), 205 (bottom left); NTI/Brian & Nina Chapple 48, 75 (top middle), 96, 172, 209 (bottom), 243 (right); NTI/Val Corbett 42, 82, 111 (top right), 126 (bottom), 138 (left), 153, 232 (left), 266 (bottom); NTI/Joe Cornish 39 (top), 83 (bottom); NTI/Roger Coulam 223 (left); NTI/

Stuart Cox 146 (left); NTI/Derek Croucher 50; NTI/Nick Dautlich 24 (middle right); NTI/Adrian Davies 264 (top right); NTI/David Dixon 25 (middle), 54 (bottom), 55 (top), 75 (middle right), 83 (top left), 107, 131, 203 (right), 205 (right), 248 (left); NTI/James Dobson 14 (right), 24 (bottom left and top right), 31 (top right), 41 (right), 60 (right), 65, 87 (right and left), 114, 116, 129 (top right), 144 (bottom), 178, 190 (bottom), 210, 211, 222, 228 (bottom), 229, 236 (left), 249 (top right), 278; NTI/John Downer 89 (left); NTI/Carole Drake 19 (top left), 27 (bottom left), 60 (left), 111 (bottom left), 123, 146 (right), 268 (bottom), 276; NTI/Rod Edwards 264 (top left); NTI/Andreas von Einsiedel 12 (bottom), 261; NTI/Simon Fraser 47; NTI/Lee Frost 75 (middle left); NTI/John Hammond 59 (left); NTI/Jerry Harpur 38; NTI/Paul Harris 25 (top middle), 34 (bottom), 75 (bottom middle and top right), 103 (bottom right), 124, 138 (right), 164 (right), 198 (top), 216, 227 (left), 238 (middle left), 263, 270 (left); NTI/Nigel Hicks 80; NTI/Ross Hoddinott 99 (bottom), 208, 255; NTI/David Hunter 204 (bottom); NTI/Jason Ingram 54 (middle); NTI/Andrea Jones 155 (bottom left); NTI/Chris Lacey 24 (top left), 28 (top), 56, 69 (middle), 78, 95, 186 (left), 189 (top middle), 235 (top right); NTI/Anthony Lambert 6 (left); NTI/Andrew Lawson 27 (middle), 34 (top right); NTI/David Levenson 26 (top left), 103 (left), 148 (right), 152, 185 (middle), 227 (right), 272 (top right and top left); NTI/John Millar 25 (top left), 32, 58 (right), 104 (bottom), 151, 176 (bottom), 190 (top right), 221, 224, 225 (top and middle), 237, 234, 252 (top), 260 (left), 265, NTI/John Miller 30, 68 (left), 106 (right), 205 (top left); NTI/Rob Matheson 67; NTI/Nick Meers 26 (middle right), 194; NTI/MMGI/Marianne Majerus 17 (bottom right and bottom left), 45, 74 (middle right and bottom right), 142 (left), 170, 274 (right and left); NTI/Paul Mogford 186 (right), 206 (top right); NTI/Robert Morris 24 (bottom right), 102, 182 (bottom right), 185 (bottom), 202 (left), 206 (left), 270 (right), 279 (right); NTI/Myles New 212 (right); NTI/NaturePL/David Kjaer 266 (right); NTI/NaturePL/Dietmar Nill 268 (top); ©NTI/NaturePL/Duncan McEwan 193 (left); NTI/NaturePL/Kim Taylor 104 (bottom right); NTI/NaturePL/Premaphotos 193 (bottom right); NTI/Clive Nichols 8 (left), 16, 37 (bottom), 46 (bottom), 76 (top), 105 (right), 106 (middle), 171; NTI/David Noton 121; NTI/Alex Ramsey 49, 61; NTI/Stephen Robson 21, 35 (middle left), 33 (left), 62, 70, 74 (top right and middle left), 75 (middle), 55 (bottom left), 75 (bottom left), 98 (bottom), 140 (left), 148 (left), 164 (left), 198 (bottom), 212 (middle), 215, 216 (left), 219 (bottom and top), 228 (top), 236 (right), 243 (left), 249 (bottom), 266 (top left); NTI/Andy Sands 260 (right); NTI/David Sellman 157, 226, 264 (bottom); NTI/Arnhel de Serra 25 (bottom right and middle right), 28 (bottom), 35 (top left), 68 (right), 214, 156 (left); NTI/Ian Shaw 8 (top right), 242 (left), 250 (middle), NTI/William Shaw 220, 212 (left), 250 (right), NTI/Gary K Smith 256; NTI/Mark Sunderland 218 (bottom); NTI/Claire Takacs 26 (bottom left), 166 (right); NTI/Megan Taylor 19 (bottom), 79 (bottom), 74 (bottom left); NTI/Penny Tweedie 57, 115 (left), 185 (top); NTI/Joe Wainwright 69 (left and right), 89 (right); NTI/Mike Warren 20; NTI/Ian West 25 (top right), 39 (bottom), 246 (bottom).

© Eddie Hyde: pages 6 (right), 22, 35 (top right and bottom right), 36, 37 (top left and top right), 40 (top left, middle left, middle right and bottom right), 43, 44, 50 (top right), 54 (top), 81 (left and right), 83 (right), 84, (bottom left and bottom right), 85, 86, 88 (right and bottom), 90 (left and right), 91 (top left, top right and middle left), 92, 93 (top and bottom), 94 (left and right), 95 (bottom), 97, 103 (top right and bottom right), 105 (left), 108 (top, middle, bottom left and bottom right) 109 (top left, top middle, top right, middle, lower left and lower right), 111 (bottom right), 118 (bottom left, top right, middle right, lower right and bottom right),119 (top, middle, bottom left and bottom right), 129 (top left, bottom left and bottom right), 132 (left and right), 133 (top and bottom), 134 (left, middle and right), 135 (left, middle and right), 136 (top left, top middle, top right, bottom left and bottom right), 137 (top left, bottom left and right), 139 (top left, top right, bottom left and bottom right), 141 (top left, top right, bottom left and bottom right), 149, 150 (left and right), 155 (top left and top right), 159 (left and right), 160 (top left, top right, middle left, middle right and bottom), 162 (left, middle and right), 163 (top left, top right, bottom left and bottom right), 167 (top right, bottom left and bottom right), 169 (left and right), 173 (left and right), 174, 175 (top left, top right, bottom left, bottom middle and bottom right), 181 (left, middle and right), 182 (top left, top right, bottom left and bottom right), 187 (left and right), 189 (bottom, far right), 190 (top left), 191 (left and right), 193 (top right), 196, 203 (left), 232 (right), 233 (top left, top right, lower left, lower right), 235 (top left), 238 (bottom left, bottom middle and bottom right), 240, 257 (top, middle and bottom), 269, 272 (bottom left, bottom middle and bottom right), 275, 277 (left and right), 279 (left).

© Alamy/Flowerphotos: pages 217 (left); © Alamy/FLPA 206 (bottom right); © Alamy/Tim Gainey 013; Alamy/Francisco Martinez 271; Alamy/JUNK TAKAHASHI/amanaimagesRF 217 (right); Alamy/Version One 218 (top).

Acknowledgements

I would like to thank Tracey Parker for her specialist and in-depth conservation and historic knowledge. She researched and wrote many of the historic articles in this book. I would also like to thank Andrea Selley and her garden staff and volunteers at Polesden Lacey for all their support.

Numerous National Trust gardeners and advisors have contributed their invaluable horticultural tips and advice including Adam Cracknell, Andy Goodwin, Andy Lewis, Chris Gaskin, Chris Trimmer, Chris Wilson, Fran Llewellyn, Colin Clark, Crispin Scott, Ed Ikin, Emma McNamara, Erica Emery, Jo Hodgkins, Kate Nicol, Mark Lamey, Martyn Pepper, Patrick Kelly, Simon Walker, Tim Parker and Paul Gallivan. Without their vast gardening knowledge, this book wouldn't have been possible.

A huge thank you to Eddie Hyde for his superb photography, battling against whatever the weather threw at him, from heavy rain to bright, glaring sunshine, and for having to tolerate the revolting smell while I did a step-by-step sequence for making stinky comfrey liquid feed.

I would also like to thank Lucy Smith and her team at Pavilion Books for their patience, creativity and editing skills, including being able to condense my exuberant horticultural notes and ramblings into something that made sense, and for creating this wonderful book. Thanks also to Lee-May Lim and Elizabeth Healey for the book design.

Finally I need to say a massive thank you to my wife Annabel and three children Guy, Lissie and Hugh for tolerating yet another year of writing a book while I locked myself away in the Garden Room and tapped away at my very well-worn keyboard!

First published in the United Kingdom in 2015 by
National Trust Books
1 Gower Street
London WC1E 6HD

An imprint of Pavilion Books Group

Text © Simon Akeroyd, 2015
Volume copyright © National Trust Books, 2015

The moral rights of the author have been asserted.

All rights reserved. No part of this publication may be reproduced, stored in a retrieval system,
or transmitted in any form or by any means, electronic, mechanical, photocopying, recording
or otherwise, without the prior written permission of the copyright owner.

ISBN: 9781909881365

A CIP catalogue record for this book is available from the British Library.

10 9 8 7 6 5 4 3 2 1

Repro by Rival Colour, UK
Printed by 1010 Printing International Ltd, China

This book can be ordered direct from the publisher
at the website: www.pavilionbooks.com, or try your local bookshop.
Also available at National Trust shops or www.shop.nationaltrust.org.uk.